Photo credits: Author's archive (152), AMX (3), Dr. Ing. h.c. F. Porsche KG (3), Rheinstahl AG (1), Carl F. W. Borgward GmbH (1), WTD 91 (1), Krauss-Maffei AG (17), Rheinmetall AG (5), Wegmann & Co. (4), MaK (2), KTS Munster (1), Ralph Zwilling (1), OTO MELARA (2), Friesecke & Höpfner (1), IABG (6), ZEISS (2), AEG-Telefunken (1), Steinheil-Lear Siegler AG (2), ELTRO (1), Texas Instruments (1), MTU (1), ZF (3), ATE (1), Blohm & Voss (1), Würth (1), Drägerwerk / Anton Piller (1), Hoesch Roethe Erde (1), SEL (1).

Other Schiffer books on related topics

The Israeli Armored Corps: History, Equipment, Operations, 1948 to 2024,
Marc Lenzin and Stefan Bühler
ISBN 978-0-7643-6906-3

Armored Forces of Russia and the Soviet Union: Tanks and Armored Vehicles, 1919–2025,
Victor Schunkow
ISBN 978-0-7643-6967-4

Originally published as *Kampfpanzer Leopard 1* by Motorbuch Verlag © 2024 Motorbuch Verlag
Translated from the German by David Johnston

Library of Congress Control Number: 2026932909

Cover design by Molly Shields
Type set in Helvetica Neue/Myriad Pro

ISBN: 978-0-7643-7162-2
eBook: 978-1-5073-0724-3

Printed in China
10 9 8 7 6 5 4 3 2 1

FSC
www.fsc.org
MIX
Paper | Supporting responsible forestry
FSC® C167893

Published by Schiffer Publishing, Ltd.
4880 Lower Valley Road
Atglen, PA 19310
Phone: (610) 593-1777; Fax: (610) 593-2002
Email: Info@schifferbooks.com
Web: www.schifferbooks.com

Contents

Foreword

In the early years, the design and development of armored fighting vehicles for the Bundeswehr took place in three major steps: In the first step, armored vehicles were purchased abroad (primarily from the United States). The second step saw armored vehicles developed and produced by foreign manufacturers to German military requirements (from France and Great Britain)—including the HS 30 and the Hotchkiss. Finally, at the end of the 1950s, the step was taken of entrusting German companies with the task of developing and producing modern and capable armored fighting vehicles. One of the first major tank projects was the Leopard 1 main battle tank, including a family of derivatives, and the SPz-neu (new infantry fighting vehicle) program.

The negative experiences associated with development of the HS 30 played a role in this plan. To avoid similar negative experiences, development of the Leopard 1 main battle tank proceeded very carefully and systematically. This approach was also necessary because at the end of the 1950s, German industry had to break new ground in the development of numerous components. There were very few workers still available with practical experience from the Second World War—as was also the case in government. To make the best possible use of existing capabilities, for the Leopard 1 program three groups of companies were commissioned to develop concept designs at the same time. Interestingly, the proposals that were submitted differed greatly in the level of technology of the components used. For example, Company Group C (Borgward, Bremen) submitted a decidedly revolutionary vehicle design. Due to the very high development risks, the client refrained from ordering corresponding prototypes. The design by Company Group B, under the leadership of the Warnecke Design Bureau of Düsseldorf, also featured new technologies in many areas (e.g., hydropneumatic suspension; hydrostatic superimposed steering gear). Despite obvious development risks, the client decided to build prototypes. In contrast, the concept design submitted by Company Group A, under the leadership of the Porsche development bureau, featured a component selection with relatively low development risks. It later turned out that this design could be brought to series production within a reasonable time and cost framework. Interestingly, the companies of "loser group" B were later assigned the SPz-neu program, from which the Marder infantry-fighting vehicle emerged.

After a tightly managed development and testing program, deliveries of the Leopard 1 main battle tank, a powerful and reliable weapon system suitable for frontline service, to the troops began on September 9, 1965, after nine years of development. Particular emphasis was placed on the system's ease of operation and—on the basis of experience gained during the Second World War—on favorable maintenance properties. The latter is reflected, among other things, in the rapid interchangeability of important assemblies.

Out of the three battle criteria of firepower, mobility, and protection, the basic concept of the Leopard 1 main battle tank gave mobility priority over protection capabilities. This decision to produce a lightweight 30-metric-ton (33-ton) standard tank was made at the end of the 1950s, since by that time, light antitank weapons were capable of penetrating virtually all available types of armor. In the case of the Leopard 1 main battle tank, the race against ammunition effectiveness was abandoned and an attempt was made to ensure acceptable survivability through agility and speed as well as a low silhouette. Outside Germany and France, this design philosophy for a main battle tank was controversial among many tank-building nations.

Although there were serious doubts as to whether the design philosophy of the Leopard 1 main battle tank would prove itself in actual combat situations, interestingly enough, a large number of nations decided to introduce this relatively light main battle tank into their armed forces. Just eight years after the start of quantity production of the Leopard 1 main battle tank, the design philosophy for a main battle tank had also changed in Germany: In 1973, during development of the Leopard 2 main battle tank, ballistic protection was augmented considerably. With this change in protection philosophy, the protection level of the Leopard 1 main battle tank was also increased through the addition of appliqué armor and the transition to spaced armor in the welded turret; this increased combat weight from 40 to 42.4 metric tons (44 to 46.7 tons). In a final, decisive improvement in protection, the threat posed by kinetic-energy penetrator ammunition was to be at least partially countered—however, in the German opinion, the associated weight increase of almost 6 metric tons (6.6 tons) could not be implemented in a system-compatible manner, particularly with regard to power transmission and chassis. In contrast, Leopard 1 main battle tanks deployed by other countries in Kosovo and Afghanistan have received a massive improvement in protection.

The original service life of the Leopard 1 main battle tank in the Bundeswehr was supposed to come to an end in the 1980s. The tactical requirements for a KPz 3 / Leopard 3 main battle tank as a successor model had been in place since April 1972. Due to serious conflicts of objectives within the military requirements as well as various problems with cooperative partners in this program (Great Britain and France), not even prototypes of the KPz 3 were built. The Leopard 1 had to remain in service for almost twice as long as originally planned!

While the Leopard 1 main battle tank left the Bundeswehr in 2003, after thirty-eight years of service, the vehicle remained in use in foreign armies for many more years. Troop reductions saw many western European nations sell off their stocks of Leopard 1s—to states such as Chile and Brazil. For those states, some of whose armed forces were still equipped with tanks from the Second World War (M3, M4, etc.), their conversion to the Leopard 1 main battle tank represented a dramatic technological advance.

This book gives the interested reader a good overview of the course of development and the technology of the Leopard 1 main battle tank. In addition to production versions, test vehicles are also presented, which were created on the basis of the Leopard 1 chassis or turret, or the technology of Leopard 1 assemblies, which were previously less well known to the public.

Rolf Hilmes
Ketsch, July 2019

Chapter 1

Development Activities

Preliminary Projects

Even in specialist circles, it is scarcely known that even before the start of development work on the Leopard 1 and SPz-neu (infantry fighting vehicle) family, German companies were already busy designing armored vehicles. As early as the beginning of 1953, the company Porsche System Engineering Ltd. of Zug (Switzerland) was working on the following designs:

- B-PS 100: a 36-metric-ton turreted tank with a 90 mm gun, loading assistance, and a crew of three
- B-PS 101 Ausf. A: a 36-metric-ton assault gun with an 88 mm gun, automatic loading and a crew of three
- B-PS 101 Ausf. B: a 36-metric-ton turreted tank with a 55 mm fast-firing gun and a crew of three
- B-PS 102: a 39.5-metric-ton turreted tank with a 90 mm tank gun and a crew of four ("India Project")

The Indian government, which since the 1950s had been negotiating with the Daimler-Benz company for the delivery of German military products, obviously showed interest in the B-PS 102 project. Its design concept was that of a conventional turreted tank, which interestingly employed several technologies taken from Wehrmacht vehicles (steering gear, suspension). Curiously, both the hull and turret (analogous to the M47 and M48) were to be made of cast steel (to be made by the Ruhrstahl company). Even though the "India Project" never came into being, this preliminary work enabled the participating companies to join in the development of the Leopard 1 relatively quickly.

The India Project

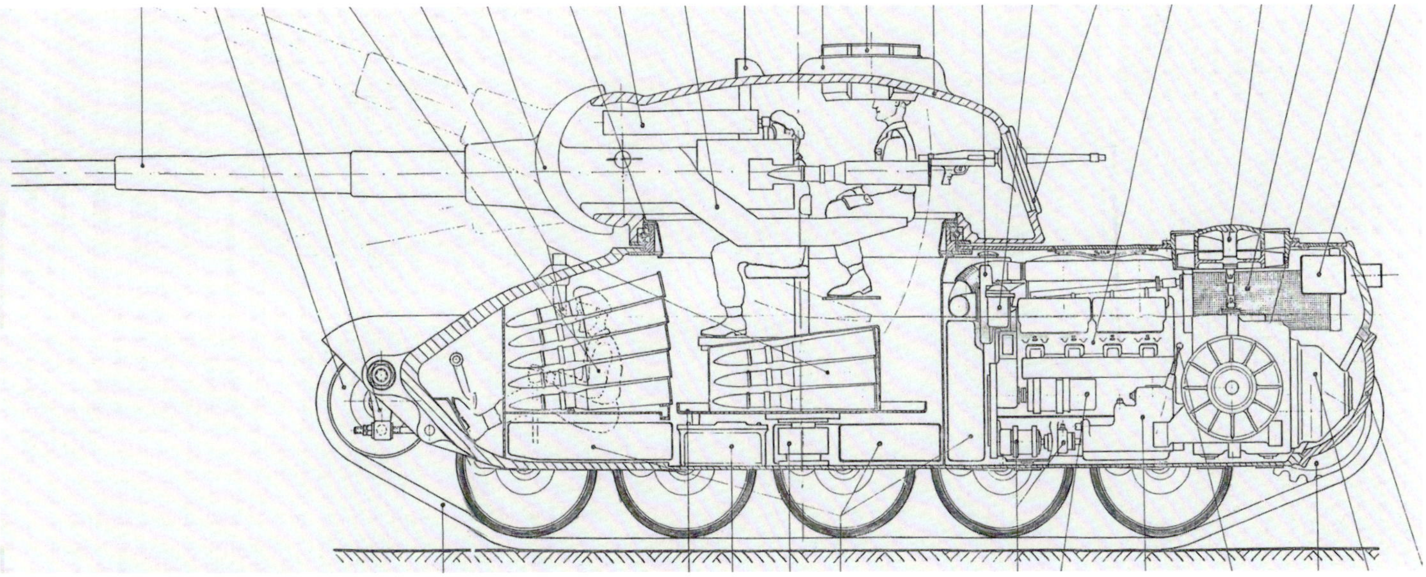

This side view shows that the turret shell is made entirely of cast homogeneous armor; the hull shell is apparently also made of cast homogeneous armor (with the exception of the floor plate and the side walls). The design of the shell is thus very similar to that of the American main battle tanks of the time. Antimine protection measures were not envisaged, since the fuel tanks and batteries were mounted directly on the hull floor. In contrast to American main battle tanks, the power transmission system was not equipped with a torque converter but with a three-disc clutch. The clutch linings could be replaced through a cover screwed into the rear section (see AMX 30). It is noticeable that the trunnion axis was not in the same plane as the barrel bore axis.

Type	India Project
Design period	1955
Crew	4
Combat weight	39.5 metric tons (43.54 tons)
Chassis length	6.2 meters (20.34 feet)
Width over tracks	3.2 meters (10.49 feet)
Height (turret roof)	no information
Main gun, caliber	90 mm
Ammunition capacity	61 rounds
Secondary weapon 1, caliber	7.62 mm mantlet machine gun
Secondary weapon 2, caliber	7.62 mm MG in rear of turret
Engine, type	MB 837 A 8-cylinder diesel
Rated output	485 kW (650.39 hp) at 2,200 rpm
Maximum speed	approx. 50 kph (31 mph)
Range on roads	450 km (279.61 mi.)
Fuel capacity	approx. 1,200 liters (317 US gal.)
Fuel consumption (on roads)	approx. 270 liters / 100 km (0.87 mpg)
Suspension	disc springs
Armor thicknesses	130 mm turret front, 90 mm glacis

Development of the Leopard 1 Begins

When the German Bundeswehr was established, the soldiers of the new Panzertruppe (armored force) were able to immediately begin tactical, gunnery, and automotive training using the American M47 main battle tank, which had been available since 1956. Nevertheless, very early on it was clear to the army operations staff in the defense ministry that

- the M47 would reach its wear limits by the mid-1960s and that the supply of spare parts could also be threatened;
- the American M47 and M48 main battle tanks were too heavy, too wide, and too tall for the geographical conditions in Germany;
- because of their gasoline engines, these main battle tanks had an excessively high rate of fuel consumption and thus an inadequate radius of action; and
- the gasoline fuel they carried posed a high risk to these main battle tanks.

Type	PT I A Prototype
Design period	1958–59
Crew	4
Combat weight	33 metric tons (36.37 tons)
Chassis length	6.52 meters (21.39 feet)
Width over tracks	3.25 meters (10.66 feet)
Height (turret roof)	2.22 meters (7.28 feet)
Main gun, caliber	90 mm
Ammunition capacity	no information
Secondary weapon 1, caliber	7.62 mm mantlet machine gun
Secondary weapon 2, caliber	—
Engine, type	MB 838 10-cylinder diesel
Rated output	611 kW (819.36 hp) at 2,400 rpm
Maximum speed	approx. 65 kph (40.38 mph)
Range on roads	365 km (226.80 mi.)
Fuel capacity	1,120 liters (295.87 US gal.)
Fuel consumption (on roads)	approx. 300 liters / 100 km (0.78 mpg)
Suspension	torsion bar
Armor thickness	50 mm glacis

Furthermore, German industry was to be placed in a position as soon as possible to establish independent development and production capabilities for armored vehicles and thus achieve parity with international standards.

An initial design to meet military requirements for a 30-metric-ton (33-ton) tank was complete by the end of 1956. The possibility subsequently arose to also meet a French requirement, and in autumn 1958 an agreement was concluded for the development of a 30-metric-ton standard tank. Italy joined the agreement as a third nation (with observer status). Great Britain declined to participate in the standard tank program in 1957, since it did not agree with the French and German military requirements concerning the level of protection and the required mobility (power-to-weight ratio of 30 hp / metric ton [33 hp/ton]).

The Porsche PT I A design, a 33-metric-ton tank, July 1959

First-Generation Prototypes (Company Group A)

To exploit industrial creativity as comprehensively as possible, in May 1959 the German side concluded corresponding development contracts with three groups of companies:

- Company Group A, consisting of the companies Porsche, Jung-Jungenthal, and Luther & Jordan
- Company Group B, consisting of the companies Ing. Büro Warnecke, Henschel, and Rheinstahl-Hanomag
- Company Group C, consisting of the Borgward company

PT I A prototype on the Stegskopf, 1961

The contracts with Company Groups A and B covered the development of prototypes and the delivery of two vehicles each. The contract with the Borgward company covered the creation of concept studies and subsequently the investigation of future-oriented technologies.

Interestingly, a contract was also concluded with the French company DEFA for the delivery of two prototypes of the French standard tank; for this, Germany paid six million deutschmarks (DM).

The first prototypes were completed in 1960. Relatively low-risk components were chosen for the drive and running gear of the Company Group A vehicle. It had a 90 mm gun made by Rheinmetall. At that time, the only available power plant was the MB 837 Ba eight-cylinder diesel engine (485 kW–650 hp). The vehicle had seven road wheels per side, with torsion bar suspension. Interestingly, the driver still sat on the left side of the vehicle. The design exceeded the prescribed weight by 4.8 metric tons (5.29 tons, equivalent to 16 percent).

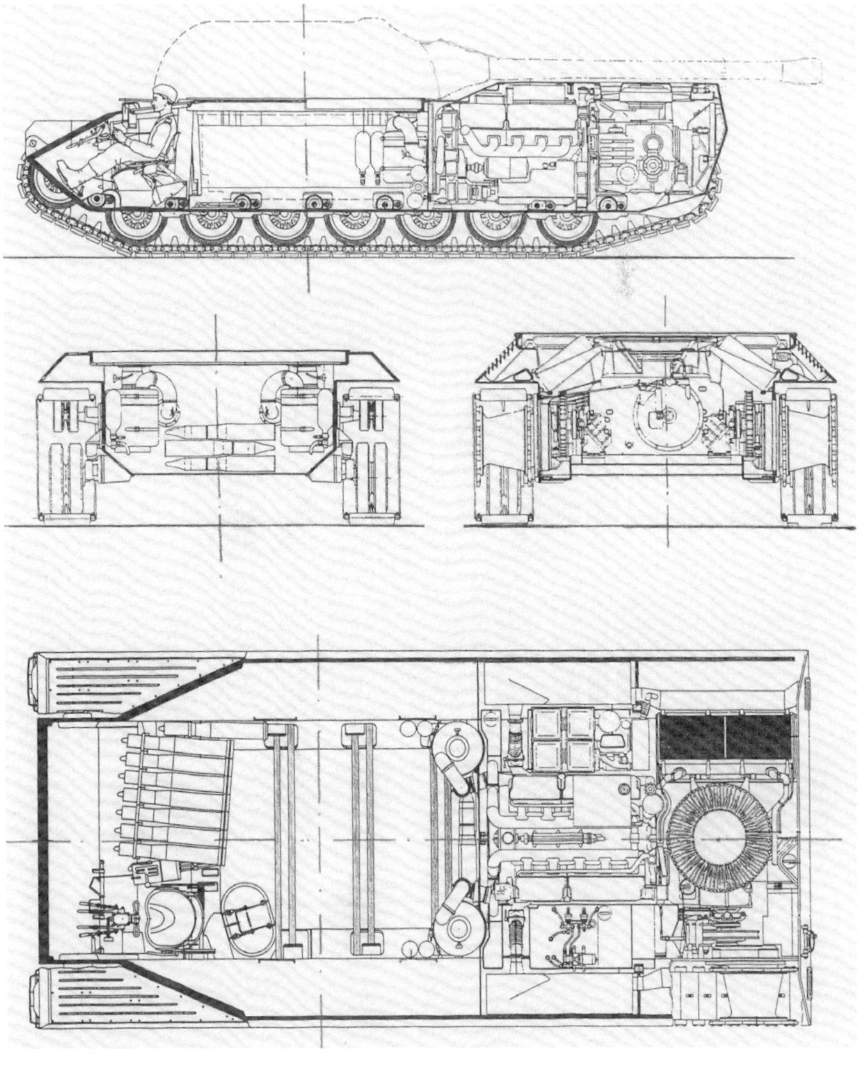

Four-view drawing of the PT I A: The two oil bath filters were housed in niches in the engine compartment bulkhead, analogous to the arrangement in the American M48 main battle tank. The two sets of batteries were placed next to the engine above the fuel tanks. This would remain unchanged until the preproduction vehicles. The inclined position of the radiators was not adopted for the second-generation PT. Remarkable is the use of inclined flange plates in the area of the swing arm bearings (fighting-compartment area). This was probably intended to provide better antimine protection (see Leopard 2 main battle tank).

Wooden model of the PT I A: Prior to the conclusion of the actual development contracts in May 1959, a number of companies worked on the concept of the "30-tonne standard tank." The first wooden models produced by the two company groups were displayed at the Erprobungsstelle E 91 testing station in Meppen in December 1959. The photo shows the wooden model from Company Group A with the 90 mm gun from the Rheinmetall company. Compared to the T-34/85, the turret height of the standard tank, which is 180 mm less, is quite noticeable.

Type	PT I A Prototype
Design period	1959–60
Crew	4
Combat weight	34.8 metric tons (38.36 tons)
Chassis length	6.71 meters (22.01 feet)
Width over tracks	3.15 meters (10.33 feet)
Height (turret roof)	2.20 meters (7.21 feet)
Main gun, caliber	90 mm Rheinmetall
Ammunition capacity	no information
Secondary weapon 1, caliber	7.62 mm mantlet machine gun
Secondary weapon 2, caliber	7.62 mm antiaircraft machine gun
Engine, type	MB 837 Ba 8-cylinder diesel
Rated output	485 kW (650.39 hp) at 2,200 rpm
Maximum speed	60 kph (37.28 mi.)
Range on roads	524 km (325.59 mi.)
Fuel capacity	1,008 liters (266.29 US gal.)
Fuel consumption (on roads)	192 liters / 100 km (1.23 mpg)
Suspension	torsion bar
Armor thickness	50 mm glacis

The first prototypes from the two company groups were completed in 1961. After brief factory trials, the vehicles were handed over to the Bundeswehr. In addition to the actual testing, the prototypes were demonstrated to various domestic and foreign delegations. The photo shows the first prototype from Company Group A with a Wegmann turret during a demonstration at Truppenübungsplatz Stegskopf (near Daaden). Note the vehicle's low silhouette (turret roof height: 2.20 meters), comparable to Soviet main battle tanks.

The openings designed to enable self-cleaning in difficult terrain are missing from the drive sprocket. Interestingly, this vehicle has already been retrofitted with the British 105 mm L7 tank gun. Germany procured this weapon in 1962, after development of a 105 mm smoothbore gun by Rheinmetall was delayed. In the area of the rear turret roof, there is a cupola for a fighting-compartment ventilator. This was later deleted because of the requirement for the tank to be able to be travel submerged (see T-55 main battle tank).

First-Generation Prototypes (Company Group B)

For the two prototypes from Company Group B, the Warnecke development office wanted to use future-oriented technologies in the drive and running-gear area. A hydrostatic superimposed steering system was planned as the transmission, which enabled stepless steering of the vehicle. The chassis was shorter than that of the prototypes produced by Company Group A, and thus six road wheels per side sufficed. Hydropneumatic suspension elements (on vehicle B I 1; Hanomag) and disk springs (on vehicle B I 2; Henschel) were used in the suspension systems. In terms of shape, the hull was more favorably designed than the prototype from Company Group A. The first prototypes surpassed the prescribed weight limit by 6.2 metric tons (6.8 tons, equivalent to 21 percent).

The first-generation prototypes were extensively tested between January 1961 and April 1962 at the Erprobungsstelle 91 testing center in Meppen. The Company Group B prototypes exhibited above-average failure rates—especially in the following components: hydropneumatic springs, hydraulic chain tensioner, steering gear, and track guidance.

While the first-generation prototypes were still being tested, contracts for the development and production of second-generation prototypes were signed with Company Groups A and B in the fall of 1961.

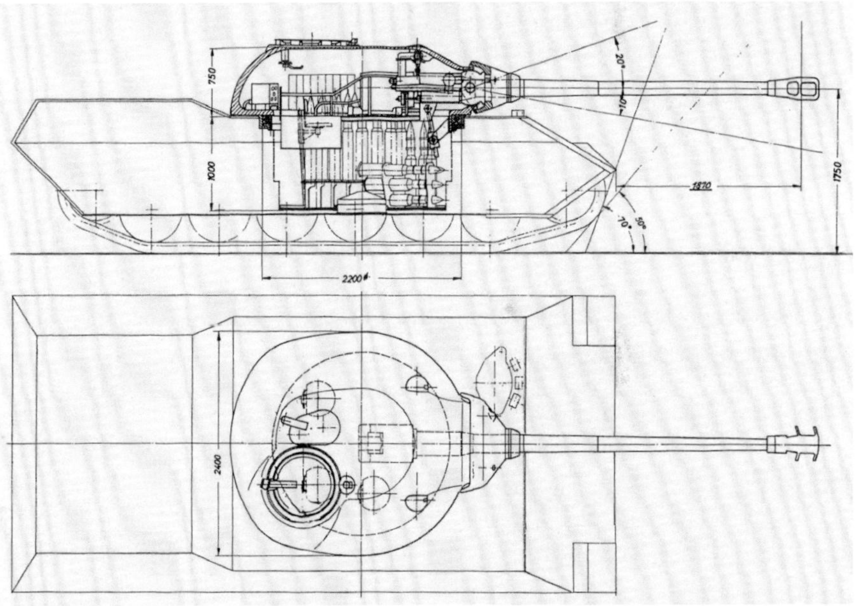

Two-view drawing of the PT I B: The 90 mm Rheinmetall gun in a Rheinmetall turret was still envisaged for the design when the drawing was made. At this design stage, the driver was still positioned on the left side. The loader's hatch was situated almost in the center of the turret, obviously to obtain a favorable turret shape—and thus directly over the shell-casing box! Also striking is the unique shape of the loader's hatch.

Wooden model of the PT I B in 1959: There was also a wooden model of Company Group B's concept available for inspection in 1959. The photo on the right shows the model next to an M48 A2 main battle tank; the difference in turret height was 53 cm (20.86 in.)! The hull front's simpler shape compared to the PT I A is noticeable. Here the driver's position has been correctly moved to the right side, giving the loader (standing on the left next to the main gun) better access to the ammunition stored in the front of the hull.

Type	PT I B Prototype
Design period	1959–60
Crew	4
Combat weight	36.2 metric tons (39.90 tons)
Chassis length	7.0 meters (22.96 feet)
Width over tracks	3.2 meters (10.49 feet)
Height (turret roof)	2.12 meters (6.95)
Main gun, caliber	90 mm Rheinmetall
Ammunition capacity	no information
Secondary weapon 1, caliber	7.62 mm mantlet machine gun
Secondary weapon 2, caliber	7.62 mm antiaircraft machine gun
Engine, type	MB 837 Ba 8-cylinder diesel
Rated output	485 kW (650.39 hp) at 2,200 rpm
Maximum speed	61 kph (37.90 mi.)
Range on roads	200 km (124.27 mi.)
Fuel capacity	420 liters (110.95 US gal.)
Fuel consumption (on roads)	210 liters / 100 km (1.12 mpg)
Suspension	hydropneumatic
Armor thickness	50 mm (glacis)

Below: **PT I B on the Stegskopf in 1961: A very favorable turret shape was achieved despite the blisters for the optical rangefinder. This was certainly due to the relatively short measuring base length (1.42 meters) of the rangefinder and the almost central position of the loader's hatch. To improve accuracy, a rangefinder with a base length of 1.72 meters was later adopted for the production version, resulting in a less favorable turret configuration.**

Below: **PT I B on the Stegskopf in 1961: Because of its greater road-wheel diameter, the PT I B got by with six road wheels per side. The drive sprockets correctly have the openings necessary for self-cleaning. There is no rear bustle on the Rheinmetall turret. This led to noticeable nose-heaviness, which would have had an unfavorable effect if the vehicle had been stabilized. Note the very shallow track rise angles at the front and rear.**

First-Generation Prototypes (Company Group C)

In the development center of the Carl F. W. Borgward company in Bremen, a comprehensive combat vehicle program was designed at the end of the 1950s—in addition to beautifully designed cars—which was characterized by the use of standardized assemblies. The 30-metric-ton battle tank design included in this program, with the designation RRV EP1-15/6, was far ahead of its time due to the selected assembly technologies and functionalities. The then head of the development center (Dipl. Ing. Erich Übelacker) planned a vehicle for this design that could move on wheels as well as on tracks (like the Russian BT tanks). The suspension would consist of hydropneumatic elements. Four six-cylinder boxer engines were planned for the drive. The three-man crew was located behind the turret. The turret, with the 105 mm tank gun, was spherically mounted and was stabilized on three axes.

The design was submitted to Company Group C for review for the Leopard 1 project. However, the client decided that no prototype should be built on this basis, since the development risks were considered extremely high. Instead, Borgward was subsequently commissioned to investigate the feasibility of a turret with three-axis stabilization.

Type	First-Generation Prototype, Company Group C
Design period	1959
Crew	3
Combat weight	approx. 30 metric tons (33 tons)
Chassis length	6.85 meters (21.58 feet)
Width over tracks	3.5 meters (11.48 feet)
Height (turret roof)	2.19 meters (7.18 feet)
Main gun, caliber	105 mm
Ammunition capacity	no information
Secondary weapon 1, caliber	20 mm cannon
Secondary weapon 2, caliber	no information
Engine, type	four 6 M 12VB 6-cylinder Boxer engines
Rated output	258 kW (345.98 hp)
Maximum speed	100 kph (62 mph) (with wheeled running gear)
Range on roads	no information
Fuel capacity	no information
Fuel consumption (on roads)	no information
Suspension	hydropneumatic

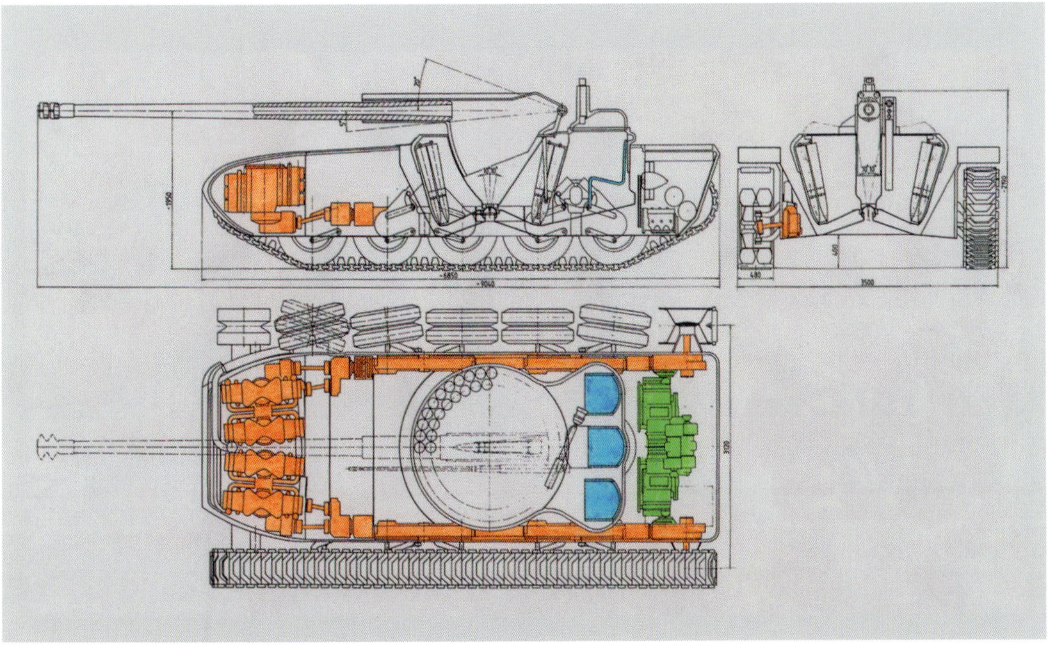

Borgward design
RRV EP-1-15

The AMX-30 Prototype

As part of the trilateral agreement among Germany, France, and Italy in September 1958, Germany also agreed to the purchase of two prototypes of the French standard tank. However, the vehicles were not delivered to Erprobungsstelle 41 in Trier until the end of 1963.

The prototypes were equipped with the French 105 mm tank gun, for which only two types of ammunition were available (a shaped-charge projectile with swirl-jacket stabilization and an explosive projectile). Compared to the German prototypes, the French vehicles were smaller, narrower, and less well armored. With a weight of 31.6 metric tons (34.8 tons), these prototypes only just exceeded the original weight requirement. At this time, the French prototypes were still all powered by a twelve-cylinder boxer engine, and they were clearly inferior to the German vehicles in terms of drive and chassis performance. Fortunately, a prototype of the AMX-30 has been preserved and is now part of the German Federal Office of Defense Technology and Procurement's Defense Technology Study Collection (Wehrtechnische Studiensammlung, or WTS), where military engineers still have the opportunity to study the unique design of the vehicle's cooling system, for example.

Type	AMX 30 Prototype
Design period	ca. 1961
Crew	4
Combat weight	31.6 metric tons (34.83 tons)
Chassis length	6.6 meters (21.65 feet)
Width over tracks	3.1 meters (10.17 feet)
Height (turret roof)	2.42 meters (7.93 feet)
Main gun, caliber	105 mm DEFA tank gun
Ammunition capacity	58 rounds
Secondary weapon 1, caliber	7.62 mm mantlet machine gun
Secondary weapon 2, caliber	no information
Engine, type	12-cylinder Boxer engine
Rated output	550 kW (737.56 hp)
Maximum speed	65 kph (40.38 mph)
Range on roads	350 km (217.47 mi.)
Fuel capacity	920 liters (243.04 US gal.)
Fuel consumption (on roads)	263 liters / 100 km (0.89 mpg)
Suspension	torsion bar
Armor thickness	40 mm (glacis)

View from above of the AMX 30 prototype: While the turret was made entirely of cast homogeneous armor (without a welded-in-place turret roof made of rolled steel), the forward part of the hull was also cast—the rear part, however, was made of welded rolled steel plates. This concept later gained favor; for example, on the turret and hull of the British Chieftain tank. The slots visible on the hull sides were used to suck in air for the radiator and engine compartment ventilation. This meant that the air ducting took up a large, unarmored space. The concept was changed in the preproduction model.

Second-Generation Prototypes (Company Group A)

After serious problems arose during development of the 90 mm tank gun by Rheinmetall, the Federal Ministry of Defense ordered 1,500 L7 tank guns (105 mm caliber) from Great Britain in the autumn of 1962. These were manufactured by the British state-owned Royal Ordnance Factory (ROF) in Nottingham. At the same time, the decision was made to procure the British 12.7 mm ranging machine gun. By installing the ranging machine gun in the turrets of the second-generation prototype, it was possible to optimize the turret shape; at the same time, it was hoped that the optical rangefinder would offer greater reliability and cost savings. With the order of 1,500 tank guns from Great Britain, there was no longer any prospect of a uniform armament for the Franco-German standard tank. The driver was now placed on the right side, so as to be able to position the ammunition magazine on the left side, directly in front of the loader. As a result of the integration of the 105 mm weapons system and taking into consideration foreign requirements, this vehicle exceeded the prescribed weight limit by 9 metric tons (9.9 tons, equivalent to 30 percent).

Type	Second-Generation Prototype, Company Group A
Design period	1960–61
Crew	4
Combat weight	39 metric tons (43 tons)
Chassis length	6.83 meters (22.40 feet)
Width over tracks	3.25 meters (10.66 feet)
Height (turret roof)	2.31 meters (7.57 feet)
Main gun, caliber	105 mm L7A3
Ammunition capacity	63 rounds
Secondary weapon 1, caliber	12.7 mm
Secondary weapon 2, caliber	7.62 mm
Engine, type	MB 838 Ca 500 10-cylinder diesel
Rated output	610 kW (818 hp)
Maximum speed	65 kph (40.38 mph)
Range on roads	600 km (372.82 mi.)
Fuel capacity	1,000 liters (264.17 US gal.)
Fuel consumption (on roads)	165 liters / 100 km (1.43 mpg)
Suspension	torsion bar
Armor thickness	70 mm (glacis)

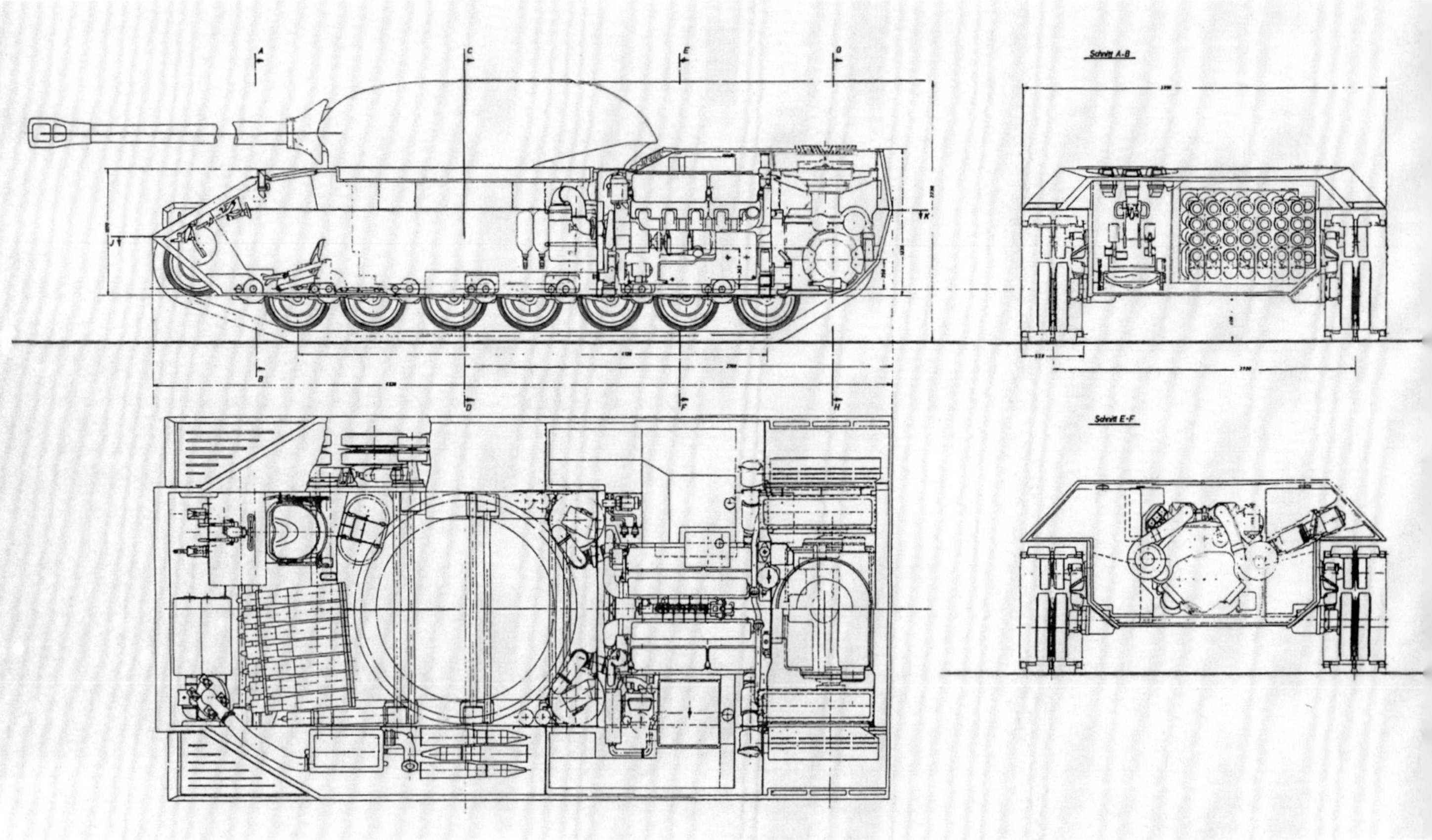

Four-view drawing of the PT II A: On the second-generation prototypes (Company Group A), the ammunition magazine was moved to the left side (loader's side)—while the driver's compartment was moved to the right. The pushed swing arms on the sixth and seventh road-wheel stations were also abandoned. The arrangement of some of the ammunition in the fighting compartment as well as the air filters and the batteries did not yet correspond to the later production version. The Rheinmetall gun was still planned in this design.

Prototype II A with Rheinmetall turret: The picture shows the M II 15 vehicle produced by MaK in Munster. In contrast to the Wegmann turret, the Rheinmetall turret is conspicuous by its lack of a prominent rear bustle. The turret also has a different mantlet design, although its shape already contains features of the later mantlet of the production turret. The British 105 mm gun was already available for installation on this prototype.

In autumn 1961 the development and production contracts for the second-generation prototypes were issued to Company Groups A and B. Company Group A was to build twenty-six vehicles, and Company Group B six vehicles. The MB 838 Ca 500 ten-cylinder diesel engine, which was later also adopted for the production tanks, was now available to power the vehicles. For the first time, the vehicles were required to be submersible to a depth of 4 meters (13 feet). Testing of the second-generation prototypes took place between 1961 and 1963.

This photo shows vehicle J II 14 produced by the Jung-Jungenthal company (Kirchen/Sieg). In this phase, a 12.7 mm zeroing machine gun was installed experimentally in place of the rangefinder, to achieve a better ballistic turret shape. The British 105 mm gun was also installed in this prototype. The forward track shields are still made of metal parts, which were often damaged when approaching obstacles (resulting in high replacement costs).

Rear view of a II A prototype with Wegmann turret: The view from the rear shows the early forms of the toolboxes and outboard intercom on the rear of the tank. The protrusion of the rear plate in relation to the track in the area of the drive sprocket is clearly visible—this feature was undesirable since it led to damaging of components attached to the rear plate when descending grades.

II A prototype with Wegmann turret: The photo shows a vehicle during a demonstration at Munster. Sikorsky H-34 helicopters can be seen taking off in the background. Note the vehicle's more favorable turret shape, achieved by deleting the rangefinder's optical heads.

Second-Generation Prototypes (Company Group B)

Due to the increasingly obvious inferiority of the vehicles from Company Group B, production was reduced from the original six vehicles to two for cost reasons. Vehicle weight rose to 39.6 metric tons (43.7 tons), partly due to the larger weapon including ammunition and a further increase in armor thickness.

The troops rejected the 12.7 mm ranging machine gun as unusable, since the trajectories of the main gun and the ranging machine gun deviated considerably, especially when firing at longer ranges. As a result, German industry was immediately commissioned to develop a new coincidence/stereoscopic rangefinder with a base length increased to 1.72 meters (5.6 feet). In contrast to the arrangement on the American main battle tanks, the rangefinder was placed next to the gunner on the turrets of the preproduction vehicles. This meant that the commander was not burdened with engaging hostile targets and could concentrate on commanding the vehicle.

Type	Second-Generation Prototype, Company Group B
Design period	1960–61
Crew	4
Combat weight	39.6 metric tons (43.65 tons)
Chassis length	6.83 meters (22.40 meters)
Width over tracks	3.25 meters (10.66 feet)
Height (turret roof)	2.31 meters (7.57 feet)
Main gun, caliber	105 mm L7A3
Ammunition capacity	63 rounds
Secondary weapon 1, caliber	12.7 mm
Secondary weapon 2, caliber	7.62 mm
Engine, type	MB 838 Ca 500 10-cylinder diesel
Rated output	610 kW (818 hp)
Maximum speed	65 kph (40.38 mph)
Range on roads	600 km (372.82 mi.)
Fuel capacity	1,000 liters (264.17 US gal.)
Fuel consumption (on roads)	165 liters / 100 km (1.43 mpg)
Suspension	hydropneumatic (B II 1) torsion bar (B II 2)
Armor thickness	70 mm (glacis)

II B prototype, running gear area: The picture shows the position of the hydropneumatic suspension elements on the road-wheel swing arms. A hydraulic cylinder was provided on the swing arm of the idler wheel to maintain the chain tension. The openings in the idler wheel, which were intended to enable better self-cleaning, are noteworthy.

II B prototype with Rheinmetall turret: The picture shows a vehicle in the WTS inventory at the Herongen storage depot (2006). As with many vehicles that were equipped with a hydropneumatic suspension, oil or gas loss occurred in the suspension elements of this suspension system after long periods of immobility, causing the vehicles to lose their ground clearance. The different design of the rear plate and the position of the exhaust air gratings (compared to the Company Group A prototype) are noteworthy.

II B prototype with Rheinmetall turret: The picture shows one of the II B prototypes with a Rheinmetall turret in the airfield at Trier-Föhren. High-speed tests were carried out there as part of the technical trials. The simpler shape of the hull in the front and side areas can be seen.

II B prototype, engine compartment: The picture provides a view of the front area of the engine compartment. On the left-hand side, next to the main engine, the auxiliary engine for power generation when the main engine is stopped can be seen. The position of the cooling-air outlets directly next to the central intake opening is less than ideal from a thermal point of view.

Leopard 1 Preproduction Version

The lessons learned from the first- and second-generation prototypes in testing and service trials were incorporated into the design of the preproduction series vehicles. Development of the preproduction model was begun in the summer of 1961. This was followed in early 1962 by an order for fifty vehicles, which were built by the Jung & Jungenthal, MaK, and Luther & Jordan companies in the 1962–64 period. The relatively large number of preproduction vehicles was necessary to test the new rangefinder in service trials and to carry out the final series of tests on the components at the testing stations.

Numerous improvements were incorporated into the preproduction version. For the first time the vehicle was fitted with active infrared equipment for night fighting. Generator output was increased to 7 kW (9.38 hp), allowing the auxiliary motor to be deleted. The turret, with mantlet, and the engine compartment cover and cold-air-exit gratings were modified compared to those of the second-generation prototypes. Combat weight reached 39.6 metric tons (43.65 tons).

Type	Leopard 1 Pre-Production
Design period	1961–62
Crew	4
Combat weight	39.6 metric tons (43.65 tons)
Chassis length	7.0 meters (22.96 feet)
Width over tracks	3.25 meters (10.66 feet)
Height (turret roof)	2.39 meters (7.84 feet)
Main gun, caliber	105 mm L7A3 L/51
Ammunition capacity	62 rounds
Secondary weapon 1, caliber	7.62 mm
Secondary weapon 2, caliber	7.62 mm
Engine, type	MB 838 Ca 500 10-cylinder diesel
Rated output	610 kW (818 hp)
Maximum speed	65 kph (40.38 mph)
Range on roads	650 km (403.89 mi.)
Fuel capacity	1,020 liters (269.46 US gal.)
Fuel consumption (on roads)	157 liters / 100 km (1.50 mpg)
Suspension	torsion bar
Armor thickness	70 mm (glacis)

Preproduction versions of the Leopard 1 and AMX 30

Preproduction vehicle climbing a sheet pile wall: The preproduction vehicle was used to carry out initial underwater-driving tests in the Kiel Fjord. For this purpose, the underwater-driving shaft was placed on the opening of the commander's hatch. The sharp upper edge of the sheet piling enabled a positive fit with the track and thus optimum traction. During this operation, the commander performed extremely large angular movements in the underwater-driving shaft—which required a correspondingly strong nervous system and a stable circulatory system.

Preproduction vehicle during deep wading: After activating the “diving hydraulics” and closing the openings for the turret’s telescopic sight, mantlet machine gun, and main gun, the preproduction vehicle was ready for deep wading after just a few minutes of preparation. A critical aspect of this operation is the risk of splash water entering the open commander’s hatch.

A preproduction Leopard 1 with HS 30 infantry-fighting vehicle: This advertising photo was supposed to demonstrate the combined use of tanks and infantry-fighting vehicles. The HS 30 was never in the position to follow the Leopard 1 main battle tanks on the battlefield (in terms of speed). There were also considerable differences in the level of protection.

Turret of a preproduction vehicle during technical trials. The picture shows a preproduction-series turret on the OBP (stationary movement platform) for testing weapon stabilization at the former E 91 test site in Meppen. On this platform, hydraulic drives were used to simulate typical movements in all three axes as they affected the turret during cross-country travel. The picture also shows the relatively large size of the mantlet—this was to be further optimized and reduced in size for the production version. A round shape was also planned for the loader's hatch in the series—this resulted in identical parts for the loader's and commander's hatches.

AMX-30 Preproduction Version

In June 1963—a few months before the official trilateral comparative trials between the German and the French models—the preproduction model of the AMX-30 was unveiled to the public in France. Compared to the prototypes, which still looked a little clunky, the pre-series version made a much more pleasing impression. The turret neck was removed, and the turret was made flatter and longer overall. In the hull, the engine compartment and cooling system, including cooling-air ducting, were made much more compact; overall, the vehicle was significantly smaller and lighter than the German model—the different ergonomic design of the crew positions was noticeable here, among other things. Remarkably, a 12.7 mm machine gun was installed in the flat commander's cupola. Of the seven preproduction vehicles, six were still equipped with the gasoline engine, while the seventh was for the first time powered by the multifuel variant of the twelve-cylinder boxer engine. In demonstrations, the vehicles impressed with their ability to travel underwater and the accuracy of their weapons. The new rangefinder, with a base length of 2 meters (6.56 feet), certainly played a decisive role in the latter.

Compared to the preproduction model of the Leopard, the AMX-30 had a maintenance-intensive centrifugal clutch (Leopard: torque converter); the driver's hatch of the AMX-30 was unfavorably located in the sloped glacis plate, and an engine change took approximately forty-five minutes (Leopard: approximately fifteen to twenty minutes).

At the time, there was an opinion among experts that the AMX-30 had the better turret and the Leopard 1 the more capable chassis.

Type	AMX 30 Preproduction
Design period	1962
Crew	4
Combat weight	32.5 metric tons (35.82 tons)
Chassis length	6.59 meters (21.62 feet)
Width over tracks	3.1 meters (10.17 feet)
Height (turret roof)	2.28 meters (7.48 feet)
Main gun, caliber	105 mm DEFA tank gun
Ammunition capacity	56 rounds
Secondary weapon 1, caliber	12.7 mm antiaircraft machine gun
Secondary weapon 2, caliber	7.62 mm mantlet machine gun
Engine, type	Sofam 12 GSdS 12-cylinder Boxer engine
Rated output	530 kW (710.74 hp) at 2,800 rpm
Maximum speed	65 kph (40.38 mph)
Range on roads	480 km (298.25 mi.)
Fuel capacity	1,200 liters (317 US gal.)
Fuel consumption (on roads)	250 liters / 100 km (0.94 mpg)
Suspension	torsion bar
Armor thickness	70 mm (glacis)

Warm-Weather Trials

To test the functions and performance of the Leopard 1 main battle tank under extreme heat and dust conditions, extensive driving and firing tests were carried out in the summer of 1964 in Veneto and on the island of Sardinia, using two preproduction vehicles—including participation by Italian tank crews.

Endurance trials showed that the cooling system allowed unrestricted engine operation up to an outside temperature of 39 degrees Celsius. The high dust concentration (sometimes over 3 g/m^3) made necessary a revision of the air filtration system. Further improvements in this respect were expected through the planned installation of side skirts. The high outside temperatures led to significantly higher wear on the rubber tires of the road wheels, and the high temperatures in the fuel system (vapor bubble formation) meant that multifuel operation of the engine was no longer possible under these conditions.

Surprisingly, firing tests showed a strong influence of solar radiation on deformation of the gun barrel; retrofitting with a thermal sleeve was urgently required. Under the arid conditions, the formation of streaks in the air layers meant that the coincidence method could not be used when using the rangefinder—in contrast, the stereoscopic method delivered better results.

Overall, the Italian tank crews were impressed by the performance and reliability of the preproduction vehicles. The hard testing in the previous years had paid off! After Belgium, the Netherlands, and Norway, Italy—the fourth NATO country—also decided to adopt the Leopard 1 main battle tank at the end of 1969.

Cold-Weather Trials

In addition to warm-weather trials, the performance of the Leopard 1 main battle tank under severe winter conditions also had to be tested under operational conditions. To this end, extensive tests were carried out at Camp Shilo (Canada) at the beginning of 1966 and the Norwegian Armored Forces School at the beginning of 1967; during the trials, the outside temperatures sometimes reached −44 degrees Celsius.

The vehicles proved to be generally suitable for winter use; nevertheless, the tests revealed the need for improvement in certain areas. For example, the fighting-compartment heating proved to be insufficiently reliable during continuous operation; heat distribution in the fighting compartment also had to be revised. When driving off-road in deep snow, the intake grille for the engine combustion air occasionally iced up completely or became clogged. Here, too, an improvement was expected with the planned side skirts.

The fully rubberized D 139 track proved itself only to a limited extent in winter conditions; especially on packed snow, aids to improve traction were absolutely necessary. In the D 640 A system track, which was already under development at the time, appropriate options for the use of snow grousers and ice studs were considered. Interestingly, in individual cases, freezing meltwater, which got from the engine compartment cover into the turret ring, caused the turret to become jammed after the vehicles had been parked outside overnight!

Tank Flotation Experiments

In 1965, information was received from Great Britain about successful experiments aimed at turning the Centurion and Chieftain main battle tanks into amphibious swimming tanks with the help of erectable folding walls (glass-fiber-reinforced plastic panels; Pearsons & Sons system), and a set of flotation equipment was ordered for the Leopard 1 main battle tank. Although these vehicles were capable of underwater travel (up to a water depth of 4 meters), flotation was seriously considered, since it was felt that the watertightness of the vehicles could not always be guaranteed after a long period of use. In addition,

The Pearson flotation system on land

The Pearson flotation system in the water

flotation was an advantage in critical conditions near the river bottom (obstacles, mud, etc.) or if there was a risk of the crossing point being mined.

In addition to advocating for the erectable folding walls of the Pearson system, Porsche suggested that the necessary buoyancy for flotation could be achieved by attaching large buoyancy bodies made of polyurethane foam to the vehicle. This solution would have been easier to install on the vehicle and also cheaper than the British system. During trials by E 41 on the Moselle River in 1967, the limits and problems of both solutions became clear relatively quickly: The floating vehicles could not be maneuvered safely in fast-moving water. In addition, both systems entailed a considerable logistical effort (transport volume). For this reason, the floating version of the Leopard 1 main battle tank was ultimately abandoned.

The Porsche flotation system on land

The Porsche flotation system in the water

Chapter 2

Bundeswehr Production Version

Delivery of the First Production Vehicle

After a development period of just nine years, on September 9, 1965, Krauss-Maffei AG of Munich delivered the first Leopard 1 production vehicle to the Bundeswehr. Krauss-Maffei AG had emerged victorious from the Federal Office of Defense Technology and Procurement's four-party competition and became general contractor for the Leopard 1 program, even though the company had not been involved in the development of the Leopard 1! (The Krauss-Maffei company had, however, built approximately two thousand half-tracks and light armored vehicles during the Second World War.) As general contractor, Krauss-Maffei AG was responsible for the overall coordination of the program. The Leopard 1 main battle tank was made up of approximately 11,400 individual parts produced by 2,700 companies; 4,600 drawings were required for production of these parts. A further 520 companies acted as direct suppliers to Krauss-Maffei AG.

Handover of the first Leopard 1 production vehicle

After the official welcoming speech, on September 5, 1965, the spokesman of the Krauss-Maffei AG Board of Management handed over the first production vehicle to the then minister of defense, Mr. Kai-Uwe von Hassel. He symbolically handed over the keys to the then inspector of the army (General de Maiziere), who then gave them to the tank crew from Panzer Lehrbataillon 93 (93rd Armored Training Battalion), based at Munster.

Thanks to systematic development and extensive testing, the Leopard was an extremely reliable, powerful, and troop-capable weapons system as delivered. Before the first production vehicle was completed, eighty-two prototypes and preproduction vehicles had been built, tested, and improved. This effort was well worth it—as the success of the Leopard 1 on the international tank market would later show. The development costs up to series production amounted to 249,030 DM. With the introduction of the Leopard 1, the M47 main battle tanks in Bundeswehr service could be successively replaced as part of a half-generational change.

Production Chassis

For production of the Leopard 1 main battle tank, Krauss-Maffei AG had built an assembly line with seventeen individual cycles in addition to a high-bay warehouse and an elaborate test track. Some of the main assemblies—including the hull shell, engine, transmission, and turret—were supplied directly to the final assembly line by subcontractors.

On cycle stand 1, the hull casing was placed on a carriage; in a first work step, torsion bars, swing arms, and road wheels were fitted. From cycle stand 2, the chassis could then move on its own wheels. In the following cycles, all individual parts and assemblies, including cabling, were installed. Some cycle stands were used exclusively for carrying out control work and functional tests as part of the quality assurance process. The tracks were fitted on the last two cycle stands, and the turret was mounted so that the vehicle could then leave the hall under its own power and drive on the test tracks. Once the vehicle had passed all the tests (including on the steep and transverse slopes and the deep wading pool), it was presented to the representative of the Bundeswehr quality inspection service for handover, which included the test reports. The assembly of a vehicle at Krauss-Maffei took approximately two days.

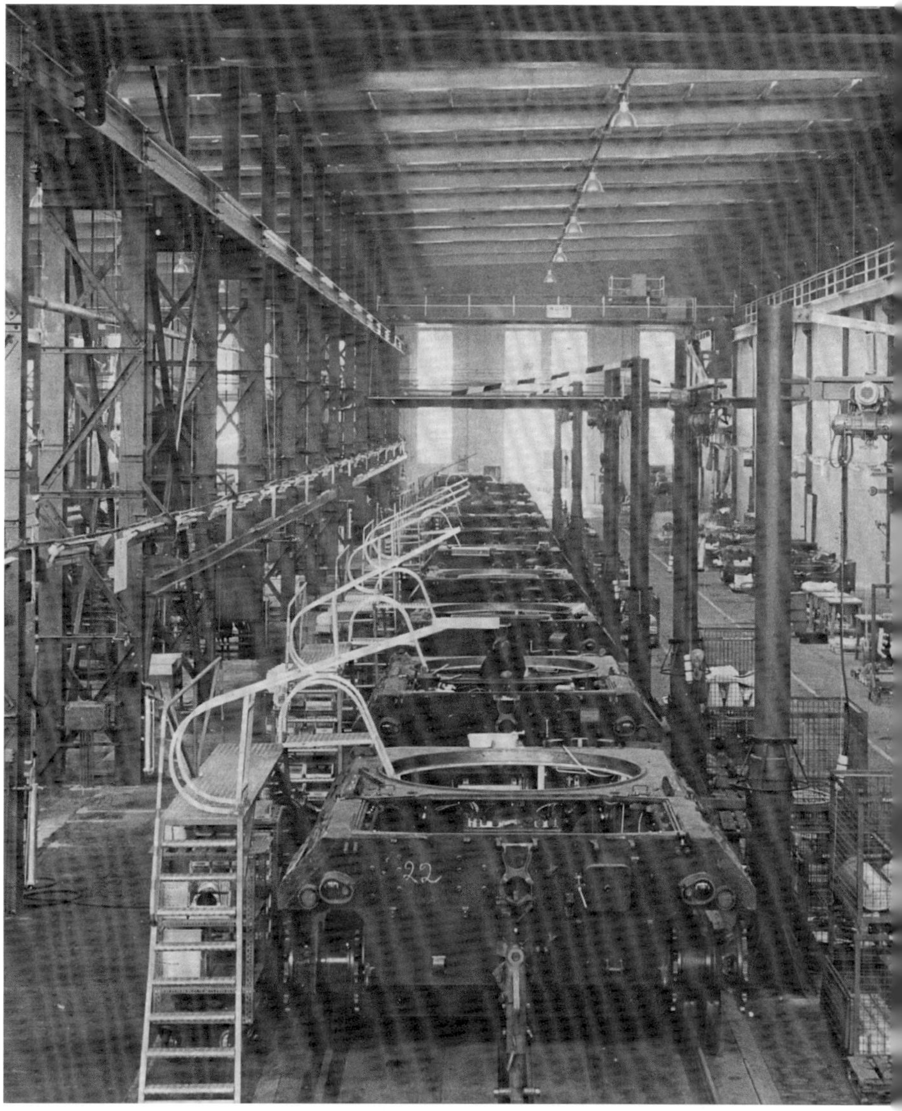

Production Turret

The turrets of the first four or five production batches of the Leopard 1 main battle tank were made of cast homogeneous steel armor. This was then-current practice, since the turrets of the Russian T-54/-55/-62 main battle tanks, the American M47/48/60 main battle tanks, and the British Centurion and Chieftain main battle tanks all were cast products. The Leopard 1's rival, the French AMX-30 main battle tank, also had a cast turret. Casting technology allowed a relatively high degree of freedom in the shaping of the components, which was reflected in the design of the turret front, including the rangefinder blisters. The ability to make a turret with varying wall thicknesses—for example, at the transitions from the turret front to the sides, or from the sides to the roof—was also an advantage.

The turret shells were supplied by various foundries to the companies Rheinmetall in Düsseldorf and Wegmann & Co. in Kassel. The mechanical machining of the turrets required very large boring mills—for example, for machining the turret ring mount (diameter: 2,200 mm). On the other hand, the machining of the mount for the main weapon (trunnion bearings) and the optics required the utmost precision. The subsequent installation of the optics, including the connecting elements to the weapon, also required the highest precision so that the required accuracy could be achieved when firing.

Even though the turret of the Leopard 1 main battle tank was basically a conventional design, the installation of the numerous turret components (e.g., elements of the elevating and traversing system, targeting and observation equipment, control elements, slip ring assemblies, cabling) proved to be a highly demanding task.

Before delivery of the turrets to Krauss-Maffei AG, the adjustment and tracking accuracy of the weapon and optics—as well as the functioning of the elements of the aiming system—were carefully checked on a turret test stand during final acceptance. The turret's empty weight was 9.1 metric tons (10 tons).

Leopard 1 Production Version

The British 105 mm L7A3 gun (L/51 caliber length) was selected as the main armament for the Leopard 1 main battle tank. At the time, this gun formed the main armament of many Western battle tanks. The Bundeswehr chose three types of ammunition for this weapon (APDS—armor-piercing discarding sabot, HEAT—high-explosive antitank, and HESH—high-explosive squash head). Aiming of the turret and gun is accomplished by means of an electrohydraulic turret drive (produced under license from Cadillac-Gage). When production began in 1965, there was no production-ready gun stabilization system available. Secondary armament consisted of two MG 3 machine guns, one firing through the mantlet and the other on the turret for use as an antiaircraft machine gun.

The Leopard 1 was equipped with a panoramic telescopic sight for the commander and an optical rangefinder and telescopic sight for the gunner. The Leopard 1 was one of the first main battle tanks to implement the so-called "hunter-killer" principle. The commander could concentrate on battlefield observation and target designation—for this he used the panoramic telescopic sight, the magnification of which could be varied from 6× to 20×. The actual target engagement was the responsibility of the gunner, who had the optical rangefinder with 16× magnification at his disposal. Range measurement could be carried out according to the stereoscopic or coincidence method. The distance measured by the gunner was transferred to the sighting mark in the optics (dependent sighting mark) via cam disks with the appropriate choice of ammunition, since the elevation angle had to be corrected. All other correction values (e.g., lead, cant, crosswind influence) had to be considered by the gunner himself.

For night fighting, the panoramic telescopic sight at the commander's position was replaced by an infrared telescopic sight. In conjunction with the IR/white-light spotlight, it was possible to fire from ranges of up to approximately 1,000 meters. It was not possible to measure distances at night; all correction values had to be calculated by the commander himself.

Leopard 1 production version, seen from the right

A production Leopard 1 during a field parade: The photo shows a production vehicle from the third batch during a field parade on the Nürburgring racetrack. The shape of the mantlet was further optimized (reduced in size) compared to the preproduction series. The side-mounted blisters of the optical range-finder led to a less-than-optimal turret configuration.

If the onboard power supply failed, a corresponding emergency (manual) mode was provided for all relevant functions (targeting, aiming, firing).

In terms of tactical and operational mobility, the Leopard 1 occupied a leading position among the main battle tanks of the time. Its powerful ten-cylinder MB 838 CaM 500 diesel engine from MTU, with a rated output of 611 kW (819 hp), resulted in an above-average power-to-weight ratio of 15.3 kW / metric ton. Since the engine was supercharged via a mechanical compressor, it also had good load response characteristics. A significant advance over the American main battle tanks was the transition to a diesel engine. This resulted not only in much more favorable fuel consumption, with 165 liters per 100 km on roads (M 48 A2: approximately 500 liters per 100 km), but also a reduced vulnerability of the vehicle. The dual-radius superimposed steering gear from ZF proved to be the best solution during the prototype tests. A wear-free torque converter provided a high starting torque when required. A capable running gear, with seven road wheels with torsion bar suspension on each side, enabled the high engine output to be converted into a high degree of maneuverability, even off-road. Total suspension travel on individual road wheels was up to 407 mm; five hydraulic telescopic shock absorbers were available on each side of the chassis to give the vehicle favorable vibration characteristics. When series production began, the vehicles were delivered with the D 139 track with rubber pads. This track had to be completely discarded when the V-shaped track pads wore out, and it and also exhibited insufficient traction in winter conditions. These disadvantages were eliminated by the D 640 A track, which was introduced later.

Since hollow-charge warheads with penetration rates of 400–500 mm of armor steel were already available in the 1960s, the Leopard 1 design abandoned the race against ammunition effectiveness and limited ballistic protection to wall thicknesses of a maximum of 70–100 mm. Protection in the extended sense was also provided by an NBC protective ventilation system and a smoke discharger system with four mortars on each side of the turret. An automatic fire-extinguishing system was also installed in the engine compartment.

The procurement costs for the first production vehicles amounted to 974,000 DM per unit. Due to retrofitting and modernization measures (as well as inflation), the unit price later rose to 2.5 million DM (Leopard 1 A4).

A production vehicle on the Krauss-Maffei company's testing grounds. In the photo can be seen the original, full-rubber D 139 track with V-shaped pads. With this track the vehicle proved uncontrollable on hard-packed snow surfaces in winter. This track was, however, lighter than the D 640 system track introduced later and produced less vibration. The shape of the emergency escape hatch can be seen in the hull floor.

Side-by-side comparison of the Leopard 1 and Chieftain main battle tanks. The photo shows the Chieftain's more powerful main gun. The different track designs are interesting: Chieftain has a hinge joint track; Leopard 1, an end link track. The Chieftain's mantletless gun mounting provided better protection for the turret front; however, removal of the main gun was a time-consuming task that took hours (the weapon was pulled out through the opened rear turret wall). Removal of the Leopard 1's main gun, on the other hand, took about thirty minutes.

Series vehicle from the third production batch (3rd Company, 93rd Tank Training Battalion) during an exercise at the Munster-North training grounds. The left front track shield has been lost or torn off. This vehicle already has the new D 640 system track with replaceable rubber pads. The rack for attaching snow grousers on the upper glacis is still missing. On the older version of this track, ice studs could be fitted in the area of the central connectors.

Comparison of the KPz 70 and Leopard 1 tanks. This photo provides an interesting comparison between the two main battle tanks. Because the driver was housed in the hull of the Leopard 1, the hull roof was higher than that of the KPz 70. Due to the KPz 70's taller turret, however, in the end there was little difference in the overall heights of the two vehicles. Note the clearly longer turret of the KPz 70, the rear of which housed an automatic loader.

Type	Leopard 1
Introduction period	1965–70
Crew	4
Combat weight	40 metric tons (44.09 tons)
Chassis length	6.94 meters (22.76 feet)
Width over tracks	3.25 meters (10.66 feet)
Height (turret roof)	2.39 meters (7.84 feet)
Main gun, caliber	105 mm L7A3 L/51
Ammunition capacity	60 rounds
Secondary weapon 1, caliber	7.62 mm mantlet machine gun
Secondary weapon 2, caliber	7.62 mm antiaircraft machine gun
Engine, type	MB 838 CaM 500 10-cylinder diesel, supercharger
Rated output	610 kW (818 hp)
Maximum speed	65 kph (40.38 mph)
Range on roads	560 km (347.96 mi.)
Fuel capacity	985 liters (260.21 US gal.)
Fuel consumption (on roads)	175 liters / 100 km (1.34 mpg)
Suspension	torsion bar
Armor thickness	70 mm (sloped at 30 degrees)

AMX-30 (Production Version)

The first AMX-30 main battle tanks were delivered to the French army in 1966, a year after production of the Leopard 1 began. Weighing in at 36 metric tons (39.7 tons), the AMX-30 was 4 metric tons (4.4 tons) lighter than the Leopard 1, but because of its less powerful engine and less capable running gear, it was also less mobile. The AMX-30 was armed with the French-designed 105 mm CN-105-F1 gun, which, with a barrel length of 56 caliber, was somewhat longer than the Leopard 1's main gun (L/51). The AMX-30's main gun was capable of firing HEAT and HESH rounds as well as illumination and smoke ammunition. The Obus G HEAT round's projectile consisted of an outer shell and a suspended inner shell, which were separated by ball bearings. This meant that the projectile spin was not transferred to the inner shell with the warhead, resulting in a relatively high penetration performance of greater than 360 mm of armor steel (regardless of range). The ammunition was extremely expensive, however. Ammunition

Type	AMX 30 Preproduction
Introduction period	1966–81
Crew	4
Combat weight	36 metric tons (39.68 tons)
Chassis length	6.59 meters (21.62 feet)
Width over tracks	3.1 meters (10.17 feet)
Height (turret roof)	2.29 meters (7.51 feet)
Main gun, caliber	CN 105 F-1 105 mm
Ammunition capacity	47 rounds
Secondary weapon 1, caliber	20 mm
Secondary weapon 2, caliber	7.62 mm
Engine, type	12-cylinder diesel
Rated output	530 kW (710.74 hp)
Maximum speed	65 kph (40.38 mph)
Range on roads	420 km (260.97 mi.)
Fuel capacity	970 liters (256.25 US gal.)
Fuel consumption (on roads)	230 liters / 100 km (1.02 mpg)
Suspension	torsion bar
Armor thickness	79 mm (sloped at 16 degrees)

capacity was forty-seven rounds, which was less than the Leopard 1 (sixty rounds). Secondary armament consisted of a 7.62 mm machine gun on the commander's cupola and a coaxial 20 mm cannon mounted to the left of the main gun. In contrast to the Leopard 1, the AMX-30's rangefinder (base length: 2 meters) was assigned to the commander, who was thus additionally burdened with tasks associated with engaging hostile targets. The tank was powered by a multifuel twelve-cylinder boxer engine with a rated output of 530 kW (710 hp). The transmission had a centrifugal clutch instead of a torque converter. The chassis was less capable than that of the Leopard 1, with five road wheels with torsion bar suspension; maximum total suspension travel was 278 mm (Leopard 1: 407 mm). To save weight, the AMX-30 was fitted with a steel track with rubber pads; since the track pins had no rubber bushings, maximum service life was 3,000 km (Leopard 1: approximately 6,000 km).

The AMX-30's turret was a one-piece casting. The "beak" at the front of the hull was also a cast part, while the rest of the hull consisted of welded armor steel plates. A total of 1,340 vehicles were produced for the French army from 1966 to 1981. Another one thousand vehicles were exported to a total of eight nations (Leopard: twelve nations).

Leopard 1 A1

With the first combat-effectiveness upgrade, numerous improvements were implemented on the Leopard 1 main battle tank, some of which had been initiated and trialed during prototype development—but did not reach production maturity until the fall of 1965. Starting in 1972, the retrofitting of the vehicles produced to date (batches 1 to 4) began with the following measures:

- Track skirts consisting of rubber-coated perforated plates were fitted in the area of the running gear, which improved protection against HEAT rounds fired from the flanks. The track skirts also reduced the dust load on the air filters. To facilitate work on the running gear (e.g., chain tensioning), the four skirt sections on each side could be folded up 180 degrees and locked in place. Interestingly, the lower edges of the track skirts were scalloped for camouflage reasons (because there are no horizontal edges in nature). In service with the army, the fourth skirt element was often cut out in the area of the drive sprocket to allow the drive sprocket to self-clean. The addition of the track skirts resulted in increase in width of 6 cm (2.36 inches) on each side, increasing overall width from 3,250 to 3,370 mm.

- The Diehl D 640 A system track, with replaceable track pads, became available for the Leopard 1 in 1972. The track pads were inserted laterally into a dovetail guide (the Bundeswehr rejected bolting the track pads for safety reasons). A safety tongue held

Type	Leopard 1 A1
Introduction period	from 1972
Crew	4
Combat weight	41.5 metric tons (45.74 tons)
Chassis length	6.94 meters (22.76 feet)
Width over tracks	3.25 meters (10.66 feet)
Height (turret roof)	2.39 meters (7.84 feet)
Main gun, caliber	105 mm L7A3 L/51
Ammunition capacity	60 rounds
Secondary weapon 1, caliber	7.62 mm mantlet machine gun
Secondary weapon 2, caliber	7.62 mm antiaircraft machine gun
Engine, type	MB 838 CaM 500 10-cylinder diesel, supercharger
Rated output	610 kW (818 hp)
Maximum speed	65 kph (40.38 mph)
Range on roads	560 km (347.96 mi.)
Fuel capacity	985 liters (260.21 US gal.)
Fuel consumption (on roads)	175 liters / 100 km (1.34 mpg)
Suspension	torsion bar
Armor thickness	70 mm (sloped at 30 degrees)

The Leopard 1 A1 main battle tank. This version was the first combat upgrade and included equipping the vehicles with running-gear skirts. The skirts yielded a slight improvement in protection in this area (especially against HEAT rounds fired at an angle). The scalloped lower edges of the skirts were intended to improve concealment, since continuous horizontal edges do not occur in nature.

the track pad securely in position during operation. For operations in winter, the track pads could be replaced by snow grousers on every eighth to tenth track link. Twenty snow grousers per vehicle was the standard issue. When not in use, the parts were stowed in racks on the glacis plate. On early versions of the D 640 A track, ice studs could also be used.

• Adoption of a weapon stabilization system (WSA-1); this considerably shortened the time in the firing halt required to get off an accurate shot. In connection with the installation of the weapon stabilization system, protective grilles were fitted to the right of the main gun in the fighting compartment, to prevent injuries to gunners and commanders during stabilized operation of the main gun. The gunner was given a control unit to carry out drift adjustment for the weapon stabilization system.

• The barrel of the main gun was fitted with thermal jacket made of light metal sections. This significantly reduced barrel distortions due to external environmental influences.

Leopard 1 A1A1

The Leopard 1 A1 version described on the previous page had only a relatively short service life, since a further retrofit program for the vehicles of batches 1 to 4 was implemented in the 1975–77 period; this led to the Leopard 1 A1A1 version. As part of this combat upgrade program, 1,225 vehicles of the Leopard A1 version were converted (vehicles of the A2 and A3 versions were not affected). The following measures were carried out as part of the conversion to the Leopard 1 A1A1 version:

- Adoption of additional armor on the turret and front. The additional armor on the glacis consisted of armor steel plates up to 40 mm thick. On the turret, the additional armor consisted of steel plates of varying thickness. The additional armor was attached to the turret and mantlet by using so-called shock mounts (rubber blocks), which were supposed to provide a certain degree of shock absorption in the event of hits. The turret basket was also covered with thinner perforated plates in a rubber lining. The forward roof slope

Type	Leopard 1 A1A1
Introduction period	from 1975
Crew	4
Combat weight	42.2 metric tons (46.51 tons)
Chassis length	6.94 meters (22.76 feet)
Width over tracks	3.25 meters (10.66 feet)
Height (turret roof)	2.39 meters (7.84 feet)
Main gun, caliber	105 mm L7A3 L/51
Ammunition capacity	60 rounds
Secondary weapon 1, caliber	7.62 mm mantlet machine gun
Secondary weapon 2, caliber	7.62 mm antiaircraft machine gun
Engine, type	MB 838 CaM 500 10-cylinder diesel, supercharger
Rated output	610 kW (818 hp)
Maximum speed	65 kph (40.38 mph)
Range on roads	560 km (347.96 mi.)
Fuel capacity	985 liters (260.21 US gal.)
Fuel consumption (on roads)	175 liters / 100 km (1.34 mpg)
Suspension	torsion bar
Armor thickness	70 mm (sloped at 30 degrees)

Leopard 1 A1A1 main battle tank. This combat upgrade saw the vehicles fitted with appliqué armor on the turret. A 40 mm steel plate was added to the mantlet armor. The added armor was intended to provide protection against rounds fired by the Soviet 100 mm tank gun from medium ranges and by the 115 mm smoothbore gun from longer ranges. The vehicle shown here was also fitted with the PZB 200 passive night vision device. The snow cleats were now placed on the upper glacis plate.

Leopard 1 A1A1 main battle tank surmounting an obstacle during a demonstration of army combat vehicles at the southern grandstand in Munster. This vehicle, with added external camouflage, climbs over a step approximately 1 meter high. The picture clearly shows the high vulnerability of the white-light/infrared searchlight. The device has no protection whatsoever and would immediately become inoperable in combat if hit by the smallest fragments.

Leopard 1 A1A1 main battle tank in a concealed position. Parked at the edge of a forest, the vehicle was optimally protected against aerial reconnaissance by the elaborate installation of a camouflage net. The carrier plate with the components of the KADAG gunnery-training device is mounted on the main gun.

A Leopard 1 A1A1 main battle tank next to an M113 A1 G armored personnel carrier. The photo illustrates the size difference between the Leopard tank and the M113. The tank's crew have stored the four tow cables between the exhaust gratings for rail transport—a common practice among the troops at that time.

of the turret was also reinforced with plates approximately 25 mm in thickness, so that protection against 100 mm APDS ammunition fired by the T-54/55 series of main battle tanks was significantly improved. The light additional armor in the rear area improved protection against HL ammunition (handheld antitank weapons) in particular. In addition to the added armor on the mantlet and turret, the following changes were carried out on the Leopard 1 A1A1 version:

- Replacement of the felt pockets in the second stage of the air filter with more-robust filter cartridges in a metal housing.
- The ability to carry a deep-wading tube (approximately 400 mm tall), which could be placed on the commander's hatch when crossing water obstacles to prevent splash water from entering the hatch during entry and exit.
- Along with the deep-wading tube, the vehicles were also equipped with longer tow cables (5 meters, or 16.4 feet). As a result, the forward cable attachment points had to be moved to the area of the track shoulders.
- In the mid-1970s, a passive night vision device was developed for the driver that worked on the principle of residual light amplification. This replaced the previously used infrared driver's unit, which always required active light sources (headlights with IR filter lenses) for operation. To ensure operation even in extreme darkness, an additional screened headlamp was introduced with the new night vision device, which was screwed into the bracket in place of the right-hand headlight. A second dummy socket was welded onto the front plate to accommodate the headlight, which was not required in this case.

The retrofitting increased the combat weight of the Leopard 1 A1A1 main battle tank from 41.5 to 42.2 tons, of which the additional armor alone weighed 660 kg.

Leopard 1 A1A1 main battle tank. This vehicle was photographed during a Bundeswehr display at WTD 51 (Bundeswehr technical center) in Coblenz-Metternich in 2005, marking the force's fifty-year anniversary. Since it has no unit insignia, it probably came from the inventory of WTD 41 (based at Trier). The mount for the PZB 200 passive targeting and observation device, including the hoop-shaped protective shield, is mounted on the gun mantlet.

Leopard 1 A1A1 NL main battle tank. A Dutch Leopard 1 A1A1 on a forest road during a demonstration at the Swiss Military Museum in Full. The generous regulations in Switzerland allow the possession of armored vehicles by selected private museums without demilitarization measures!

Leopard 1 A2

The first 232 vehicles of the fifth production batch were produced in the period from April 1972 to May 1973 and were given a new cast turret with a thicker mantlet and increased armor protection in the forward area. The result was the Leopard 1 A2. Insiders recognize this version by its oval-shaped rangefinder blisters. The Leopard 1 A2 was delivered from the factory with the following components:

- traverse and elevation system with weapon stabilization
- thermal jacket on the gun barrel
- D 640 A track
- side skirts
- exhaust gratings consisting of eight extruded profiles instead of the previous cast version (this new form of exhaust grating had already been used in the vehicles of the fourth production batch)

Type	Leopard 1 A2
Introduction period	1972–73
Crew	4
Combat weight	42 metric tons (46.29 tons)
Chassis length	6.94 meters (22.76 feet)
Width over tracks	3.25 meters (10.66 feet)
Height (turret roof)	2.39 meters (7.84 feet)
Main gun, caliber	105 mm L7A3 L/51
Ammunition capacity	60 rounds
Secondary weapon 1, caliber	7.62 mm mantlet machine gun
Secondary weapon 2, caliber	7.62 mm antiaircraft machine gun
Engine, type	MB 838 CaM 500 10-cylinder diesel, supercharger
Rated output	610 kW (818 hp)
Maximum speed	65 kph (40.38 mph)
Range on roads	560 km (347.96 mi.)
Fuel capacity	985 liters (260.21 US gal.)
Fuel consumption (on roads)	175 liters / 100 km (1.34 mpg)
Suspension	torsion bar
Armor thickness	70 mm (sloped at 30 degrees)

Further improvements and changes flowed into the Leopard 1 A2 version:

- New NBC defense system (compact system) with more-effective filters
- Improved air filtration system
- Replacement of the driver's infrared system with an image intensifier unit (BiV). A shielded headlamp had to be installed on the driver's side for illumination in extreme darkness. An additional dummy socket was fitted on the upper glacis plate for the headlamp, which was then not required.
- Since the smoke discharger system was often damaged during training and maneuver missions, a protective bracket / bar deflector was fitted to the cups of the smoke discharger system on the A2 version.

Leopard 1 A3

A new delivery contract was necessary for the remaining 110 vehicles of the fifth production batch, since they were fitted with a completely new welded turret. This version was assigned the designation Leopard 1 A3. The basic concept of the turret with spaced armor covering the forward sides had been developed in 1968 as part of the experimental program. Its shape was also the inspiration for the prototypes of the first generation of the Leopard 2 main battle tank. The spacing of the armor steel plates resulted in a slight improvement in protection against APDS and HEAT ammunition, with no increase in weight. The production of the turrets for the vehicles of the fifth and sixth construction batches was divided equally between these companies:

- Blohm & Voss, Hamburg
- Rheinstahlwerke, Witten-Annen

The new turret concept increased the size of the fighting compartment by 1.5 cubic meters (53 cubic feet). Instead of the stowage basket

Type	Leopard 1 A3
Introduction period	1973
Crew	4
Combat weight	42.4 metric tons (46.73 tons)
Chassis length	6.94 meters (22.76 feet)
Width over tracks	3.25 meters (10.66 feet)
Height (turret roof)	2.39 meters (7.84 feet)
Main gun, caliber	105 mm L7A3 L/51
Ammunition capacity	60 rounds
Secondary weapon 1, caliber	7.62 mm mantlet machine gun
Secondary weapon 2, caliber	7.62 mm antiaircraft machine gun
Engine, type	MB 838 CaM 500 10-cylinder diesel, supercharger
Rated output	610 kW (818 hp)
Maximum speed	65 kph (40.38 mph)
Range on roads	560 km (347.96 mi.)
Fuel capacity	985 liters (260.21 US gal.)
Fuel consumption (on roads)	175 liters / 100 km (1.34 mpg)
Suspension	torsion bar
Armor thickness	70 mm (sloped at 30 degrees)

on the rear of the turret, corresponding stowage boxes were integrated into the turret shape to accommodate the searchlight and accessories (e.g., camouflage net). As a side effect of this, there was a significant increase in protection against HEAT ammunition in the rear of the turret.

In the welded-turret variant, the gunner was provided with a periscope in a rotating and tilting mount.

As an interesting innovation, the welded turrets of the Leopard 1 A3 version received an opening (diameter approximately 350 mm) in the turret roof behind the loader's hatch to accommodate a mortar (close-defense weapon). This device is known from the Königstiger (King Tiger) and Jagdpanther from the Second World War, among others. When the vehicles were delivered, the opening was covered by a bolted plate. However, serious problems arose during trials with the ammunition, so that the defensive mortar was not fitted in the turrets later (this opening was omitted in the welded turrets of the Leopard 1 A4 version).

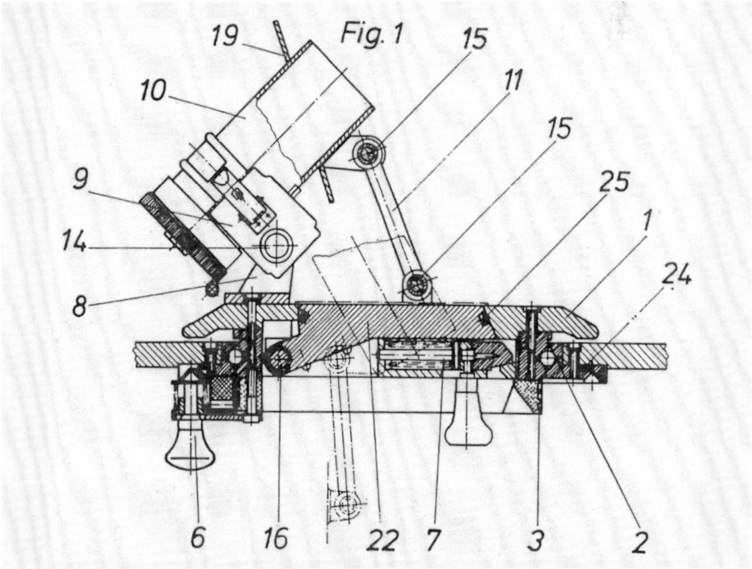

Diagram of the defensive mortar system: The image shows the layout of the mortar system (patent specification by the Wegmann company). For reloading, the mortar was lowered by a lever mechanism through an inward-opening hatch into the fighting compartment. The mortar was mounted in the turret roof in such a way as to allow it to be rotated by 360 degrees. Reloading under NBC conditions was therefore not possible.

Leopard 1 A3 at a Bundeswehr display. A Leopard 1 A3 main battle tank was included at the display by Wehrtechnische Dienststelle 51 at Coblenz-Metternich in 2005, marking the fiftieth anniversary of the Bundeswehr. The last segment of the running-gear skirt in the area of the drive sprocket has been cut off, to enable it to self-clean.

Leopard 1 A3 AUS main battle tank in a jump: "Army long-distance flying championships" were very popular among the troops. Such experiments were not without danger for the crews as well as for the vehicle. The picture shows an Australian Leopard 1 A3 main battle tank after "dynamically overcoming" a knoll.

The planned defensive mortar system on the turret rood of a Leopard 1 A3 main battle tank. It was originally planned to install a mortar system behind the loader's hatch of the Leopard 1 A3 version for close-in defense. This weapon, which was loaded from inside the turret, had been a feature of several armored vehicles of the former German Wehrmacht. The weapon was not adopted for service use for safety reasons, and the opening in the turret roof was covered with a plate.

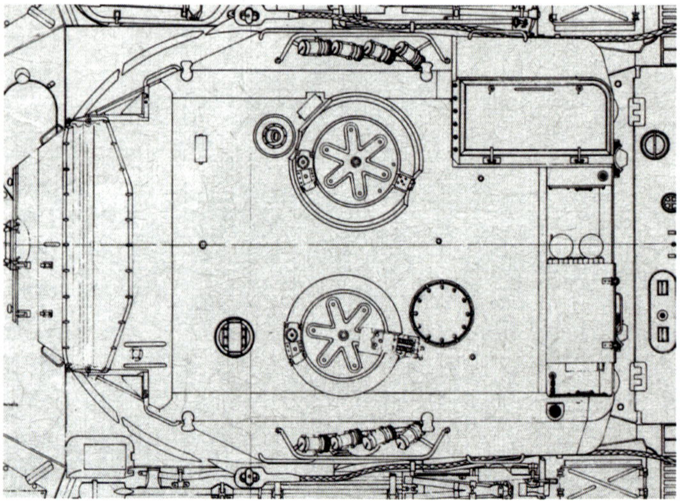

Leopard 1 A4

Fire control systems with analog computers (Galileo; Arenco) had previously been tested in several preproduction vehicles; however, none of these systems met requirements in the early 1960s. It was not until the 1970s that a fire control computer suitable for tanks became available. It was subsequently decided to equip the sixth production batch with a computer-controlled fire control system and improved observation and targeting equipment. These components had already been installed in the prototypes of the Leopard 2 main battle tank since 1972. The new integrated fire control system was also installed in the Leopard 1 main battle tank, and the resulting variant was designated the Leopard 1 A4. A total of 250 tanks of this type were produced between August 1974 and March 1976.

Although logistical equality with the other versions would have been desirable, no consideration was given to retrofitting this modern fire control system to the older vehicles. To simplify logistical support, the 250 Leopard 1 A4 main battle tanks were delivered mainly to the tank battalions of the 10th Armored Division (based at Stetten am kalten Markt).

Type	Leopard 1 A4
Introduction period	1974–76
Crew	4
Combat weight	42.4 metric tons (46.73 tons)
Chassis length	6.94 meters (22.76 feet)
Width over tracks	3.25 meters (10.66 feet)
Height (turret roof)	2.39 meters (7.84 feet)
Main gun, caliber	105 mm L7A3 L/51
Ammunition capacity	55 rounds
Secondary weapon 1, caliber	7.62 mm mantlet machine gun
Secondary weapon 2, caliber	7.62 mm antiaircraft machine gun
Engine, type	MB 838 CaM 500 10-cylinder diesel, supercharger
Rated output	610 kW (818 hp)
Maximum speed	65 kph (40.38 mph)
Range on roads	560 km (347.96 mi.)
Fuel capacity	985 liters (260.21 US gal.)
Fuel consumption (on Roads)	175 liters / 100 km (1.34 mpg)
Suspension	torsion bar
Armor thickness	70 mm (sloped at 30 degrees)

The welded turret was also used for the Leopard 1 A4 version; the most striking difference between it and the A3 version is the large viewing head of the new PERI-R 12 panoramic periscope, with two side-mounted protective bars.

As a further improvement, the Leopard 1 A4 received a new gear selector lever, which enabled automatic transmission shifting; this made driving the tank significantly easier.

Leopard 1 A4 main battle tank, view from the front. This vehicle was part of the ***50 Years of the Army*** **display at Munster / Camp Kohlebissen in May 2006. The tank belonged to the 4th Company, 293rd Armored Battalion, based at Stetten am kalten Markt, and was sent from there to the tank museum. The only external difference between the A4 and the earlier A3 version is the former's larger PERI-R-12 panoramic periscope.**

Taken at the Swiss Military Museum at Full, this photo provides a good size comparison between the Leopard 2 main battle tank and the Leopard 1 A4. While both types have almost the same hull construction height, the Leopard 2's hull roof is about 75 mm (2.95 in.) higher due to the tank's greater ground clearance. Despite its larger main gun, the overall height of the Leopard 2 is only 90 mm (3.54 in.) greater.

Y 947809

Photo taken during comparative trials between the Leopard 1 A4 main battle tank and the Russian T-62. The photo provides a diagonal view of both vehicles. The US Army (Vilseck) provided the T-62 that took part in the trials. The two hinged hatches in the T-62's turret are much less favorable in combat situations than, for example, the commander's lift and swing hatch in the turret of the Leopard 1 A4 main battle tank.

Overhead view of the Leopard 1 A4 main battle tank. This vehicle is on display in the Swiss Military Museum in Full. The top view shows the relatively large dimensions of the welded turret. The grating over the air intake of the NBC protective ventilation system is located in the area of the left track shoulder on the horizontal surface in front of the turret. Farther back, the protective hood for the engine's combustion air intake can be seen on the left-hand side at the transition to the engine compartment cover.

Leopard 1 A5

The components for conducting a firefight installed in the vehicles of production batches 1 to 5 were based on the technologies available in the early 1960s. More than ten years of use led to increasing signs of wear and tear and thus to increasing material maintenance costs. In addition, the rangefinder was showing increasingly poor adjustment stability (resulting in, among other things, higher ammunition consumption during gunnery training)! For this reason, the first research into equipping the older vehicles with a more modern and efficient fire control system began in 1976. A tactical requirement was issued in 1981, on the basis of which three companies offered corresponding systems. The following systems were subjected to a competitive trial:

- LEMSTAR-M fire control system with EMES 17 from the AEG company
- FLP-10 fire control system with EMES 18 from the KAE company
- AFS-L fire control system with EMES 12 A 3 from the Karl Zeiss company

After extensive testing of the three fire control systems, the FLP-10 system from Krupp-Atlas Electronics (Bremen) was selected

Type	Leopard 1 A5
Introduction period	1986–92
Crew	4
Combat weight	42.2 metric tons (46.51 tons)
Chassis length	6.94 meters (22.76 feet)
Width over tracks	3.25 meters (10.66 feet)
Height (turret roof)	2.39 meters (7.84 feet)
Main gun, caliber	105 mm L7A3 L/51
Ammunition capacity	60 rounds
Secondary weapon 1, caliber	7.62 mm mantlet machine gun
Secondary weapon 2, caliber	7.62 mm antiaircraft machine gun
Engine, type	MB 838 CaM 500 10-cylinder diesel, supercharger
Rated output	610 kW (818 hp)
Maximum speed	65 kph (40.38 mph)
Range on roads	560 km (347.96 mi.)
Fuel capacity	985 liters (260.21 US gal.)
Fuel consumption (on Roads)	175 liters / 100 km (1.34 mpg)
Suspension	torsion bar
Armor thickness	70 mm (sloped at 30 degrees)

Side-by-side comparison of the Leopard 1 A5 with the M48 A2 main battle tanks. The photo illustrates very well the different design philosophies of the two vehicles. The silhouette of the Leopard 1 main battle tank was specifically optimized as a measure to improve survivability on the battlefield. The difference in turret roof height between the two vehicles is 260 mm (10.23 in.). The silhouette of the M48 A2 main battle tank was heightened by a further 440 mm (17.32 in.), thanks to the raised commander's cupola. As battles in the Middle East wars have shown, the commander's cupola tends to have a negative effect on the survivability of the tank commander, in particular.

Side-by-side comparison of the Leopard 2 A6 and the Leopard 1A5 main battle tanks. The photo was taken in September 2005 at Defense Technology Center 41 in Trier during festivities marking the fiftieth anniversary of the formation of the Bundeswehr. The difference in turret roof heights between the two vehicles was 90 mm (3.54 in.). Regarding the camouflage, the unfavorable shadow formation on the undersides of the forward turret modules can be seen in the photograph.

for the conversion program at the end of 1983. In the 1986–93 period, 1,225 vehicles were converted. These vehicles were given the designation Leopard 1 A5.

The main elements of the FLP-10 fire control system were as follows:

- The EMES 18 primary sight for the gunner with day and night channels (thermal imaging device) as well as a laser transmitter and receiver. The sighting line was primarily stabilized, and the weapon tracked the line of sight.
- The fire control (ballistic) computer for determining the correction values for the tangent elevation and lead angles for the selected ammunition type. The computer processes the following input parameters, among others:
- range to the target measured by the laser rangefinder
- cant (plumb gyro)
- air values
- lead when firing at a moving target
- system error of the weapon system

A converted M48 A2 GA2 main battle tank, on which the earlier commander's cupola was replaced by a massive ring made of cast homogeneous armor

A Leopard 1 A5 main battle tank negotiating a step. The photo was taken during a demonstration at the south grandstand in Munster. If an experienced driver accelerates hard shortly after climbing the step, the relatively steep angle of attack seen here can be achieved for a short time. The weight of the vehicle then rests briefly on the two rear road wheels. Due to the relatively low-rated speed of the engine, the Leopard 1 main battle tank always impresses spectators at such demonstrations with the powerful and low-frequency sound of the engine. No other tank achieves this impressive effect!

The following changes were also made to the 1 A5 version of vehicles:

- The commander's panoramic periscope and the TRP sight were raised to clear the EMES 18 sight housing.
- Installation of new batteries (100 Ah; Dryfit)
- Installation of new trunnion bearings (roller bearings) with resolver (angle encoder) for the EMES 18
- Installation of a field adjustment system
- Retrofitting with new gear selector lever for automatic transmission shifting
- Adaptations for installation of the 120 mm smoothbore gun (relocation of the trunnion bearings and cutout in the upper area of the turret muzzle)
- Installation of high-pressure washers for the driver's observation periscopes
- With the use of the thermal-imaging device, the gunnery searchlight was eliminated from the Leopard 1 A5.

The vehicles of the Leopard 1 A5 version remained in service the longest. The last combat firing was carried out by the 74th Armored Battalion (Altenwalde) in July 2003 at the Bergen-Hohne training area. PzBtl 74 was disbanded at the end of December 2003—shortly before this, its Leopards had been transferred to the Siegelsbach depot. This marked the end of the era of the Leopard 1 main battle tank in the Bundeswehr in 2003 after thirty-eight years of service!

Side-by-side comparison of the Spähpanzer 2 A2 Luchs (Lynx) wheeled amphibious reconnaissance armored fighting vehicle with the Leopard 1 A5 main battle tank. Although reconnaissance vehicles should ideally be low in profile and inconspicuous, the Spähpanzer Luchs has a turret roof height of 2,800 mm (110.23 in.) due to its chassis design with rigid axles. It is thus 410 mm (16.14 in.) taller than the Leopard 1 A5 main battle tank.

A Leopard 1 A5 main battle tank during winter maneuvers. The photo depicts a Leopard 1 A5 of the 413th Armored Battalion with minimal winter camouflage. To avoid damage to the track skirts during off-road driving, almost all skirt sections have been removed. Only one skirt section in the area of the commander's hatch was left on the vehicle to facilitate his ascent. The placement of the tactical number on the toolbox is unusual.

Leopard 1 A6

In the design philosophy for the Leopard 1 main battle tank, a conscious decision was made in 1956 to abandon the race between protection and ammunition effectiveness, and this initially gave the Leopard 1 relatively modest armor protection. One of the most important lessons learned from the battles of the Yom Kippur War in 1973 was that the tank's level of protection is absolutely crucial for survival in combat. As an initial reaction to these clear findings, the protection level of the prototypes of the Leopard 2 main battle tank was raised in 1974. When it became clear at the beginning of the 1980s that the introduction of the planned PzKW 2000 (and thus the replacement of the Leopard 1 main battle tank) would be considerably delayed, it was also decided to conduct research to significantly improve the protection level of the Leopard 1 main battle tank (especially against kinetic-energy penetrator ammunition).

At the end of 1986, the Krauss-Maffei company was awarded a contract to construct two test vehicles, which were to have the following equipment:

VT 5:
- 120 mm smoothbore gun
- new RTW 90 panoramic periscope with day and night channels for tank commanders
- additional armor (for protection against kinetic-energy penetrators) on the front and sides of the turret
- fire suppression system in the fighting compartment

VT 2:
- 120 mm smoothbore gun
- additional armor (for protection against kinetic-energy penetrators) on the front and on the flanks of the hull and turret for protection of the fighting compartment
- measures to reduce the IR signature in the area of the engine compartment
- fire suppression system in the fighting compartment

The two test vehicles were completed in 1987 and underwent extensive trials at WTD 91 in Meppen. The added armor and the 120 mm gun resulted in a weight increase of just under 6 metric tons (6.6 tons) for the VT 2. This raised the gross weight to more than 47 metric tons (51.8 tons). The high combat weight alone was very problematic; however, even worse was the fact that the weight increase was concentrated in the forward parts of the turret and hull! This resulted in a significant increase in

The VT 2 test vehicle

the unbalanced moment of the turret—with considerable effects on the aiming system and stabilization. The entire vehicle also showed a pronounced nose-heaviness, with unfavorable consequences for driving dynamics and negotiating obstacles.

A standard retrofit was therefore out of the question from an overall systems-engineering perspective. It went no further than the two test vehicles, of which the turret of the VT 5 now lives a somewhat sad existence in the Rheinmetall factory museum in Unterlüß.

VT 2 test vehicle with complete IR camouflage measures: In the further course of the investigations, the VT 2 received an extension of the running-gear skirts as well as rear-ventilated panels on the road wheels. In addition to reducing the IR signature, these measures were also intended to reduce the tank's radar signature (reduction of the radar reflective surface, or RCS).

Parallel to the conversion of the demonstrators to the Leopard 1 A6 version (unofficial designation), investigations were carried out at WTD 41 into the effects of the higher combat weight on the drive and chassis assemblies. The picture shows a converted test vehicle with additional weights on the turret sides on the off-road track on the Grüneberg. The testing of the vehicles had to be rough, tough, and realistic, since otherwise, weak points would be carried over into series production and service use. Eliminating the previously unrecognized problem areas would then have involved extremely high costs.

Leopard 1 with 120 mm Smoothbore Gun

As early as 1982, Rheinmetall offered to equip two Leopard 1 main battle tanks with the 120 mm smoothbore gun at its own expense and to carry out corresponding factory trials. One of the reasons given was that even the DM 23 105 mm APDSFS ammunition could no longer penetrate the T-72 main battle tank (1981 model) head on. In addition, this could create logistical parity with the Leopard 2 main battle tank. As a result, the Bundeswehr provided a Leopard 1 A5 with cast turret and a Leopard 1 A3 with welded turret for conversion in 1983. In connection with the installation of the 120 mm weapon system, the following modifications were required on both vehicles:

Turret:

- additional cutout in the upper area of the turret front for the installation and removal of the larger weapon system
- relocation of the trunnion bearings
- use of a new mantlet
- changes to the elevation control cylinder due to new geometric conditions
- changes to the weapon stabilization system (controller)
- changes to the fire control computer
- installation of new ammunition racks
- modifications to periscope array on the commander's hatch
- enlargement of the ammunition hatch

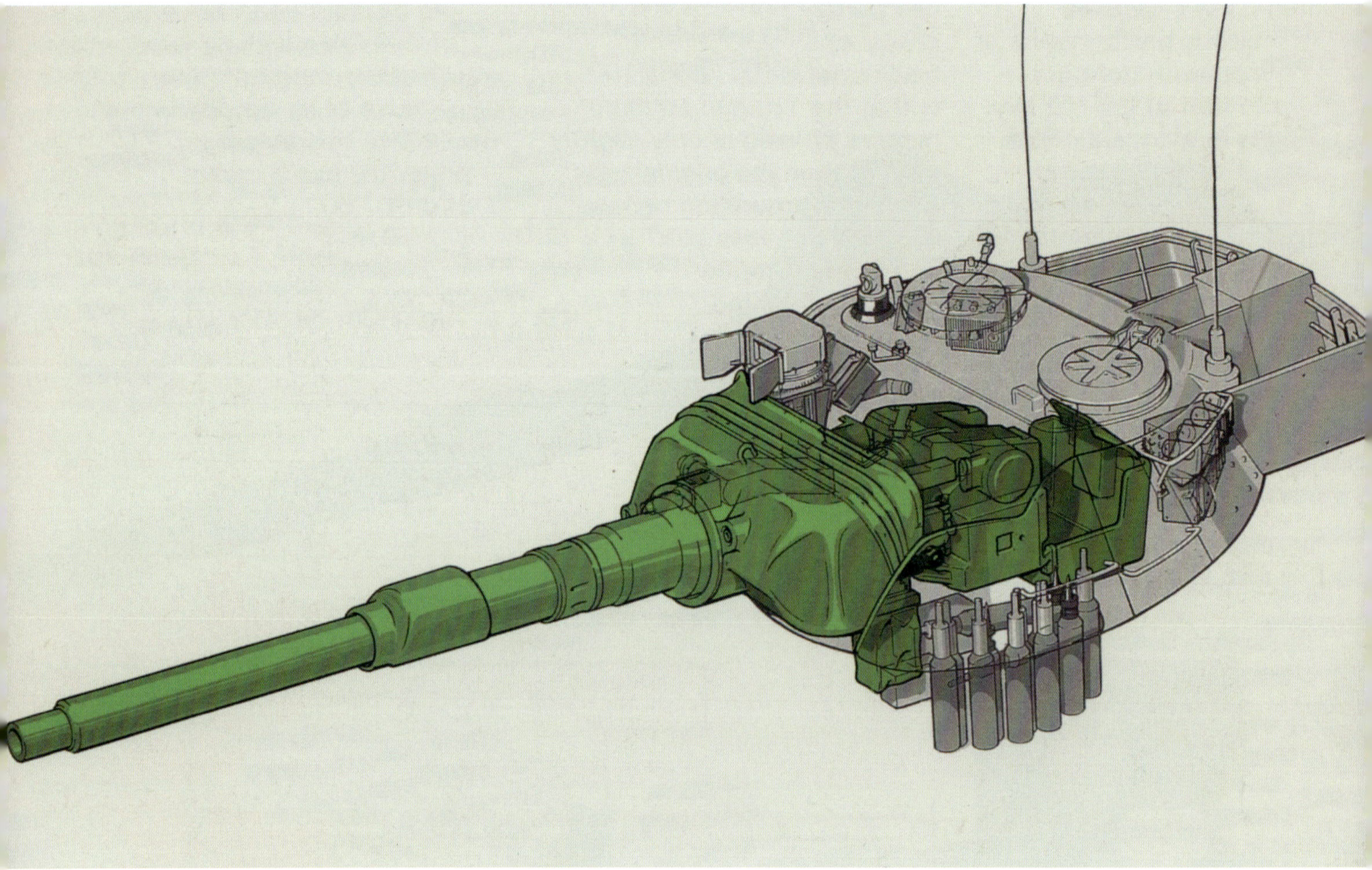

Drawing illustrating the installation of the 120 mm smoothbore gun

Chassis:
- installation of new ammunition racks
- new barrel lock on the rear of the tank

The larger ammunition reduced ammunition capacity from 60 to 42 rounds. The additional weight resulting from the conversion amounted to 1.35 metric tons (1.48 tons). It led to an increase in the imbalance of the turret and to a slight shift of the center of gravity of the overall vehicle to the front. The conversion would have cost around 500,000 DM per vehicle. Factory testing was carried out in 1985, followed by official testing at WTD 91 in Meppen in 1986.

Although the mechanical modifications necessary to accommodate the 120 mm weapon system were considered when the turret of the Leopard 1 A5 was converted, the larger weapon system was not fitted as standard (presumably for cost reasons).

Chapter 3

Export Versions

Belgium: Leopard 1 BE

At the end of the 1960s, the Belgian army began searching for a replacement for its M47 main battle tanks. The types considered were the M60 A1, AMX-30, Chieftain, and Leopard 1. The final candidates were the AMX-30 and Leopard 1. The latter finally won out due to more-favorable procurement costs and a generous compensation package. Although the decision was made in mid-1956, due to financial difficulties the order for 334 vehicles was not finalized until 1967. The Belgian vehicles were largely identical to the Leopard 1s from the third and fourth production batches, the only changes being the installation of FN machine guns as secondary weapons and side-mounted toolboxes.

A major combat upgrade program was implemented starting in 1974, which saw the introduction of a gun stabilization system and a more modern fire control system (SABCA). This system had a laser rangefinder and an

Type	Leopard 1 BE
Introduction period	May 1968–March 1971
Crew	4
Combat weight	40 metric tons (44.09 tons)
Chassis length	6.94 meters (22.76 feet)
Width over tracks	3.25 meters (10.66 feet)
Height (turret roof)	2.39 meters (7.84 feet)
Main gun, caliber	105 mm L7A3 L/51
Ammunition capacity	60 rounds
Secondary weapon 1, caliber	7.62 mm mantlet machine gun
Secondary weapon 2, caliber	7.62 mm antiaircraft machine gun
Engine, type	MB 838 CaM 500 10-cylinder diesel, supercharger
Rated output	610 kW (818 hp)
Maximum speed	65 kph (40.38 mph)
Range on roads	560 km (347.96 mi.)
Fuel capacity	985 liters (260.21 US gal.)
Fuel consumption (on roads)	175 liters / 100 km (1.34 mpg)
Suspension	torsion bar
Armor thickness	70 mm (sloped at 30 degrees)

Leopard 1 A5 ABL side view: In addition to added MEXAS turret armor from IBD Diesenroth Engineering (Lohmar), this technology demonstrator also received revised running-gear skirts—probably made of ceramic. The Canadians were the only ones to adopt this innovation, however. The Belgians retired the last of their Leopards in 2014 and since then have had no main battle tanks.

The appliqué armor seen here, mounted on rubber blocks, was not adopted by the Belgians. The gunner's vision devices are striking.

analog computer that could process various parameters for firing correction. The function of field adjustment of the weapon could also be carried out with this version. A further modernization program was approved in 1985 and saw the tanks retrofitted with a thermal-imaging system, an electrical aiming system (Honeywell), and ceramic side skirts. The retrofitted vehicles received an enlarged optical head on the right side of the turret. However, this upgrade affected just 132 vehicles from the entire fleet. The conversions were carried out in 1994–95, and the new version was given the designation Leopard 1 A5 BE.

The number of Leopard 1s in service with the Belgian army was steadily reduced from about 2010, and the last vehicles were finally retired in 2014. Some of the Belgian Leopard 1 A5 BE tanks were purchased by a Belgian businessman and placed in storage. Thirty of these have since been refurbished and sent to the Ukraine (see section on Ukraine below).

Leopard 1 tanks of the Belgian Lancers 1st Regiment driving past the royal tribune on the Place des Palais in Brussels during the parade held on July 21, 1989. *Photo: © Jean-Pol Grandmont, cc-bvy-sa 4.0*

Netherlands: Leopard 1 NL

The Netherlands had to find a replacement for its Centurion main battle tanks purchased in the 1950s. After a comparative study (1967–68) between the Chieftain and Leopard 1 main battle tanks, the decision was made at the end of 1968 in favor of the Leopard 1. By 1972, the Dutch armored force had received a total of 468 vehicles. In principle, these were vehicles from the fourth production batch—with minor modifications, such as the following:

- FN-MAG machine guns were used as secondary weapons.
- A Dutch-made product was used for the smoke discharger system.
- Additional stowage boxes were attached to the hull sides.

Interestingly, the Dutch insisted that the vehicles be equipped with the old D 139 track. As part of the first combat upgrade program in

Leopard 1-V (verberted, improved) of the Dutch armed forces during an exercise, circa 1985. *Photo: Koninklijke Landmacht*

Type	Leopard 1 NL
Introduction period	October 1969–March 1972
Crew	4
Combat weight	40 metric tons (44.09 tons)
Chassis length	6.94 meters (22.76 feet)
Width over tracks	3.25 meters (10.66 feet)
Height (turret roof)	2.39 meters (7.84 feet)
Main gun, caliber	105 mm L7A3 L/51
Ammunition capacity	60 rounds
Secondary weapon 1, caliber	7.62 mm mantlet machine gun
Secondary weapon 2, caliber	7.62 mm antiaircraft machine gun
Engine, type	MB 838 CaM 500 10-cylinder diesel, supercharger
Rated output	610 kW (818 hp)
Maximum speed	65 kph (40.38 mph)
Range on roads	560 km (347.96 mi.)
Fuel capacity	985 liters (260.21 US gal.)
Fuel consumption (on roads)	175 liters / 100 km (1.34 mpg)
Suspension	torsion bar
Armor thickness	70 mm (sloped at 30 degrees)

the mid-1980s, the vehicles were fitted with added turret armor (like the Leopard 1 A1A1) and a new fire control system (AFSL-2 [NL]) from the Zeiss company. The EMES 12 A3 fire control system was retained and was supplemented by a laser rangefinder; a ballistic computer was installed to process the correction values. The previous aiming system was upgraded to a gun stabilization system with corresponding elements from Honeywell. Preparations were made for the installation of a thermal-imaging device from Phillips. This version was given the designation Leopard 1-V (the V standing for "verbertert," or improved).

A further modernization program with the installation of the FLP 10 integrated fire control system (with EMES 18 like the German A5) was launched in 1988 but was implemented on only two vehicles and then not pursued further. In total, 168 of the Leopard 1-Vs were handed over to Greece in 1993, together with the two A5 prototypes. In 1998, 202 Leopard 1-V main battle tanks were sold to Chile.

The Royal Netherlands Army decided to procure the Leopard 1 following extensive comparative trials between the British Challenger (*right*) and the German Leopard (*left*). The photo was taken at the Leusderheide testing grounds on February 26, 1968.
Photo: Erich Koch / Anefo, cc-by-sa 3.0

KU92-60
40

Norway: Leopard 1 NO

In Norway, following comparative trials between the Swedish Stridsvagn 103 S and the Leopard 1 in 1966–67, the decision was made in favor of the Leopard 1 main battle tank. It was initially decided to purchase seventy-eight vehicles in 1968. They corresponded to the fourth production batch—only the rubber tires of the road wheels were widened, and a thermal jacket was fitted to the main gun. Later, a large storage box was added to the upper glacis plate to accommodate the snow grousers.

At the beginning of the 1990s, the Norwegian main battle tank inventory was increased to a total of 170 vehicles because of the delivery of ninety-two vehicles from the Bundeswehr inventory (fifty-nine vehicles of the Leo 1 A1A1 and thirty-three vehicles of the Leo 1 A5 version).

In 1994, the seventy-eight vehicles from the initial purchase were upgraded to the Leopard 1 A5 standard and retrofitted with the EMES 18 fire control system; the hydraulic gun control system was replaced by the GEARDRIVE 90 BL electric gun stabilization system from Telefunken Systemtechnik. The converted main battle tanks

Type	Leopard 1 NO
Introduction period	January 1971–July 1971
Crew	4
Combat weight	40 metric tons (44.09 tons)
Chassis length	6.94 meters (22.76 feet)
Width over tracks	3.25 meters (10.66 feet)
Height (turret roof)	2.39 meters (7.84 feet)
Main gun, caliber	105 mm L7A3 L/51
Ammunition capacity	60 rounds
Secondary weapon 1, caliber	7.62 mm mantlet machine gun
Secondary weapon 2, caliber	7.62 mm antiaircraft machine gun
Engine, type	MB 838 CaM 500 10-cylinder diesel, supercharger
Rated output	610 kW (818 hp)
Maximum speed	65 kph (40.38 mph)
Range on roads	560 km (347.96 mi.)
Fuel capacity	985 liters (260.21 US gal.)
Fuel consumption (on roads)	175 liters / 100 km (1.34 mpg)
Suspension	torsion bar
Armor thickness	70 mm (sloped at 30 degrees)

Norwegian Leopard 1 tanks in winter camouflage during the NATO Exercise Alloy Express in spring 1982. *Photo: © PD*

were given the designation Leopard 1 A5 NO. An interesting feature of the Norwegian Leopards is the shielding of the side exhaust outlets by a plastic hood (Thercam), which was intended to reduce the vehicle's IR signature.

The Norwegian Leopard 1s were gradually withdrawn from service, leaving only Leopard 2s. According to reports, parts of decommissioned vehicles were sunk off the Norwegian coast.

Italy: Leone

In the spring of 1976, the formation of a consortium between various German defense companies and the Italian company OTO Melara was announced. As part of this cooperative effort, the German side was to build a standard chassis in the 43-metric-ton class, on which a turret from OTO Melara was to be mounted in a first step. The first prototype was completed in 1977 and underwent factory trials at OTO Melara in La Spezia.

The chassis was based on the engine and running-gear assemblies of the Leopard 1 main battle tank. The hull had to be redesigned (size and arrangement of the gratings) due to changed requirements, in particular for use in special climatic conditions.

This vehicle, known as the Leone main battle tank, was probably intended less for the needs of the Italian armed forces than for export. Series production of the Leone, which was planned from 1978, did not take place.

On closer examination, the later C-1 Ariete main battle tank (120 mm gun) borrowed a great deal from the Leopard 1.

Type	Leone
Year produced	1977
Crew	4
Combat weight	43 metric tons (47.39 tons)
Chassis length	6.73 meters (22.08 feet)
Width over tracks	3.25 meters (10.66 feet)
Height (turret roof)	2.39 meters (7.84 feet)
Main gun, caliber	105 mm L7A3 L/51
Ammunition capacity	60 rounds
Secondary weapon 1, caliber	7.62 mm mantlet machine gun
Secondary weapon 2, caliber	7.62 mm antiaircraft machine gun
Engine, type	MB 838 CaM 500 10-cylinder diesel, supercharger
Rated output	610 kW (818 hp)
Maximum speed	65 kph (40.38 mph)
Range on roads	600 km (372.82 mi.)
Fuel capacity	1,000 liters (264.17 US gal.)
Fuel consumption (on roads)	170 liters / 100 km (1.38 mpg)
Suspension	torsion bar
Armor thickness	no information

EI · 118798
59

Italy: Leopard 1 IT / 1A5 IT

Although Italy had been involved in Leopard development as an observer since 1958, it was not until 1964 that a comparative trial among the M60, AMX-30, and Leopard 1 main battle tanks was carried out at the Camp Teulada training area in Sardinia. Because, on the one hand, there was an urgent need to replace the obsolete M47 main battle tank, and, on the other hand, deliveries of the Leopard 1 had to be spread over a longer period, it was spontaneously decided to purchase seven hundred M60 main battle tanks from the Americans. Since this type of main battle tank did not prove itself during service trials, the purchase contract was reduced to two hundred vehicles in 1966.

In further comparative trials between the AMX-30 and Leopard 1 main battle tanks in the fall of 1969, the Leopard proved to be not only the less expensive but also the better tank. At the beginning of 1970, it was finally decided to order eight hundred Leopard 1s for the Italian army—two hundred of these vehicles would be built in Germany, while the remaining six hundred Leopard 1s would be manufactured by OTO Melara in Italy. These vehicles corresponded to those from the fourth and fifth production batches. This was followed in 1977 by a further delivery of 120 Italian-made vehicles (production batch 5—Leopard 1 A2 IT). Starting in 1983, all vehicles—at least those that were not already so equipped—were fitted with the thicker cast turret of the Leopard 1 A2; interestingly, they were not retrofitted with a gun stabilization system!

Type	Leopard 1 IT
Introduction period	September 1971–July 1972
Crew	4
Combat weight	40 metric tons (44.09 tons)
Chassis length	6.94 meters (22.76 feet)
Width over tracks	3.25 meters (10.66 feet)
Height (turret roof)	2.39 meters (7.84 feet)
Main gun, caliber	105 mm L7A3 L/51
Ammunition capacity	60 rounds
Secondary weapon 1, caliber	7.62 mm mantlet machine gun
Secondary weapon 2, caliber	7.62 mm antiaircraft machine gun
Engine, type	MB 838 CaM 500 10-cylinder diesel, supercharger
Rated output	610 kW (818 hp)
Maximum speed	65 kph (40.38 mph)
Range on roads	560 km (347.96 mi.)
Fuel capacity	985 liters (260.21 US gal.)
Fuel consumption (on roads)	175 liters / 100 km (1.34 mpg)
Suspension	torsion bar
Armor thickness	70 mm (sloped at 30 degrees)

After the German phase-out of the Leopard 1 A5, Italy purchased 120 examples of that version's turret from the Bundeswehr in 1995 and mounted them on Italian chassis. The result was the Leopard 1 A5 IT version. Due to a new army structure, only one hundred Leopard 1 A5 IT main battle tanks remained in service from the year 2000—in addition to two hundred C-1 Ariete main battle tanks. Italy deployed Leopard 1s with KFOR. A sensor mast was seen in the rear turret area. It is not known whether the data collected by the mast initially had to be entered into the fire control system manually by the crew, or whether the data were entered automatically. The Leopard 1 A5 IT tanks were later also decommissioned and taken out of service. They

Handover of five new Leopard 1s to the 132nd Armored Brigade "Manin" formed in 1975. During reorganization in 1986, it was renamed the 132 a Brigata Corazzata "Ariete." Taken in 1977, the photo shows the vehicles on their way to the firing range at Maniago. *Photo: © PD*

were presumably sold to the Swiss company RUAG but remained in Italy. As part of the effort to support Ukraine following the attack by Russia on February 22, 2022, consideration was given to selling them to that nation.

Denmark: Leopard 1 / 1A5 DK

With a view to replacing its Centurion main battle tanks, the Danish armed forces carried out a comparative study between the Stridsvagn 103 S and the Leopard 1 at the end of the 1960s. The decision was made in favor of the Leopard 1 main battle tank, of which Denmark ordered 120 units in 1974. The vehicles corresponded to the fifth production batch (welded-turret variant). The turrets still had the optical rangefinder but were already prepared to accommodate the FLP-10 integrated fire control system with the EMES 18. Interestingly, Denmark experimented for several years with special camouflage mats that had a rough surface and reduced the vehicle's IR signature. Since the critical IR signature in the area of the exhaust gas and exhaust air grids could not be influenced, and considerable problems arose during cleaning and any necessary decontamination, they were removed over time.

Type	Leopard 1 DK
Introduction period	February 1976–August 1978
Crew	4
Combat weight	42.4 metric tons (46.73 tons)
Chassis length	6.73 meters (22.08 feet)
Width over tracks	3.25 meters (10.66 feet)
Height (turret roof)	2.39 meters (7.84 feet)
Main gun, caliber	105 mm L7A3 L/51
Ammunition capacity	59 rounds
Secondary weapon 1, caliber	7.62 mm mantlet machine gun
Secondary weapon 2, caliber	7.62 mm antiaircraft machine gun
Engine, type	MB 838 CaM 500 10-cylinder diesel, supercharger
Rated output	610 kW (818 hp)
Maximum speed	65 kph (40.38 mph)
Range on roads	560 km (347.96 mi.)
Fuel capacity	985 liters (260.21 US gal.)
Fuel consumption (on roads)	175 liters / 100 km (1.34 mpg)
Suspension	torsion bar
Armor thickness	70 mm (sloped at 30 degrees)

A Leopard 1A5DK with IFOR markings crushes a Serbian M55 A4 B1 20 mm antiaircraft carriage during Operation Joint Endeavour at the Danish Camp DANBAT in Doboj, Bosnia-Herzegovina. *Photo: © PD*

In the mid-1990s, the Leopard 1 DK was converted to the FLP-10 integrated fire control system, resulting in the Leopard 1 A5 DK version. One hundred Leopard 1 A3s and ten Leopard 1 A4s were purchased from the Bundeswehr in the 1992–94 period and converted into the Leopard 1 A5 DK version. All Danish vehicles were prepared to accommodate a dozer blade; however, the dozer blade was permanently installed on only one vehicle per platoon.

In the mid-1990s, thirty-five vehicles were equipped with a fighting-compartment cooling system, including a power generator system for missions overseas—this version was given the designation Leopard 1 A5 DK-1.

Denmark's first deployment of tanks on a UN mission saw it dispatch vehicles with white paintwork and large "UN" markings. A tank company with ten vehicles took part in the UNPROFOR mission. These were later transferred to IFOR and SFOR—after having been painted green again. With the influx of A4s equipped to Leopard 2A5 standard from Bundeswehr stocks and a further wave of force reductions, all Leopard 1 A5 DKs were withdrawn from service. The FFG company in Flensburg bought almost a hundred of them and placed them in storage. This stock now forms the basis for the delivery of Leopard 1 main battle tanks to the Ukraine.

Australia: Leopard AS 1

In the mid-1970s the Australian land forces were also obliged to seek a modern main battle tank to replace their aging Centurions. A study examined the Chieftain, Vickers, AMX-30, M60 A1, and Leopard 1 tanks. The M60 A1 and the Leopard 1 were shortlisted, and the Australian armed forces carried out extensive trials with both types in 1972. The decision was made in favor of the Leopard 1, ninety of which were ordered in 1975. The vehicles were given the designation Leopard 1 AS 1 and corresponded to vehicles from the fifth production batch (welded-turret variant). Due to Australian requirements, however, they were delivered with numerous changes compared to the Leopard 1 A3. These changes included, among other things,

- installation of a tropical kit for improved cooling and to ensure engine operation at high ambient temperatures;
- installation of a SABCA fire control system with laser rangefinder and a ballistic computer, including the corresponding sensors;
- provision of additional stowage boxes on the hull sides; and
- the use of hydraulic end stops in place of truncated cone springs.

Type	Leopard AS 1
Introduction period	June 1976–November 1978
Crew	4
Combat weight	42.4 metric tons (46.73 tons)
Chassis length	6.73 meters (22.08 feet)
Width over tracks	3.25 meters (10.66 feet)
Height (turret roof)	2.39 meters (7.84 feet)
Main gun, caliber	105 mm L7A3 L/51
Ammunition capacity	59 rounds
Secondary weapon 1, caliber	7.62 mm mantlet machine gun
Secondary weapon 2, caliber	7.62 mm antiaircraft machine gun
Engine, type	MB 838 CaM 500 10-cylinder diesel, supercharger
Rated output	610 kW (818 hp)
Maximum speed	65 kph (40.38 mph)
Range on roads	560 km (347.96 mi.)
Fuel capacity	985 liters (260.21 US gal.)
Fuel consumption (on roads)	175 liters / 100 km (1.34 mpg)
Suspension	torsion bar
Armor thickness	70 mm (sloped at 30 degrees)

Further upgrades were made to the vehicles in the course of their service life, including additional stowage boxes at the rear of the turret, a camouflage kit from Barracuda, and the option to mount a dozer blade or a mine plow.

Although the Australian armored force preferred the Leopard 2, for political reasons the Australian government purchased fifty-nine M1 A1 AIM Abrams tanks from the United States in 2004, and these replaced the Leopard 1.

Dockers in the port of Gladstone lift out Leopard main battle tanks from the hold of the *Scan Atlantic* on May 2, 2001. The ship also carried several artillery pieces, light armored vehicles (LAVs), and M113 tanks as part of Exercise Tandem Thrust, a joint United States and Australian military exercise near the Shoalwater Bay training area in Queensland. Canadian units made up the enemy force. *Photo: © PD*

A Leopard AS1 of the Australian 1st Armoured Regiment (1ARMD) during Exercise Talisman Sabre 2005 at the Shoalwater Bay training area, Queensland, Australia. Mounted on the front of the tank is the TWMP (Track-Width Mine Plough) originally developed for the Canadian army. It was produced by the Israeli company RAMTA, a division of Israeli Aircraft Industries. The plow can be adjusted in width and clears the space in front of the tracks and to the left and right, while any explosive devices are detonated on the approximately 1.5-meter-wide middle track. The unit is controlled via the EEJK (Engineer Equipment Interface Kit), developed by Krauss-Maffei. For this purpose, there is a welded-on cover with two sockets on the hull roof. The TWMP uses the mount that was developed for the dozer blade. *Photo: © PD*

Canada: Leopard C1/C2

In 1976, Canada decided to replace its Centurion main battle tanks with the Leopard 1 and awarded a contract for delivery of 114 vehicles to be designated Leopard 1 C1. The Leopard 1 C1 was essentially similar to the Leopard 1 A3 version (fifth production batch), but with the following changes:

- Installation of the SABCA fire control system with laser rangefinder and ballistic computer
- Adoption of the PZB 200 passive image intensification system, which was mounted on the mantlet. Several years later, a thermal-imaging system (IRS 100) was installed next to the PZB 200.
- Installation of Belgian FN machine guns
- Installation of a compact white light spotlight in the rangefinder's left blister
- Fittings to accommodate a dozer blade

During the Leopard 1 C1's service life, Canada investigated further measures to increase combat effectiveness—including the installation of a more powerful 105 mm tank gun (IWS) or the use of hydropneumatic suspension elements (Laser Engineering Ltd.)—however, none of these measures were subsequently implemented as standard. Only the equipping of the vehicle with comprehensive additional armor, which, among other things, offered protection against RPG-7 rocket-propelled grenades, was implemented on twenty-six vehicles starting in 1978; these vehicles were then given the designation Leopard 1 C1 A1.

Further modernization of the fleet was made possible by the purchase of 123 Leopard 1 A5 turrets from the Bundeswehr. These conversions took place in the 1999–2001 period; the vehicles with the FLP-10 fire control system were given the designation Leopard 1 C2. In addition to the modified optical head, this version was also recognizable by the significantly longer stowage boxes at the rear of the turret. Canada also ordered twenty-six sets of the additional armor for this cast turret version in 2000; the designation of these converted vehicles was Leopard 1 C2 A1.

Type	Leopard 1 C1
Introduction period	July 1978–June 1979
Crew	4
Combat weight	42.4 metric tons (46.73 tons)
Chassis length	6.73 meters (22.08 feet)
Width over tracks	3.25 meters (10.66 feet)
Height (turret roof)	2.39 meters (7.84 feet)
Main gun, caliber	105 mm L7A3 L/51
Ammunition capacity	59 rounds
Secondary weapon 1, caliber	7.62 mm mantlet machine gun
Secondary weapon 2, caliber	7.62 mm antiaircraft machine gun
Engine, type	MB 838 CaM 500 10-cylinder diesel, supercharger
Rated output	610 kW (818 hp)
Maximum speed	65 kph (40.38 mph)
Range on roads	560 km (347.96 mi.)
Fuel capacity	985 liters (260.21 US gal.)
Fuel consumption (on roads)	175 liters / 100 km (1.34 mpg)
Suspension	torsion bar
Armor thickness	70 mm (sloped at 30 degrees)

Loading a Canadian Leopard C2 A1 onto a C-17 on October 7, 2006, for transport from Manas Air Base in Kyrgyzstan to Kandahar Air Base in Afghanistan. The C-17 Globemaster III bears the name "Spirit of McChord" and entered service in 1999.

In the mid-2000s the Canadian government decided to decommission all main battle tanks without replacement. In doing so, it was following a general trend, particularly in western European countries. However, during the increasingly heated deployment in Afghanistan, it was discovered that the wheeled vehicles deployed there were too weakly armed, were unable to cope with the waterways, and were rather helpless in the face of IED attacks. The phaseout of the Leopard C2 was stopped with vehicle 66, and around twenty of them were quickly deployed with the protection kit fitted and successfully committed. Nevertheless, the Leopard 1 was considered unsustainable, and efforts were made to replace it with the Leopard 2. After these were delivered, the Leopard C2s were still used for training purposes until the lack of spare parts that could no longer be procured put a natural end to this.

Turkey: Leopard T1

After Krauss-Maffei halted production of the Leopard 1 main battle tank in the summer of 1979 due to the start of Leopard 2 production, in the fall of 1982 the production line for the Leopard 1 had to be reopened to fill orders placed by Turkey and Greece.

As part of German-Turkish military aid, Turkey received seventy-seven Leopard 1 T1 main battle tanks, which—apart from the following modifications—corresponded to the Leopard 1 A3 version of the fifth production batch:

- A laser component was added to the EMES 12 A3 rangefinder.
- The PZB 200 passive image intensification system replaced the active infrared system.

In a further delivery in the 1990–92 period, the Turkish armed forces received a further 150 Leopard 1 main battle tanks from Bundeswehr stocks (Leopard 1 A4s, which were converted to the Leopard 1 T1 version). A further eighty-five vehicles from Bundeswehr stocks followed in the mid-1990s.

Type	Leopard 1 T1
Introduction period	September 1983–December 1983
Crew	4
Combat weight	42.4 metric tons (46.73 tons)
Chassis length	6.73 meters (22.08 feet)
Width over tracks	3.25 meters (10.66 feet)
Height (Turret roof)	2.39 meters (7.84 feet)
Main gun, caliber	105 mm L7A3 L/51
Ammunition capacity	60 rounds
Secondary weapon 1, caliber	7.62 mm mantlet machine gun
Secondary weapon 2, caliber	7.62 mm antiaircraft machine gun
Engine, type	MB 838 CaM 500 10-cylinder diesel, supercharger
Rated output	610 kW (818 hp)
Maximum speed	65 kph (40.38 mph)
Range on roads	560 km (347.96 mi.)
Fuel capacity	985 liters (260.21 US gal.)
Fuel consumption (on roads)	175 liters / 100 km (1.34 mpg)
Suspension	torsion bar
Armor thickness	70 mm (sloped at 30 degrees)

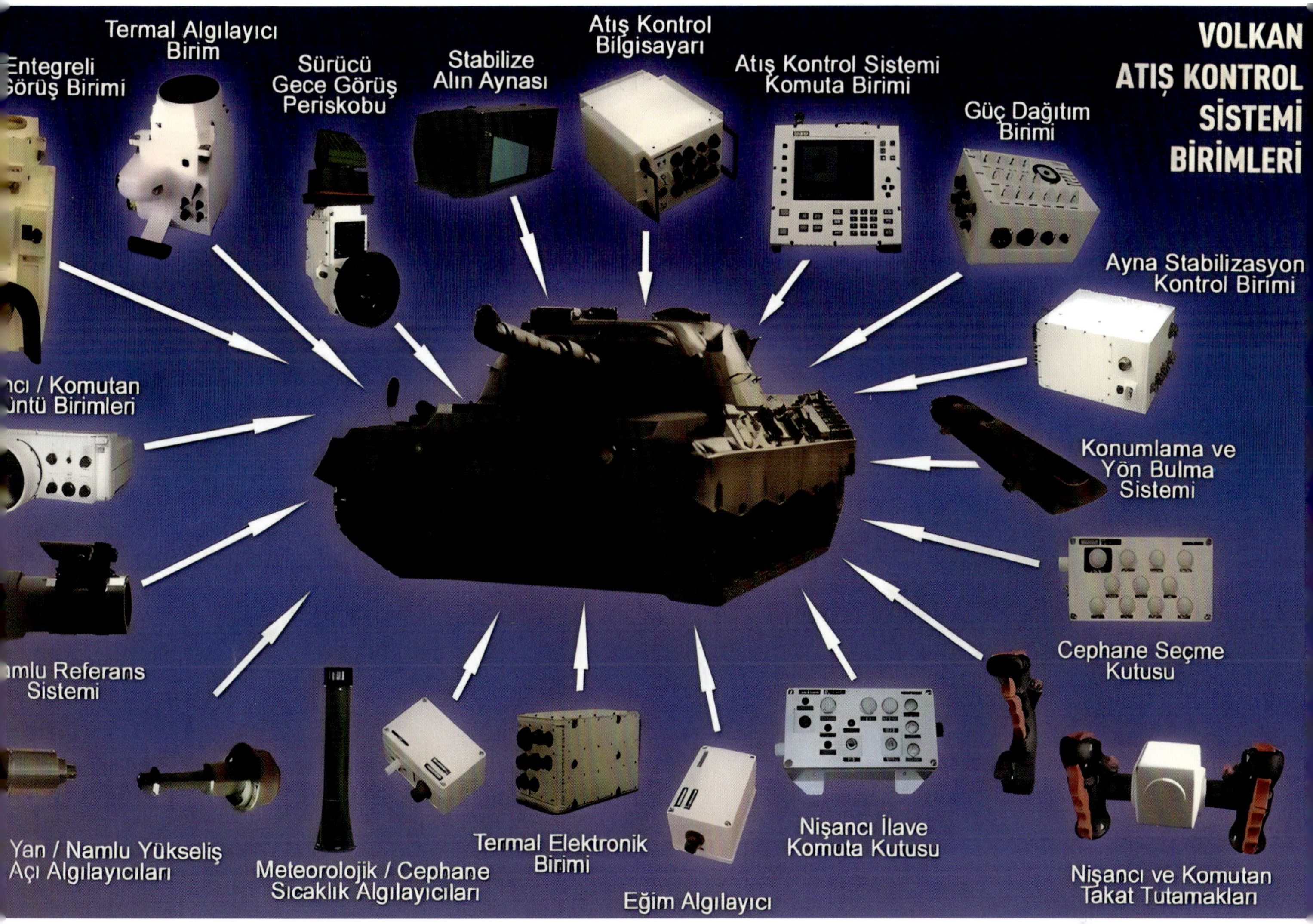

An overview of the conversion package. All elements are now standard components of modern fire control systems.

Turkey received seventy-seven Leopard T1s at the same time as Greece in the early 1980s. Externally, these corresponded to the A3 version due to the commander's TRP zoom periscope, with a modified A4 fire control system (EMES 12A3).

After the reduction of the Bundeswehr A4 fleet at the end of the 1980s, 150 of these were converted to the T1 version and were also given to Turkey. The RERI R14 was dropped in favor of the TRP, which certainly represented a step backward but increased uniformity in terms of supply and training. This version is also known as the Leopard 1TU, 1A3TU, or 1A3T1.

After further force reductions in the early 1990s, a further 170 Leopard 1s were handed

A Leopard 1T (ex-A1/A1A4). After some delays, the vehicles were accepted into service.

over to Turkey from the stock of Bundeswehr versions A1A1 to A1A4. This time, however, they remained unchanged and were therefore designated A1/A1A4.

In 2002 the Turkish company ASELSAN received the order to modernize the Leopard 1A1/A1A4 fleet in terms of fire control and night combat capability—understandable, since these are the primary weaknesses of the main battle tank. While propulsion and protection can be modified only at great expense, with results that could not bc guaranteed, the optical rangefinder (TEM) was considered to be outdated, slow, and not precise enough, and its use caused night blindness. This shortcoming was compounded by weaknesses when firing on the move, especially at moving targets.

The project, which was initially planned for a good four years, was then extended to around eight years before the last Leopard 1T retrofitted with the VOLKAN fire control system was delivered. In principle, the resulting tank is similar to the German Leopard 1A5 but is more comprehensive and technically more up to date. There are also external similarities, since the gunner's sight is located in the same place but is not as tall as the EMES 18 of the Leopard 1A5. The VOLKAN fire control system also includes a sensor mast in the middle of the turret rear area. It appears that the hydraulic gun control system has been retained, which may not be entirely advantageous.

According to the sources, 162 ex-A1/A1A4 (cast turret with additional armor) and nine ex-T1/A3T1 (welded turret) were converted to the Leopard 1T version. Nothing is known about any further orders. The following inventory of the Turkish Leopard 1 fleet can therefore be assumed, unless other circumstances (accidents, war losses, conversions, or similar) led to further write-offs:

- 218 T1/A3T1s
- 171 examples 1T (162 ex-A1, 9 ex-T1/A3T1)

218 Exemplare T1/A3T1
171 Exemplare 1T (162 ex-A1, 9 ex-T1/A3T1)

A Leopard 1T (ex-T1/A3T1). Few of the welded-turret versions were converted. The periscopes can again be seen.

Greece: Leopard GR 1

The last production series of the Leopard 1 main battle tank was manufactured by the Krauss-Maffei and MaK companies in the period from February 1983 to April 1984. Greece received 106 examples of the Leopard GR 1 version, which basically corresponded to the Leopard 1 A3 version from the fifth production batch. Modifications required by the Greek army included

- a laser rangefinder added to the EMES 12 A 1,
- installation of the PZB 200 passive image intensification system in place of the active IR system,
- addition of a collimator on the gun muzzle for the field adjustment system,
- installation of a tropical kit for improved cooling performance and increased engine output in high ambient temperatures,
- hydraulic end stops in place of the truncated cone springs on the road wheels, and
- special four-color camouflage scheme to Greek specifications.

Type	Leopard GR 1
Introduction period	February 1983–April 1984
Crew	4
Combat weight	42.4 metric tons (46.73 tons)
Chassis length	6.73 meters (22.08 feet)
Width over tracks	3.25 meters (10.66 feet)
Height (turret roof)	2.39 meters (7.84 feet)
Main gun, caliber	105 mm L7A3 L/51
Ammunition capacity	60 rounds
Secondary weapon 1, caliber	7.62 mm mantlet machine gun
Secondary weapon 2, caliber	7.62 mm antiaircraft machine gun
Engine, type	MB 838 CaM 500 10-cylinder diesel, supercharger
Rated output	610 kW (818 hp)
Maximum speed	65 kph (40.38 mph)
Range on roads	560 km (347.96 mi.)
Fuel capacity	985 liters (260.21 US gal.)
Fuel consumption (on roads)	175 liters / 100 km (1.34 mpg)
Suspension	torsion bar
Armor thickness	70 mm (sloped at 30 degrees)

In 1992, Greece received 168 vehicles of the Leopard 1-V version from the Netherlands. At the end of 1993, seventy-five Leopard 1 A5 main battle tanks were supplied to the Greek military from Bundeswehr stocks and there were

Leopard GR 2 main battle tank. At the end of 1993, seventy-five Leopard 1 A5 main battle tanks from Bundeswehr stocks were sold to Greece, and 170 more followed in 1998. There the vehicles were given the designation Leopard GR 2. As the photo illustrates, the colors selected for the variegated camouflage scheme were optimally matched to the conditions of the Greek terrain.

designated the Leopard GR 2. Finally, in autumn 1998, a further agreement was reached with Germany for delivery of 170 Leopard 1 A5 main battle tanks.

Greece operated the Leopard 1 main battle tank without significant changes. Some Leopard 1-Vs were converted into mine-clearing / combat engineer vehicles by removing the 105 mm gun and fitting a Pearson mine sweeper. Without the gun, they are no longer considered main battle tanks. The Leopard 1-Vs received from the Dutch are probably no longer in service as main battle tanks. While the status of the GR 1s (A3 turret with EMES 12) is unclear, the GR 2s / 1A5s that were received from the Bundeswehr are still in use.

Brazil: Leopard 1 A1 BE / 1A5

Due to the increasing number of European nations equipping their land forces with the Leopard 2 main battle tank, more and more used Leopard 1s were offered for sale on the world market in the 1990s. The armed forces of some of the countries that showed interest in the Leopard 1 were still equipped with battle tank models from the Second World War (e.g., M4 Sherman). For these militaries, the purchase of the Leopard 1 meant a huge modernization boost! These countries included Chile and Brazil.

Both countries were offered used Leopard 1 main battle tanks by the Netherlands and Belgium. Belgium apparently made the more favorable offer to Brazil in 1997, as a result of which Brazil purchased eighty-seven Leopard 1 BE main battle tanks from Belgium to replace its M 60s. This was later followed by a further purchase of forty-one Belgian main battle tanks. As far as is known, no technical modifications were made to the vehicles.

Type	Leopard 1 A1
Introduction period	1997–98
Crew	4
Combat weight	40 metric tons (44.09 tons)
Chassis length	6.73 meters (22.08 feet)
Width over tracks	3.25 meters (10.66 feet)
Height (turret roof)	2.39 meters (7.84 feet)
Main gun, caliber	105 mm L7A3 L/51
Ammunition capacity	60 rounds
Secondary weapon 1, caliber	7.62 mm mantlet machine gun
Secondary weapon 2, caliber	7.62 mm antiaircraft machine gun
Engine, type	MB 838 CaM 500 10-cylinder diesel, supercharger
Rated output	610 kW (818 hp)
Maximum speed	65 kph (40.38 mph)
Range on roads	560 km (347.96 mi.)
Fuel capacity	985 liters (260.21 US gal.)
Fuel consumption (on roads)	175 liters / 100 km (1.34 mpg)
Suspension	torsion bar
Armor thickness	70 mm (sloped at 30 degrees)

On September 7, Brazil's Independence Day (here: 2019), tens of thousands flock to the Esplanada dos Ministérios in Brasília to attend the traditional parade. According to Defense Express, Brazil is planning to upgrade a total of fifty-two Leopard 1 A5s by 2030. At the time of the announcement in January 2023, two options were being considered: The "small solution" includes the replacement or modernization of the fire control system, the integration of the basic command system (C2), and the replacement of optical-electronic devices and the air-conditioning system. The "major solution" also provides for the replacement of hydraulic mechanisms in the turret, a laser threat detection system, an inertial navigation system, an automatic fire-extinguishing system, and other improvements. The aim is to extend the service life of the weapon system by at least fifteen years. *Photo: © Keven Kobalchini, Ministério da Defensa, cc-by-sa 2.0*

Brazil had been in negotiations with Russia for the delivery of T-72 S tanks since 1994. Remarkably, Brazil then decided to purchase the Leopard 1, even though the T-72's performance was superior in certain respects (e.g., firepower, protection).

In 2006, Brazil signed a contract with Germany for the delivery of 220 Leopard 1 A5 main battle tanks; delivery of the 220 tanks and other support vehicles took place between 2009 and 2012. The more modern version was intended to replace the vehicles procured from Belgium serving with the armored regiments. The older Belgian main battle tanks would be assigned to the reconnaissance regiments.

This river crossing by armored vehicles of the 6th Armored Infantry Brigade took place during Operation Laçador. It was attached to the 6th Army Division during the operation (source); however, normally it is part of the 3rd Army Division. *Photo: Jorge Cardoso, Ministério da Defensa*

Leopard wading through a river as part of Operation Laçador. *Photo: Jorge Cardoso, Ministério da Defesa*

Chile: Leopard 1-V

Chile's armed forces were still operating M50 Shermans and M41 light tanks when, in 1998, the opportunity arose to purchase 202 used Leopard 1-V main battle tanks from the Netherlands. This was sufficient to equip three armored regiments. Prior to delivery, the vehicles were equipped with the PZB 200 passive image intensification system. In Chile, some of the tanks were finished in a new camouflage that suited the desertlike character of large areas of Chile.

Apparently, Chile has had very good experiences with German tank designs, since it subsequently developed into an interesting customer for the Bundeswehr. In 2004, Chile purchased 140 Leopard 2 A4s. Then, in 2008, the decision was made to purchase thirty Flakpanzer Gepard self-propelled antiaircraft guns, and in 2009 the delivery of two hundred Marder infantry-fighting vehicles to Chile began. The number of Leopard 1s in service was reduced, and finally there were increasing problems with the supply of spare parts.

In 2005 it was announced that thirty Chilean Leopard 1-V main battle tanks would be sold to Ecuador after they were replaced by Leopard 2s. The author has no confirmation, including in picture form, that the vehicles were in fact transferred to Ecuador.

Type	Leopard 1-V
Introduction period	1999–2000
Crew	4
Combat weight	40 metric tons (44.09 tons)
Chassis length	6.73 meters (22.08 feet)
Width over tracks	3.25 meters (10.66 feet)
Height (turret roof)	2.39 meters (7.84 feet)
Main gun, caliber	105 mm L7A3 L/51
Ammunition capacity	60 rounds
Secondary weapon 1, caliber	7.62 mm mantlet machine gun
Secondary weapon 2, caliber	7.62 mm antiaircraft machine gun
Engine, type	MB 838 CaM 500 10-cylinder diesel, supercharger
Rated output	610 kW (818 hp)
Maximum speed	65 kph (40.38 mph)
Range on roads	560 km (347.96 mi.)
Fuel capacity	985 liters (260.21 US gal.)
Fuel consumption (on roads)	175 liters / 100 km (1.34 mpg)
Suspension	torsion bar
Armor thickness	70 mm (sloped at 30 degrees)

Ukraine

Equipping Ukraine with Western military equipment after the Russian invasion in violation of international law initially depended heavily on the nature of the equipment. The Gepard self-propelled antitank gun system came into play relatively early on. Due to its basic "defense mission" (i.e., a defensive role), it was very easy for politicians to approve it.

When it came to main battle tanks, the situation was somewhat different.

It was only after around eleven months had passed that other nations were allowed to give Leopard 2 main battle tanks to the Ukrainians, and the Federal Republic of Germany also donated some. These were taken from the active stocks of almost all nations. The majority of these were A4 versions. In a multilateral trade process, further Leopard 2s were given to countries, which in turn donated a large number of T-72 tanks to Ukraine. Once no more Leopard 2s were available through this or other channels, the focus shifted to older types. This brought the Leopard 1 back into the discussion. It was no longer in service with any armed forces in central and northern Europe, and the only available examples were owned by companies or private individuals.

The FFG company of Flensburg had purchased ninety-nine Leopard 1s from the Danish army after they were decommissioned, without any concrete marketing prospects, and then placed most of them in weather-protected storage. These were the 1A5DK version, in some cases also the 1A5DK-1, with a generator in the

turret rear and other minor modifications. These main battle tanks therefore had the EMES 18 fire control system, with thermal-imaging device. Attempts to market these vehicles came to nothing. The temporary oversupply of Leopard 2s and the relatively strict export restrictions set narrow limits on success, so that scrapping was already being considered. These vehicles, together with other Leopards still available in Denmark, are now earmarked for delivery to Ukraine. The KMW company (now renamed KNDS) is repairing the turrets, while FFG itself is overhauling the chassis. In this way, over 130 Leopard 1A5 main battle tanks, ex-DK, are to be made available to Ukraine.

In 2016 the Swiss-government-owned armaments company RUAG purchased one hundred Leopard 1 main battle tanks of the A5 version from Italy. Of these, ninety-six are still available, which Rheinmetall offered to Ukraine in spring 2023, apparently without conclusively clarifying their feasibility. Even before that (2019), twenty-five of these tanks were sold to the German company GLS but were not picked up by them. Due to the situation regarding export options and ownership, which has yet to be clarified, it remains unclear whether these tanks will find their way to Ukraine at all.

Rheinmetall was more successful with the purchase of former Belgian army Leopard 1s from the Belgian company OIP Land Systems, which in turn had acquired the vehicles from the Belgian state in 2014. In a project financed by Germany, a total of thirty of the fifty Leopard 1 A5BEs are being refurbished. However, one special feature of these vehicles is the SABCA fire control system, which is good but not widely used. This is probably the main reason why twenty of the vehicles are being used to recover spare parts.

The Leopard 1 Main Battle Tanks in Service in Ukraine

It was to be expected that the Leopard 1 would not play a role in classic battle tank operations: The tank's armor is simply too weak, and, unlike the equally venerable T-models of Russian design, it has not been retrofitted with reactive armor. Its mobility is good, if not outstanding, but the tank can hardly be used in an offensive role in the current warfare. The Leopard 1's mobility is helpful in evading drone attacks. The range and accuracy of Leopard 1's gun is welcomed, and while there are plenty of targets for its rather small 105 mm caliber gun, it would not be sufficient against more modern T-72 and T-90 tanks. The thermal-imaging device is a major advantage. It also allows night movement and combat, when the threat from drones is reduced. The general age of the vehicles should also not be underestimated. Failures of various assemblies are not uncommon, and spare parts are in short supply.

The opinion expressed by some "experts," that the Leopard 1 would be of little help to Ukraine, is not shared here. Any tank is still better than no tank at all. This comes from statements by Ukrainian people, who on a daily basis have experienced the change in warfare brought about by drones.

In November 2023, Rheinmetall announced the delivery of additional Leopard 1 systems to the Ukraine. The contract covers twenty-five Leopard 1A5 main battle tanks, five recovery vehicles (Bergepanzer 2), and three driver-training tanks. The message was accompanied by a photo of this ex-Bundeswehr Leopard 1 A5, even though, as far as is known, only Leopard 1 A5BE tanks refurbished by or by way of Rheinmetall have so far been delivered. *Photo: © Rheinmetall*

Chapter 4

Experimental Vehicles Based on the Leopard 1

ETF Suspension Test Bed

In tank development, newly developed components—such as engines, transmissions, running-gear elements, etc.—are subjected to test bench trials for functional and performance verification. Driving tests are then essential to determine the behavior of the new components under influences from the overall system and the effects of real-world operating conditions. For these purposes, test vehicles are used, which, for cost reasons, often have their origins in prototypes or preproduction vehicles from previous tank projects.

A number of Leopard 1 preproduction vehicles were used in the KPz 70 program, in particular for testing new running-gear elements. One example is the testing of hydropneumatic suspension elements with regard to their mechanical durability, tightness, and thermal behavior. The picture shows a converted preproduction vehicle (L II 5; manufacturer: Luther & Jordan; Brunswick), which served as a suspension test vehicle (ETF) for testing the hydropneumatic elements of the first generation of the

KPz 70 program in the 1966–68 period. New ground had to be broken both with the suspension elements and with the entire electrical control system for level control.

In addition, the entire system was very complex, so experience showed that there would be numerous defects and failures during the initial tests. The KPz 70 program was discontinued at the end of 1969, and the hydropneumatic suspension never became ready for series production. After the start of development of the Leopard 1 main battle tank, some of Company Group B's prototypes were again equipped with a hydropneumatic suspension. To date, it has not been possible to develop the hydropneumatic suspension into a production- and service-ready component in Germany, neither during the Leopard 1 program nor in the SPz-neu project nor in the course of the Leopard 2 program.

T III F Turret with Three-Axis Stabilization

In 1958, Company Group C (Borgward) presented a concept with a three-axis stabilized turret as part of the prototype designs. The design was not pursued further for the Leopard 1 because the development risks were too high at the time. However, it was decided to investigate the technology of the three-axis stabilized turret in more detail with a functional prototype. With a three-axis stabilized turret, accuracy could be improved when firing with the vehicle in a tilted position.

In the mid-1960s, Rheinstahl-Hanomag received an order to build a functional prototype; the electric drive and controls were supplied by AEG-Telefunken (Hamburg). The T III F turret housed a 105 mm tank gun as well as a coaxial 30 mm automatic cannon and a 7.62 mm machine gun for use by the tank commander. The lower half of the turret was spherical so that the turret could be moved in three axes. Three crew members were accommodated in the left half of the turret, while the right half housed the ammunition supply and an automatic loader. At the rear of the turret was a cooling system for the fighting compartment; the turret weighed 17.75 metric tons (19.56 tons) when fully equipped.

The turret was mounted on a chassis that, for logistical reasons, incorporated drive and running-gear elements from the Leopard 1. The hull was made of mild steel and was 3.51 meters (11.51 feet) wide. An auxiliary engine (74 kW, or 99 hp) was housed in the chassis to supply the stabilization system. The driver's position was located in the center of the vehicle's nose in front of the turret. If necessary, the vehicle could also be driven from the turret—a camera was installed on the upper glacis plate for this purpose.

No information is available about the level of accuracy that was achieved in trials. However, it can be assumed that the complex turret drive was prone to frequent failures. The drive elements were extremely difficult to access. Both for technical and cost reasons, this concept was not implemented in series production. Today, modern battle tanks use a gyroscope (vertical sensor) to compensate for tilting, which feeds the current position of the vehicle in relation to the ground-based system into the computer with high dynamics.

GVT Battlefield Test Bed

After the first laser simulators (TALLISSI) and multichannel telemetry systems became available in the early 1970s, it was possible to carry out field trials. In these practice-oriented tests, relevant combat data—such as reaction times, hit probabilities, and hit positions—could be determined under real conditions. On behalf of the BMVg (West German Federal Ministry of Defense), five battlefield test vehicles (GVT 01-05) were built in the 1970s to provide information on the feasibility of combat with highly maneuverable, double-barrel casemate tanks.

For logistical reasons, the drive and running-gear elements of the Leopard 1 were used in the construction of these vehicles. To increase their tactical mobility, track ground contact length was kept as short as possible. The engine's rated power was increased through the use of exhaust-driven turbosuperchargers and increasing the engine speed. The five GVTs were deployed in cooperation with the Combat Data Acquisition System (GDEA), mainly on the IABG premises in Lichtenau near Paderborn. With the GVT 05 and the VT 1-2 double-barrel casemate test vehicle, service trials were also carried out in the fall of 1975 at the former armored-forces school in Munster. The armored troops were not very enthusiastic about the revolutionary tank concept, and consequently most of these vehicles ended up as interesting exhibits in various museums.

Type	GVT Battlefield Test Bed
Year produced	1976
Crew	3
Combat weight	30.2 metric tons (33.28 tons)
Chassis length	6.30 meters (20.66 feet)
Width over tracks	3.69 meters (12.10 feet)
Height (turret roof)	2.03 meters (6.66 feet)
Main gun, caliber	2 × 120 mm (mockups)
Ammunition capacity	—
Secondary weapon 1, caliber	—
Secondary weapon 2, caliber	—
Engine, type	MB 838 Ka 500 10-cylinder diesel
Rated output	920 kW (1,233.74 hp)
Maximum speed	68 kph (42.25 mph)
Range on roads	no information
Fuel capacity	350 liters (92.46 US gal.)
Fuel consumption (on roads)	no information
Suspension	torsion bar with switching memory

Experimental Development (KPz Keiler)

Even before series production of the Leopard 1 main battle tank began in the fall of 1965, the Porsche company had drawn up a study with possible measures to increase its combat effectiveness. The aim was to come up with suggestions for improving all three combat-effectiveness criteria (firepower, mobility, and protection). Two test vehicles (ET 01, ET02) were built in the 1969–71 period as part of the Experimental Development Project to test the new components; these vehicles were also temporarily referred to as KPz Keiler (Wild Boar main battle tanks). The two test vehicles were eventually fitted with assemblies that

- could have been retrofitted to the Leopard 1 main battle tank to improve its combat capabilities without major costs or effort and
- reflected progress in the relevant component technology as part of a fundamental development.

The two test vehicles were equipped for the first time with a welded turret of bulkhead construction, which was later used in a similar form on the Leopard 1 A3 and A4 main battle tanks and the prototypes of the Leopard 2. The

Type	KPz Keiler
Year produced	1970
Crew	4
Combat weight	46.2 metric tons (50.92 tons)
Chassis length	7.58 meters (24.86 feet)
Width over tracks	3.42 meters (11.22 feet)
Height (turret roof)	2.43 meters (7.97 feet)
Main gun, caliber	105 mm smoothbore L/51
Ammunition capacity	no information
Secondary weapon 1, caliber	7.62 mm antiaircraft machine gun
Secondary weapon 2, caliber	7.62 mm mantlet machine gun
Engine, type	MB 872 Ka 500 10-cylinder diesel
Rated output	920 kW (1,233.74 hp)
Maximum speed	65 kph (40.38 mph)
Range on roads	450 km (279.61 mi.)
Fuel capacity	no information
Fuel consumption (on roads)	no information
Suspension	torsion bar

exhaust / exhaust air gratings were relocated to the vehicle's rear plate due to the more powerful engine and the modified cooling system. At the end of 1969, while the two test vehicles were still under construction, the bilateral KPz 70 tank program, which had been ongoing for seven years, was canceled. This created a completely new situation for the Bundeswehr overnight, since Germany now had to develop a main battle tank to replace the M48 entirely on its own. For time and cost reasons, assemblies from the experimental development as well as parts from the KPz 70 program were adopted for the subsequent Leopard 2 program.

Total Protection Test Bed (VTGS)

After the mass production of infrared sensors with the associated peripherals became possible in the early 1970s, this technology was increasingly used for reconnaissance (thermal-imaging devices) as well as for the automatic guidance of missiles and artillery ammunition. In conjunction with radar equipment, it was possible to significantly reduce the number of false targets, so that the first "intelligent artillery ammunition" became available at the beginning of the 1980s. This intelligent ammunition posed a new and serious threat to armored vehicles. In return, measures were developed on the vehicle side to reduce their infrared and radar signatures in order to make reconnaissance and target acquisition more difficult.

For this purpose, the Bundeswehr built and tested the Versuchsträger Gesamtschutz (VTGS), or Total Protection Test Bed. The vehicle was based on a Leopard 1 main battle tank chassis with a welded turret. The transmission was modified so that a ring cooling system could be installed in place of the flat radiators on the sides. This enabled a shielded exhaust and cooling-air outlet at the rear. In addition to infrared suppression measures, the radar signature was also reduced, which was achieved mainly through special shaping and coatings. The special armor elements (dummies) were also adapted to fit the hull with rubber mounting blocks. The VTGS was built in the mid-1980s at the Pietzsch GmbH branch facility in Schlangen (near Paderborn).

The lessons learned from these basic investigations were later incorporated into the design of the Boxer and Puma armored fighting vehicles.

Thermal image of a Leopard 1 main battle tank. Despite mixing the exhaust gases with the cooling air, the Leopard 1 still has a pronounced "hotspot" in the area of the exhaust grating when viewed with a thermal-imaging device. Another problem is the engine compartment ventilation: Here the heated air flows upward from the gratings in the front engine compartment cover and heats either the lower edge of the turret (with the turret in the twelve o'clock position) or (as here) the main gun's thermal sleeve.

Side view of the Total Protection Test Bed (VTGS). Special design precautions were taken to significantly reduce both the IR and radar signatures on the VTGS. By using a ring radiator, it was possible to create an exhaust air / exhaust gas outlet in the rear of the vehicle, which was additionally covered by a panel. The picture also shows the special shaping measures to reduce the vehicle's radar reflective cross section (RCS).

The picture shows a view from below into the cover plate at the rear of the vehicle. Since the acoustic signature should also be reduced, the VTGS has a muffler. The large opening in the rear of the tub for the cooling-air outlet from the ring radiator is clearly visible. The rear wall of the panel was provided with an insulating layer on the inside.

Thermal image of the VTGS. The hotspots on the hull sides were avoided thanks to the IR camouflage measures. The vehicle was also being heated by the sun when the photo was taken—the lower heat capacity of the GRP panels used in the rear part of the vehicle is noticeable here due to a slightly higher temperature. A small section of the clearly heated side wall of the engine compartment can be seen in front of the drive sprocket.

Jagdpanzer (JPz) Panther (Panther Tank Destroyer)

At the beginning of the 1980s, the Bundeswehr developed a new equipment concept for its armored forces. At the heart of this was the Kampfwagen 90 (KW 90) project, of which the following vehicle variants were to be developed:

- infantry fighting vehicle
- tank destroyer
- antihelicopter tank
- antitank combat vehicle
- mortar carrier

The Panther tank destroyer was supposed to replace the Jaguar tank destroyer in the antitank units; this vehicle was later also given the task of antihelicopter defense. An unusual feature of this new tank destroyer was an elevating platform (the question of whether it would be manned or unmanned was later decided in favor of the unmanned version). The elevated platform was expected to increase combat effectiveness, particularly with regard to battlefield observation and target reconnaissance. In the mid-1980s, several companies submitted various concept ideas on wheeled and tracked chassis for this vehicle. Following an official evaluation, the proposal from Wegmann & Co. for the Panther tank destroyer was selected as the most cost-effective solution in 1988. Wegmann had planned a Leopard 1 main battle tank chassis as the carrier vehicle. A fighting-compartment module was inserted into the rotating frame, which—in addition to two control stations for the commander and

Wooden model of the Panther Tank Destroyer. As part of the Kampfwagen 90 (KW 90) project in the mid-1980s, a tank destroyer with an elevatable weapon platform was planned as the successor to the Jaguar 1 and Jaguar 2 tank destroyers. Wegmann & Co. in Kassel had the attractive and cost-effective idea of using the chassis of the Leopard 1 main battle tank, which had become available for the vehicle, and attaching the fighting-compartment module, including the elevating device and the weapon platform, to the turret.

the gunner—housed the lifting device and the platform with the sensors and the launcher. The platform could be swiveled through 90 degrees to be able to remove the engine.

After reunification in 1989 and the associated elimination of the tank threat from the East, the KW 90 program was discontinued. The Puma infantry-fighting vehicle survived as the only version of the planned vehicle range. Another consequence of the elimination of the massive tank threat from Warsaw Pact units was the complete dissolution of the tank destroyer force in the German army. Some of the Jaguars were sold to Austria—but the majority of these vehicles were scrapped.

Trilateral Test Bed (TVT)

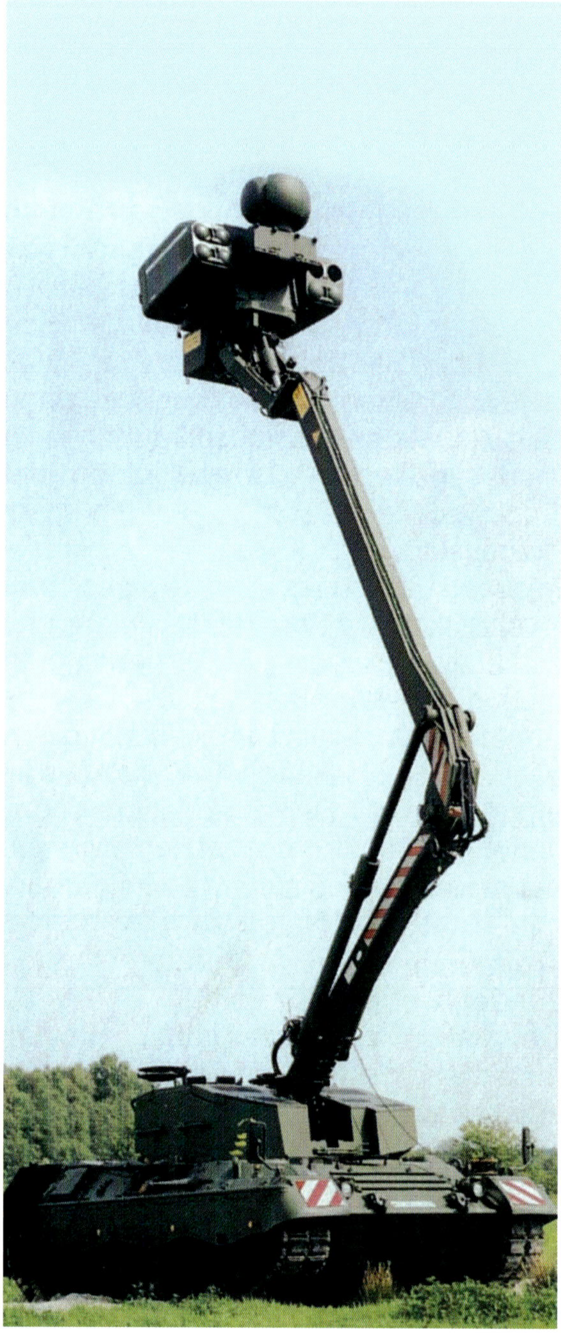

In 1981, France, Great Britain, and Germany agreed to jointly develop the PARS 3 LR missile (Anti-Tank Missile System 3–Long Range), which was to replace the HOT guided missile in the 1990s. The missile was to be deployable from helicopters as well as from vehicles. Proof of these capabilities was to be provided at the end of development.

Interestingly, the three nations agreed in 1991 to use the German concept for the Panther tank destroyer to demonstrate the system's ability to be launched from a ground-based platform. This concept provided for the launch of the missile from an elevatable platform. A Leopard 1 main battle tank served as the carrier vehicle, with a fighting-compartment module inserted in its rotating frame; this accommodated the control stations and the lifting device with the platform.

The trilateral test vehicle was completed in 1995 and had a combat weight of 41.5 metric tons (45.75 tons). The platform could be raised to a height of 12.5 meters in less than thirty seconds by using an articulated mast. Two control stations (commander and gunner) were located in the fighting-compartment module. From there, monitors were used for battlefield observation, target reconnaissance, target selection, and briefing of the selected missile. The platform was equipped with an OSIRIS sight with a stabilized-view mirror, and launchers for a total of eight missiles.

The firing tests conducted at the Wehrtechnische Dienststelle 91 (Meppen) in 1996 were successful. The overall PARS 3 LR program was less successful, with the UK announcing its withdrawal in 1993 and France postponing the procurement of the missiles indefinitely in 2005.

After a good thirty years (!) of development and overcoming numerous technical problems, series production of the PARS 3 LR began at MBDA (Schrobenhausen) in November 2015. According to the contract, 674 missiles were ordered; the system price is expected to be around 560,000 euros per missile.

Type	TVT
Introduction period (planned)	2009–14
Combat range (max.)	5,000 m (5,468 yards)
Missile length	1.60 m (62.99 in.)
Missile diameter	15.5 cm (6.10 in.)
Missile weight	41 kg (90.38 lbs.)
Velocity	290 m/sec. (951.44 ft./sec.)
Time to 4,500 m	14.5 sec
Warhead	tandem hollow charge
Guidance method	IR target location (fire and forget)

Leopard 1 Turret on the Puma Chassis

In 1983 the Krauss-Maffei and Diehl companies began initial conceptual studies for a light tracked-vehicle family. Three years later, the first prototype chassis was ready and presented to the public under the name Puma. The chassis was designed as a front-wheel-drive vehicle, thus providing favorable conditions for the creation of a complete vehicle family. The vehicles were to cover a weight range of 16–34 metric tons (17.6–37.48 tons); various engines and chassis with four, five, and six road wheels were planned. The design objective of all vehicles was to optimize costs, since the original intention of the manufacturers was to replace the M113 fleets in the various armed forces with a modern and efficient vehicle by the end of the 1980s.

At the end of 1993, a variant with a turret of the Leopard 1 A5 main battle tank was also unveiled; its combat weight was 36 metric tons (39.68 tons). Due to its relatively low level of protection, this vehicle was assigned the role of a tank destroyer. Comparable basic concepts (turret tank with front-mounted engine) were the light Argentinian TAM tank on the chassis of the Marder infantry-fighting vehicle and the Israeli Merkava main battle tank. Although a number of prototypes of the Puma family were tested by the German armed forces as well as in Turkey, Norway, and Switzerland, no production orders were placed.

Battlefield Test Containers

In the mid-1970s, results from practical field trials were successfully obtained from the battlefield test vehicles (GVT; see below), using laser gunnery simulators and telemetry systems. While the aim of the trials with the GVTs was to investigate the possible uses of twin-barrel casemate tanks and the associated targeting procedure in target engagement, the armaments division also wanted to extend the field trials in the early 1980s to obtain generally valid combat data. To this end, several "containers" were built that could be inserted into the rotating crane frame of a Leopard 1 chassis. The containers represented a fighting compartment and were equipped with laser weapon simulators as well as optical and optronic sighting devices. The type of simulated weaponry as well as the means of aiming and the distribution of tasks within the crew could be varied. The aim of the field trials with the containers was to find new concepts for future main battle tanks, which in particular could be expected to have a shorter reaction time when engaging targets.

The tests were carried out in the 1980s mainly at the IABG test site at Lichtenau near Paderborn.

Chapter 5

Inside the Leopard 1

General Fighting-Compartment Layout

The layout of the Leopard 1 main battle tank followed that of the standard concept for a turreted tank, with a crew of four and a rear-mounted engine. Three members of the crew (commander, gunner, and loader) were accommodated in the turret. The loader determined the overall placement of the crew, because ideally he was right-handed and positioned to the left of the main gun. This meant that the commander and gunner had to be on the right side of the turret. Because of the round shape of the turret ring and basket, ergonomic conditions for these two crew members were less than ideal.

The ready ammunition (thirteen rounds) is stored (standing) in ready racks at the edge of the turret platform on the left side of the turret, within easy reach of the loader; further ammunition racks are located beneath the main gun and in the rear of the turret. So that the gunner can also reach the ammunition stored in the ammunition magazine relatively easily, the ammunition racks (forty-two rounds) were housed in the left side of the hull front. The driver's position therefore had to be moved to the right side—mirroring the arrangement in British tanks.

When the Leopard 1 A1 version was retrofitted with gun stabilization, large protective screens had to be fitted to the right of the weapon to prevent the commander and gunner from being injured by the stabilized gun. This crew arrangement proved itself relatively well and was later retained by the Leopard 2 main battle tank.

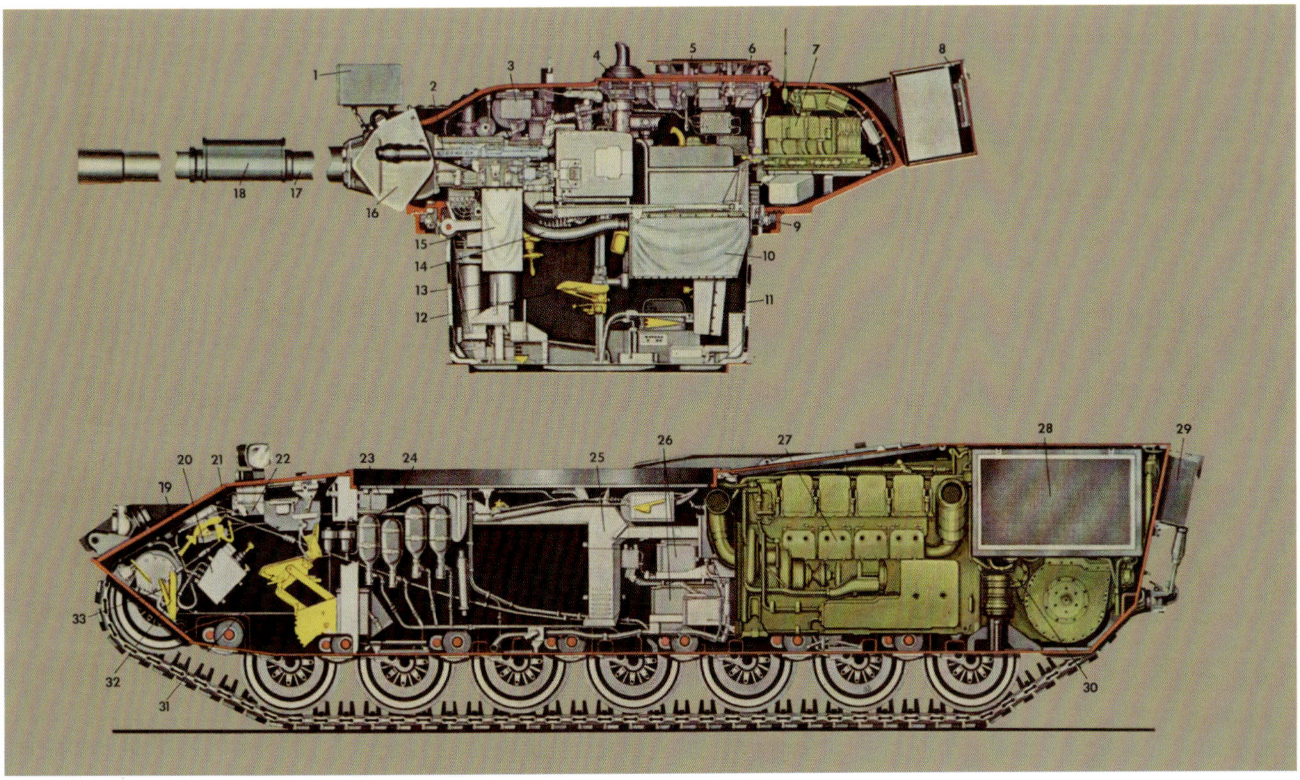

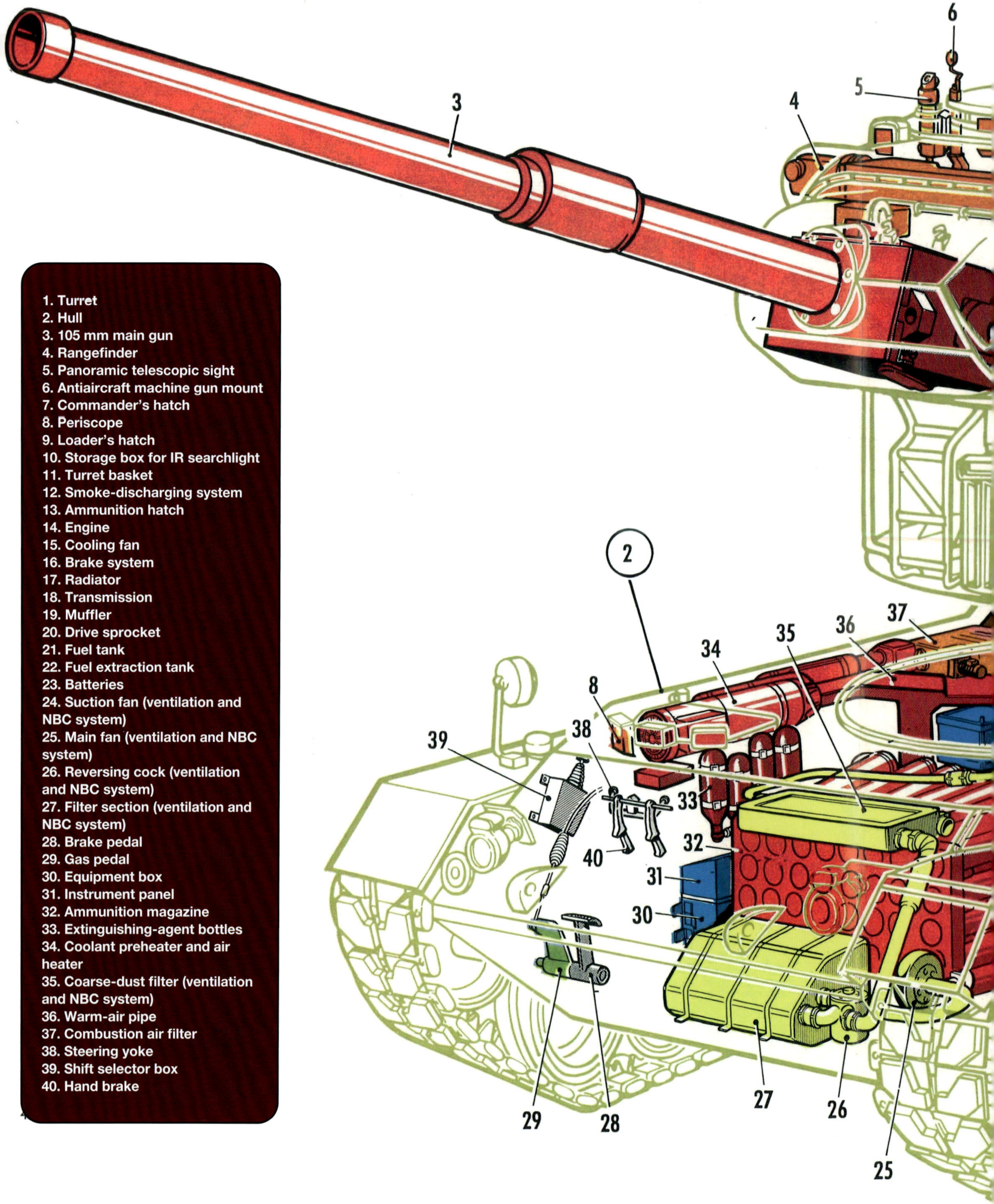

1. Turret
2. Hull
3. 105 mm main gun
4. Rangefinder
5. Panoramic telescopic sight
6. Antiaircraft machine gun mount
7. Commander's hatch
8. Periscope
9. Loader's hatch
10. Storage box for IR searchlight
11. Turret basket
12. Smoke-discharging system
13. Ammunition hatch
14. Engine
15. Cooling fan
16. Brake system
17. Radiator
18. Transmission
19. Muffler
20. Drive sprocket
21. Fuel tank
22. Fuel extraction tank
23. Batteries
24. Suction fan (ventilation and NBC system)
25. Main fan (ventilation and NBC system)
26. Reversing cock (ventilation and NBC system)
27. Filter section (ventilation and NBC system)
28. Brake pedal
29. Gas pedal
30. Equipment box
31. Instrument panel
32. Ammunition magazine
33. Extinguishing-agent bottles
34. Coolant preheater and air heater
35. Coarse-dust filter (ventilation and NBC system)
36. Warm-air pipe
37. Combustion air filter
38. Steering yoke
39. Shift selector box
40. Hand brake

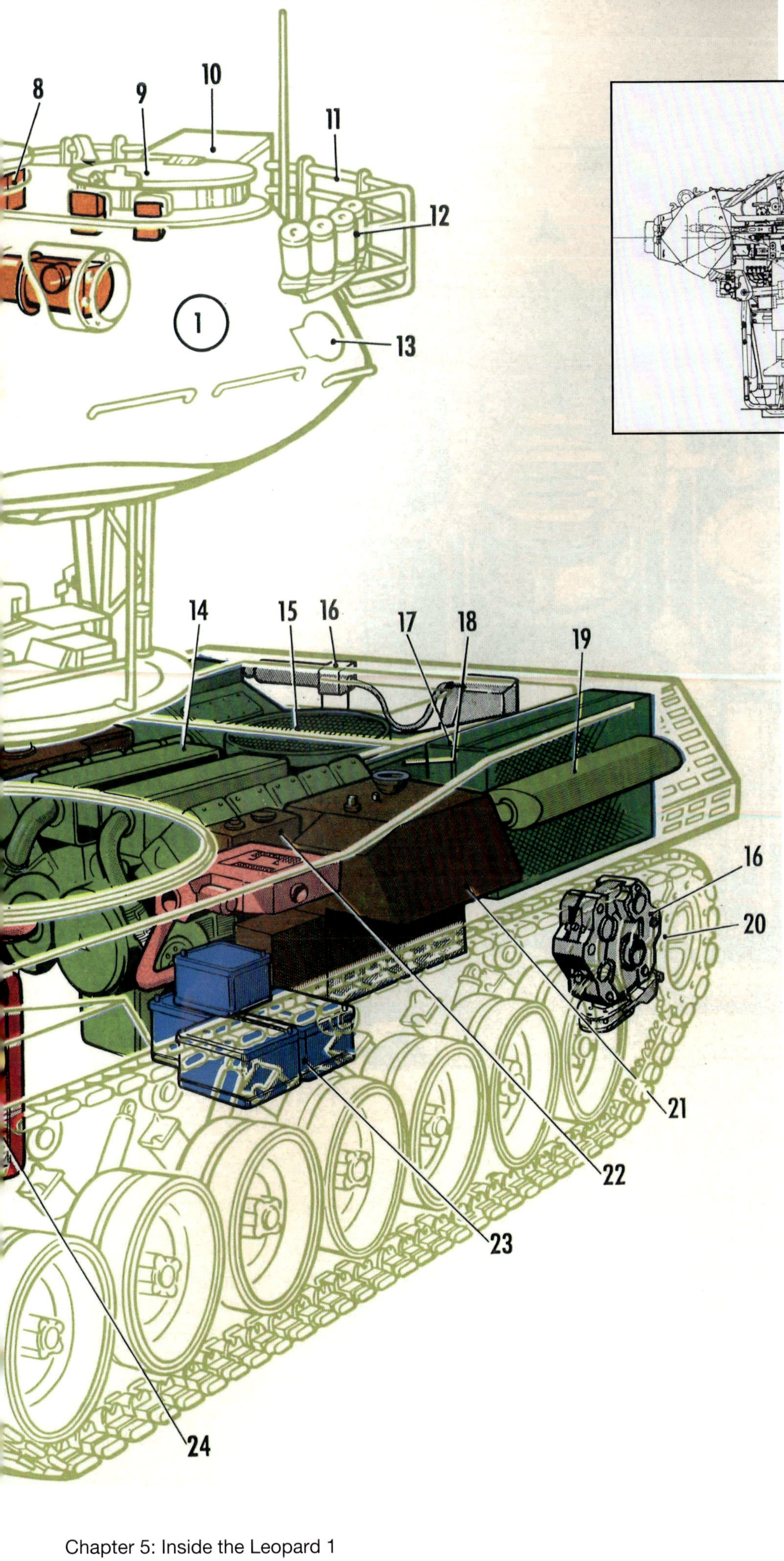

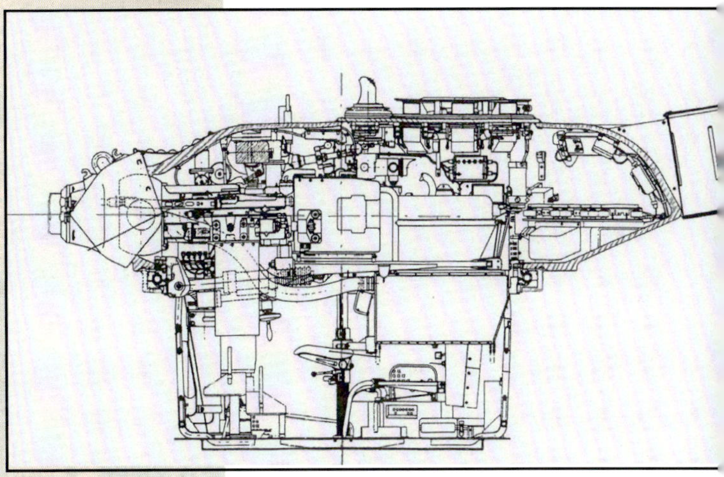

Cast turret cross section. The 20 mm thick rolled steel plate welded onto the turret roof is clearly visible. This made it possible to easily machine the openings for the turret hatches and the panoramic periscope without having to clamp the entire turret. The drawing still shows the older form of the container for the empty shell casings. A flexible hose was used to extract the remaining gases created when the gun was fired from the container, and to transport them outside.

Three-dimensional image of a Leopard 1 main battle tank, showing the internal components. The individual parts of the NBC ventilation system are colored in yellow. The placement of the filters inside the fighting compartment in front of the ammunition rack proved to be a disadvantage. This meant that contaminated filter elements had to be transported through the fighting compartment to the outside via the driver's hatch. The position of the batteries (*colored blue*) in the niches in front of the bulkhead to the engine compartment also proved to be disadvantageous in later use. This made access difficult, so that in practice the acid level was often not checked regularly.

Commander's and Gunner's Positions

The commander and gunner have their seats on the right-hand side of the turret; the commander sits behind the gunner in an elevated position. He has his own hatch with a ring of seven periscopes. The height of the commander's seat can be adjusted hydraulically by using a lever. The monocular eyepiece of the panoramic zoom telescopic sight is located in front of the commander. The one-handed handle for controlling the weapon and turret is located on the right-hand side. This enables the commander to assign a target to the gunner or to engage the target himself in an emergency.

The gunner is situated in front of the commander in a lower position in the forward area of the turret cage. Directly in front of him is the binocular eyepiece of the turret rangefinder sight, and below it the two aiming handles for rotating the turret and aiming the weapon. Firing pawls and a palm switch as a safety element are located on both aiming handles.

If the 24-volt (V) onboard power supply fails, the gunner is still able to engage a target. Aiming is carried out with the telescopic sight, whereby all relevant parameters (engagement distance, lead, cant, etc.) must be estimated by the gunner. The turret and weapon can be moved manually (at lower speeds) by using the traverse or elevation hand controller. For emergency firing, the gunner can generate the necessary power surge for the propellant charge igniter in the cartridge base via a manually movable magnetic core within an induction coil.

The space available for the commander and gunner is severely restricted, resulting in more or less unfavorable joint flexion angles for these two crew members in all seating positions.

Commander's and gunner's position: The picture provides a view of the right turret side of a Leopard 1 main battle tank from the third production batch. The vehicle had not yet been retrofitted with the weapon stabilization system—the corresponding protective grilles are missing. In the area of the commander's position, the commander's seat (seat surface folded up), the lower part of the panoramic periscope with the monocular view, and the traverse mechanism with the override handle can be seen. In the area of the gunner's position, the sight of the turret telescope and the front support of the rangefinder's sight can be seen. On the right-hand side of the gunner's position are the azimuth circle as well as a switch box and the turret lashing.

***Right:* Gunner's position in the turret of a Leopard 1 A5 main battle tank: The use of the new EMES 18 main gunner's sight resulted in the installation of new control units at the gunner's position. The control unit for the thermal-imaging device was located on the right above the aiming handles. The picture also allows a view down to the driver's position and parts of the emergency exit hatch.**

HÖHE
LUFTTEMP.
PULVERTEMP.
DRIFT
BELEUCHTUNG H2F
PRÜFUNG
LAMPEN
VOR
BELEUCHTUNG
WÄRMEBILDGERÄT
GROSS
KLEIN
SCHARFSTELLUNG
STRICHBILD
WAFFE
MG

Loader's Position

During normal training activities, the loader on the left side of the turret has the most generous amount of space in the turret area. With the aid of a parka, the loader can even create a comfortable resting place for tankers on the floor of the turret platform. However, this situation changes dramatically when the eleven ready positions along the turret ring are filled with ammunition. The gunner then also has very limited room to move and must constantly ensure that he does not enter the main gun's recoil range. The situation is exacerbated when driving with the gun stabilized. A safety screen is not practical at the gunner's position.

The 105 mm cartridges (weighing 18–21 kg and approximately 1,000 mm in length) are still relatively easy to handle, and loading is made considerably easier by the 105 mm weapon's breech, with horizontally sliding breechblock. In addition to loading the main weapon, the loader is responsible for the proper functioning (barrel change, ammunition feed, etc.) of the coaxial machine gun. Practitioners know that the greatest disruptive effect for the loader when loading the main weapon is caused by the connecting cable from the intercom system to the control box on his chest.

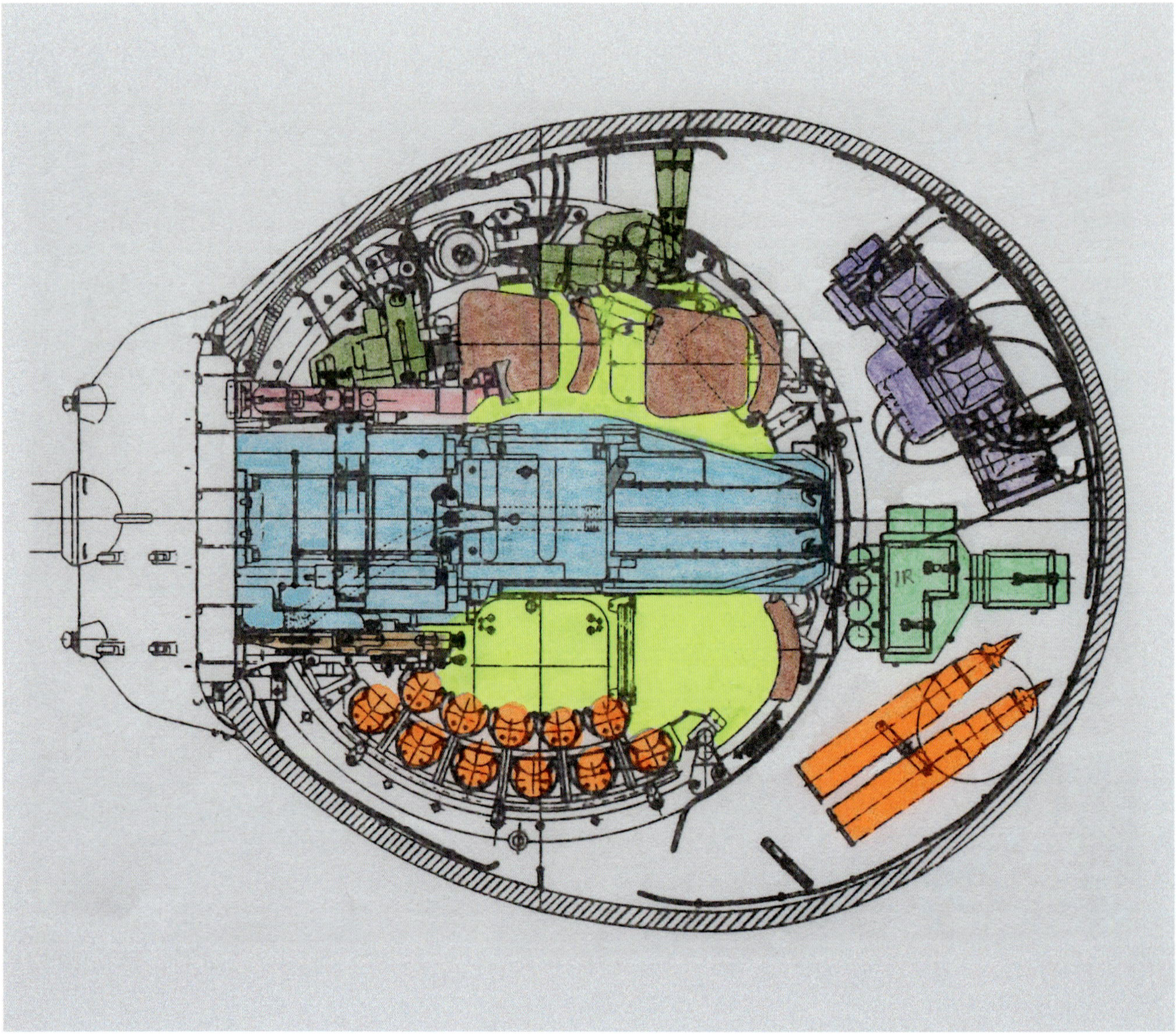

Loader's position: This remarkable photo shows the left side of the turret with filled ammunition racks. The cartridges with the ogive projectile heads are squash-head projectiles. The cartridges with the peculiarly shaped cylindrical parts are shaped-charge projectiles. The cylindrical part ("spike") serves as a spacer element through which the warhead is ignited shortly before the impact of the insert. This was intended to ensure that the hollow-charge spike was formed before the insert was destroyed. The way the machine gun ammunition is stored does not comply with the regulations at all but was probably intended to reinforce the atmosphere in a combat-ready vehicle.

The loader's position in a Leopard 1 A5 main battle tank: The picture conveys the supposed impression of the generous space available for the gunner—but such a picture presents itself only when the ammunition racks were empty and folded up! In the loader's workspace, the racks for the ready ammunition were arranged on the left side of the turret as well as the ammunition magazine in the hull front. Four boxes for the 7.62 mm machine gun ammunition were also placed in the forward area of the gunner's position. The loader has access to further boxes of machine gun ammunition through the flap on the floor of the rotating platform. The ready ammunition for the mantlet machine gun on the left side of the gun cradle (not installed here) was located in the white box on the left turret side wall.

Driver's Position

The driver is housed separately from the turret crew in the front right of the forward hull. He has a steering yoke with which to steer the tank. Using the steering yoke is easier than steering with two steering levers, as was the case with older armored vehicles (M113, Hotchkiss, etc.). However, driving the Leopard 1 main battle tank also requires careful training since, for example, the minimum turning radii depend on the gear selected. The brake and accelerator pedals are located in the footwell in front of the driver's seat. Since the transmission has a torque converter, a clutch pedal is no longer required. However, the driver still has to shift gears himself in the vehicles from production batches 1 to 5, since the automatic gearshift was retrofitted only later (installed at the factory in vehicles from the sixth production batch). The driver's compartment is also noticeably cramped; the driver's seat, for example, is only 490 mm wide. To the left of the driver's seat is a large equipment compartment (electronics) with an instrument panel above it. To the right of the driver's seat are the gear selector and the direction selector levers. The driver is also assigned the control units for the heater and the fire-extinguishing system.

The three periscopes above the steering wheel offer only a relatively small field of vision and initially caused considerable problems, especially for inexperienced drivers when driving with the hatch closed. The small periscopes often limit the speed off-road—even if the engine and chassis would allow a higher speed!

The emergency exit hatch (52 × 35 cm, or 20.5 × 13.77 in.) is recessed into the floor of the hull behind the driver's seat; it can be reached much more quickly by the driver than by the turret crew. However, with a ground clearance of 440 mm, only slender contortionists will be able to disembark quickly and gallantly.

Engine Compartment with Engine

Engine installed: A look at the installed power pack reveals the high component density in the engine compartment. This is the result of the need to reduce or minimize the armored space (weight saving). On the other hand, the high component density makes access to various components more difficult. For example, the entire engine has to be removed to change a glow plug. The fan wheel can be seen in the middle of the rear section. Below it is the so-called air duct box, which pushes the sucked-in air through the two radiators arranged on the side.

Engine on the hook of a Bergepanzer 2 armored recovery vehicle: The Bergepanzer 2 (standard armored recovery vehicle) is optimized for work on the Leopard 1 main battle tank. The crane system was designed in such a way that the ARV can drive through an open hangar door with an engine on the hook. It is also possible to use the Bergepanzer 2 to pick up a turret of the main battle tank and set it down in front of the vehicle. The picture shows the two superchargers on the front of the engine. When development of the MB 837 engine series began in the mid-1950s, the technology of exhaust-driven turbochargers for tank engines was not yet ready for use.

In contrast to Russian main battle tanks, the Leopard 1's engine, transmission, cooling system, and other assemblies are combined into a single power pack. After removing the engine compartment cover, the following tasks must be carried out to remove the power pack:

- Loosen four bolts in the engine mount.
- Separate the transmission and final drives (sliding sleeve).
- Disconnect the actuating cables.
- Disconnect electrical connections.
- Disconnect the fuel line.
- Disconnect the brake hydraulics line.
- Disconnect the air intake (compressors) and exhaust lines.

The complete power pack weighs approximately 4.7 metric tons (5.18 tons); four lifting lugs are provided for extraction.

To save weight in tank construction, the aim is to achieve a high component density within the armored housing volume. For this reason, only 2–3 cm (0.8–1.2 in.) of free space remains between the power pack and the assemblies in the engine compartment (e.g., fuel tanks). In order to avoid damaging these components when installing the power pack, appropriate guide elements are provided to hold the power pack securely in place until it has reached its final position in the engine mounts. Due to the high component density, unacceptably high temperatures would occur in the engine compartment during engine operation. To avoid the risk of overheating, the engine compartment is constantly flushed with cooling air. In the Leopard 1, this air is taken from the air duct box in front of the radiators and exits from the two grilles in the forward engine compartment cover, below the turret rear, after passing through the engine compartment. During deep wading and underwater travel, the engine compartment remains dry—only the air-ducting box with the radiators is flooded.

Engine Compartment Without Engine

When the engine is removed, the vehicle's brake system, which consists of the service brake and the parking brake, remains in the engine compartment. This also includes the brake valve block, including the reservoir on the rear wall of the engine compartment. The mechanical connection between the transmission output and the brake / final drive is established by an internally toothed sliding sleeve. Before the drive unit is pulled, the sliding sleeve is pulled into the final drive via the hollow shaft of the drive wheel, using a special tool.

The fuel tanks are located to the left and right of the engine (475 liter, 480 liter, and 30-liter extraction tank). A small free space remains on the hull floor between the engine and gearbox, which is used to accommodate the bilge pump; the water outlet is located in the rear wall.

The engine compartment is separated from the fighting compartment by a gastight and watertight bulkhead. The spray pipes of the fire-extinguishing system are also installed in the engine compartment. Two extinguishing agent cylinders are automatically triggered by a so-called fire-warning wire, which triggers the extinguishing process at temperatures above 180 degrees Celsius. The fire-warning wire is laid in critical areas within the engine compartment.

Chapter 6

Components

Firepower-Defining Components

The 105 mm Main Gun

The British 105 mm L7 tank gun was chosen as the primary weapon for the Leopard 1 main battle tank. The gun consists of a one-piece barrel, which is fitted with three bayonet lugs at the end of the propellant chamber to attach the base piece. The barrel has twenty-eight grooves and fields with a constant right-hand twist. This causes the projectiles to spin (at approximately 100,000 rpm) until they exit the barrel, which serves to stabilize them during the flight phase. A bore evacuator is located halfway down the length of the barrel and is used to extract the remaining gases in the rear part of the tube after the projectile has exited, and to expel them to the front. To reduce barrel distortion due to the effects of weather, a thermal sleeve was retrofitted starting in 1972. If, however, barrel distortion occurred after firing several shots in a few minutes due to residual thermal stress, the gunner was able to improve accuracy by using the field adjustment system (FJA), retrofitted to the Leopard 1 A5 version starting in 1986.

The horizontally sliding breechblock in the breech opens automatically after firing, as

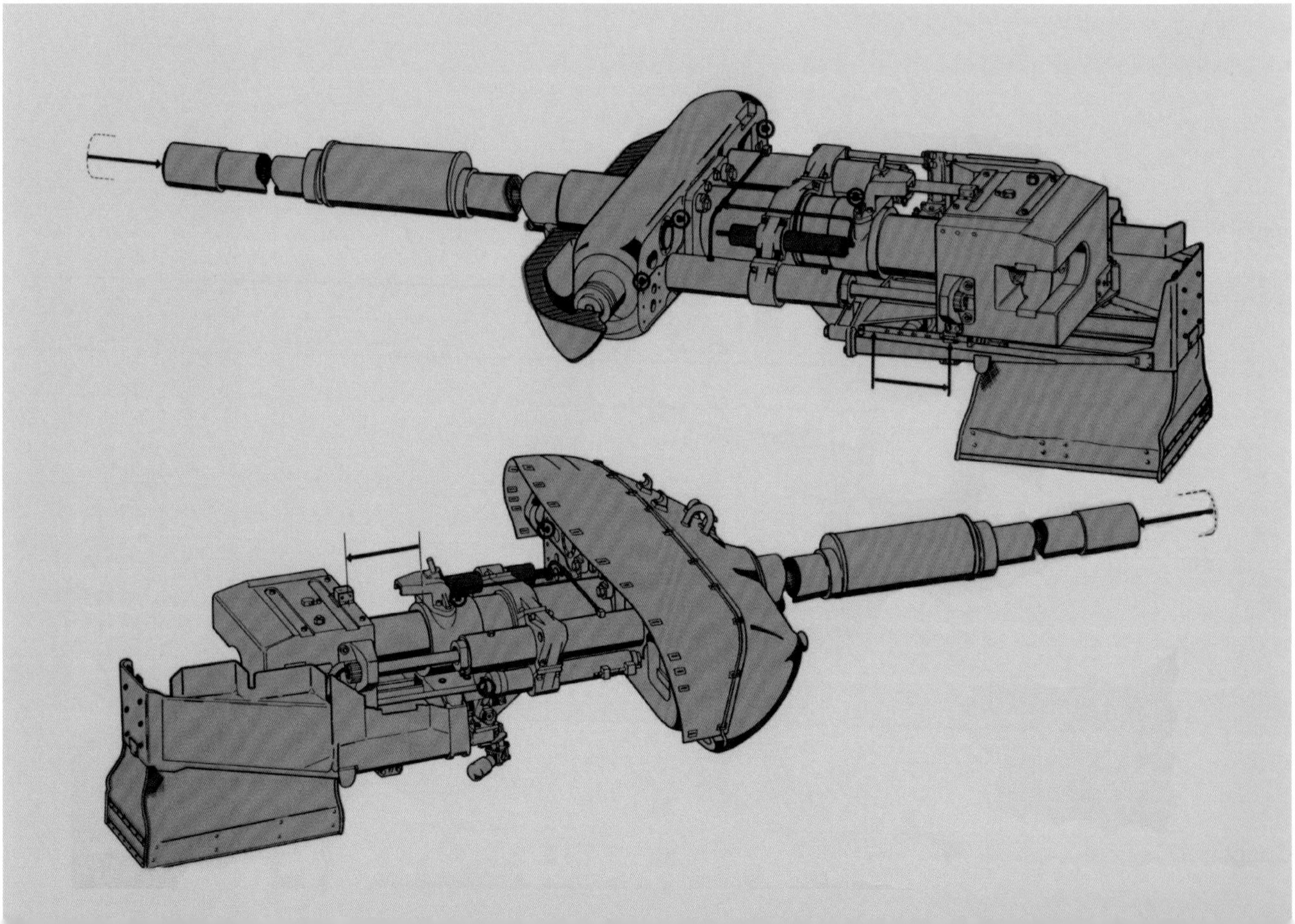

the gun returns to battery from full recoil. At the same time, the empty cartridge case is ejected by the ejector claws and falls into the case catcher. When a new cartridge is loaded, the ejector claws are pushed forward again—this unlocks the breechblock and closes by spring pressure.

The recoil parts of the weapon system are mounted in the cradle tube; the recoil energy is absorbed by two hydraulic tube brakes. With a maximum braking force of 600 kN (= 60 tons), the tube return is 280 mm (11 in.). The tube is then pushed back into the forward position by a pneumatic recuperator.

Main Gun	Specification
Caliber	105 mm
Caliber lengths	50.9
Barrel length	5,347 mm (17.54 ft.)
Barrel length with breech	5,588 mm (18.33 ft.)
Number of grooves	28
Twist angle	9°54', right-hand twist
Design gas pressure	5,210 bar
Service gas pressure	4,250 bar
Barrel recoil	280 mm (11 in.)
Weight of barrel	760 kg (1,675.51 lbs.)
Weight of breech	496 kg (1,093.49 lbs.)
Weight of weapon system without mantlet 1,285 kg (2,832.94 lbs.)	496 kg
Weight of weapon system with mantlet	2,300 kg (5,070.63 lbs.)
Gewicht Waffenanlage m. Blende	2300 kg

105 mm Armor-Piercing Discarding Sabot (APDS) Ammunition

In the 1960s, a so-called hard-core projectile with sabots of the type L 28—later L 52 A1—became available for engaging armored targets. The projectile was spin-stabilized and made of relatively brittle tungsten carbide. Compared to the previously used full-caliber projectiles, the subcaliber sabot represented a clear advantage for the conditions of the time. The projectile itself consisted of the actual core (penetrator), which had a relatively small diameter (45 mm, or 1.77 in.) to reduce air resistance. Three sabot segments made of a light metal alloy (7075) were used to center the core in the barrel. This allowed the gas pressure in the tube to act on the full cross-sectional area. After the projectile left the barrel, the sabot segments were thrown outward by the centrifugal forces and separated from the actual projectile (core). The small cross section of the core had a positive effect both on the trajectory (low loss of velocity) and armor penetration (concentration of kinetic energy on a small cross section).

A disadvantage was that the sabot segments had to be accelerated as a "dead weight" and flew up to 700 meters (765 yards) after the projectile left the barrel. It was therefore not possible to fire over friendly troops with this type of ammunition. Another disadvantage of APDS ammunition was its high angular sensitivity on impact and the loss of effect on the target if the target structure consisted of spaced or special armor.

APDS Ammunition	Specification
Cartridge designation	105 × 617 DM 13
Cartridge length	838 mm (33 in.)
Cartridge weight	18.6 kg (41 lbs.)
Projectile length	274 mm (10.78 in.)
Projectile weight	5.85 kg (12.90 lbs.)
Explosive charge weight	—
Projectile core diameter	45 mm (1.77 in.)
Projectile core weight	2.73 kg (12.9 lbs.)
L/D	3.2:1
Propellant charge weight	6.5 kg (14.33 lbs.)
Muzzle velocity	1,478 m/sec. (4,849 ft./sec.)
Speed drop	approx. 100 m/sec. (328 ft/sec) at 1,000 m
Maximum gas pressure	3,500 bar
Armor penetration	approx. 260 mm at 1,000 m

APDS cartridge

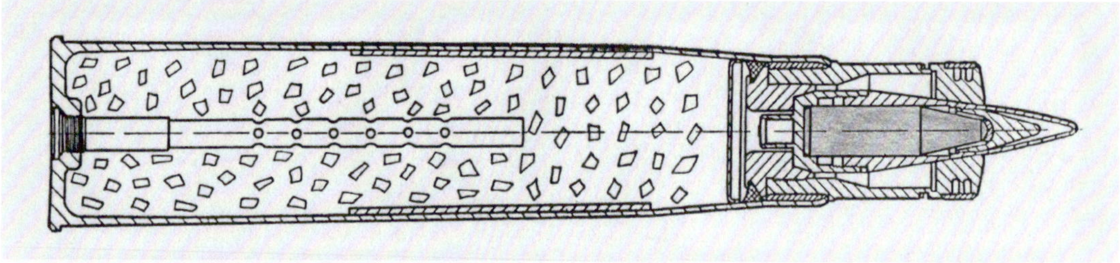

APDS projectile

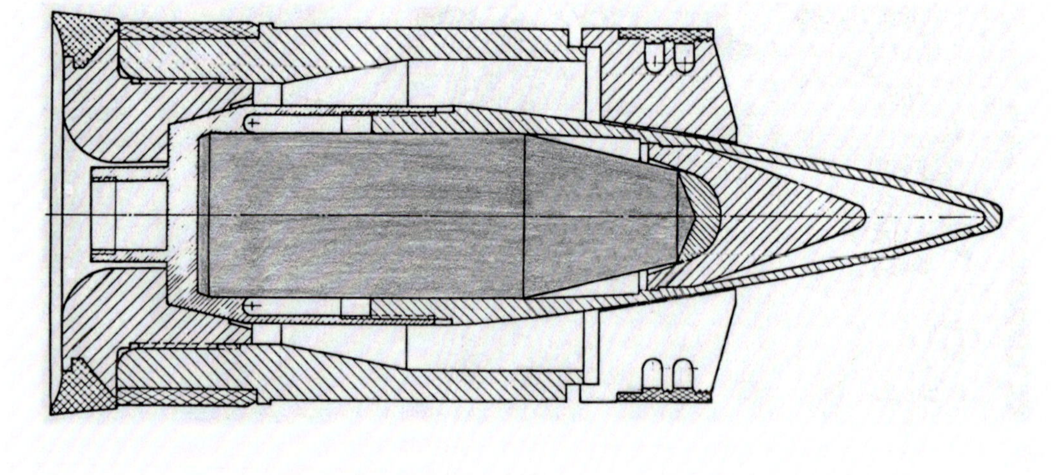

105 mm Armor-Piercing Discarding Sabot, Fin-Stabilized (APDSFS) Ammunition

The APDS projectile became obsolete at the latest with the appearance of the T-72 main battle tank in 1973 and its multilayered special armor on the front of the vehicle. Further development of the spin-stabilized sabot projectile led to fin-stabilized dart ammunition (APDSFS) in the 1970s. The transition to fin stabilization meant that the projectile could be made longer—which had a positive effect on the achievable penetration rate. The elimination of spin (and thus the centrifugal forces) now also enabled effective use against spaced armor. Due to the slimmer projectile, a tungsten heavy-metal alloy was used as the penetrator material for the dart projectiles, which exhibited significantly more ductile behavior with high strength. The dart ammunition also exhibited significantly better penetration characteristics when striking heavily sloped armor.

The basic projectile design corresponds to the sabot projectile—that is, the penetrator, with a relatively small cross section, is centered by three sabot segments during acceleration in the barrel. After projectile exit, the three segments separate from the penetrator.

At the beginning of the 1980s, the Bundeswehr ordered around 100,000 rounds of this new type of ammunition from Israel (DM 13) and a further 100,000 rounds of an improved model (DM 23) at the end of 1983. With the new dart ammunition and the modern fire control system, the Leopard 1 A5 main battle tank, in particular, demonstrated acceptable firepower in the 1980s.

APDS Ammunition	Specification
Cartridge designation	105 × 617 DM 13 AP-DS-FS
Cartridge length	884 mm (34.80 in.)
Cartridge weight	18.8 kg (41.45 lbs.)
Projectile length	390 mm (15.35 in.)
Projectile weight	6.27 kg (13.82 lbs.)
Explosive charge weight	—
Projectile core diameter	33 mm (1.3 in.)
Projectile core weight	4.18 kg (9.21 lbs.)
L/D	11.8:1
Propellant charge weight	5.7 kg (12.56 lbs.)
Muzzle velocity	1,450 m/sec. (4,757.21 ft./sec.)
Speed drop	approx. 44 m/sec. at 1,000 m
Maximum gas pressure	no information
Armor penetration	approx. 360 mm at 1,000 m

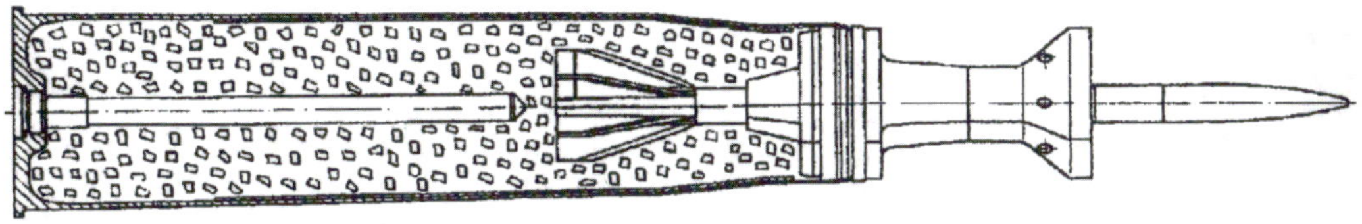

Kinetic-energy cartridge

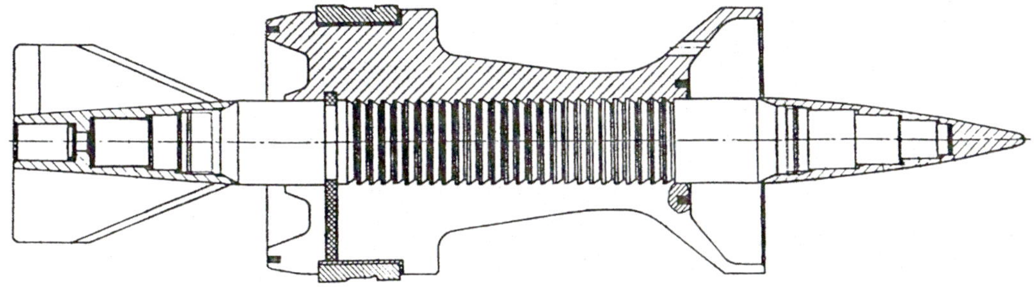

Kinetic-energy projectile

105 mm Hollow-Charge (HEAT) Ammunition

This American-made shaped-charge projectile for the Leopard 1's 105 mm tank gun is fin-stabilized. To prevent the transmission of spin to the projectile as far as possible, the projectile has a slipping plastic guide band. With a muzzle velocity of 1,173 meters/second, the projectile loses approximately 275 meters/second over the first 1,000 meters of flight due to the unfavorable projectile shape. In contrast to the APDS projectile, the impact velocity on the target does not play a role here, since the penetration performance of the shaped charge is independent of range. The penetration rate is subject to a certain amount of variation; it is approximately 430 mm (16.9 in.) in homogeneous armor steel.

The projectile has a so-called "spike" containing a piezo detonator so that the shaped charge spike can form on impact with a target. When the head fuse strikes, a power surge initiates the bottom fuse, located at the rear end of the warhead, which detonates the projectile's explosive charge. The detonation front of the explosive compresses the conical insert in the projectile head so that the hollow-charge spike is formed when all the particles of the insert collide along the longitudinal axis of the projectile.

(HEAT: High-explosive anti-tank)

Hollow-Charge Ammunition	Specification
Cartridge designation	105 × 617 HEAT M 456
Cartridge length	988 mm (38.89 in.)
Cartridge weight	21 kg (46.30 lbs.)
Projectile length	673 mm (26.50 in.)
Projectile weight	10.14 kg (22.35 lbs.)
Explosive charge weight	1.04 kg (2.29 lbs.)
Propellant charge weight	5.2 kg (11.46 lbs.)
Muzzle velocity	1,173 m/sec. (3,848.42 ft./sec.)
Speed drop	approx. 275 m/sec. at 1,000 m
Maximum gas pressure	3,750 bar
Armor penetration	approx. 400–460 mm depending on range

HEAT cartridge

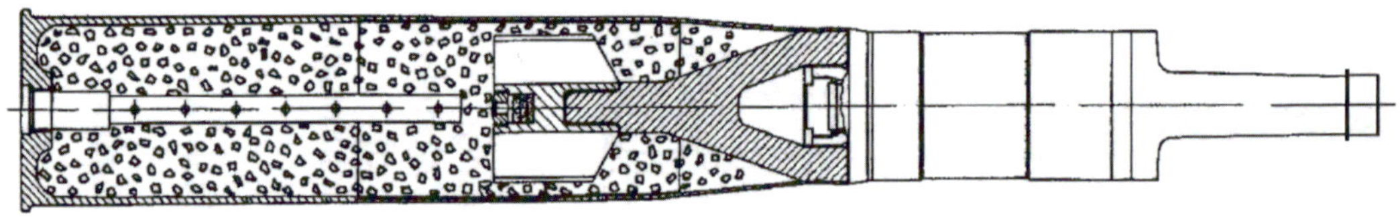

HEAT projectile

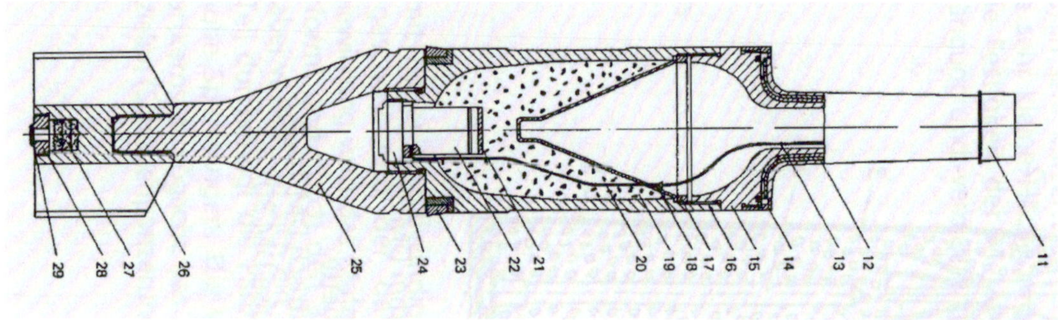

105 mm Squash-Head (HESH/HEP) Ammunition

The third type of ammunition that can be fired from the 105 mm tank gun is the so-called squash-head round. It is used to engage lightly armored and area targets. This is an explosive projectile with a thin-walled shell and a charge of plastically deformable, highly explosive material. The thin-walled projectile casing limits the permissible load when firing; the muzzle velocity is therefore only 731 meters/second.

This type of ammunition was produced for the 105 mm tank gun both in the United States and in Great Britain; this resulted in slightly different designations:

- US production: HEP (high-explosive plastic)
- UK production: HESH (high-explosive squash head)

Squash-Head Ammunition	Specification
Cartridge designation	105 × 617 HESH DM 512
Cartridge length	937 mm (36.88 in.)
Cartridge weight	21.2 kg (46.74 lbs.)
Projectile length	411 mm (16.18 in.)
Projectile weight	11.25 kg (24.80 lbs.)
Explosive charge weight	2.40 kg (5.30 lbs.)
Propellant charge weight	2.70 kg (5.95 lbs.)
Muzzle velocity	731 m/sec. (2,398.30 ft./sec.)
Maximum gas pressure	3,750 bar
Speed drop	171 m/sec. at 1,000 m
Armor penetration	max. of 80 mm at 1,000 m

HEP cartridge

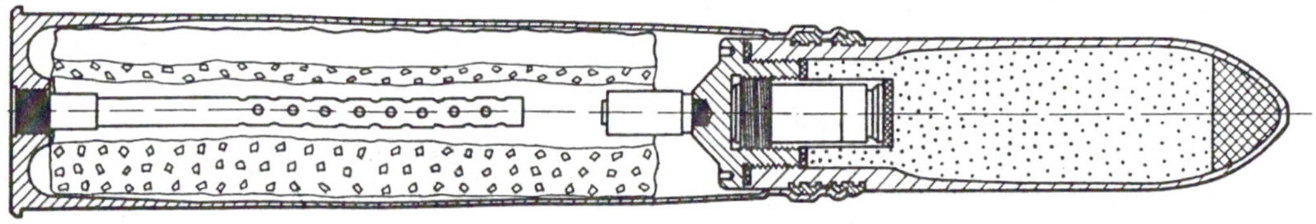

HEP projectile

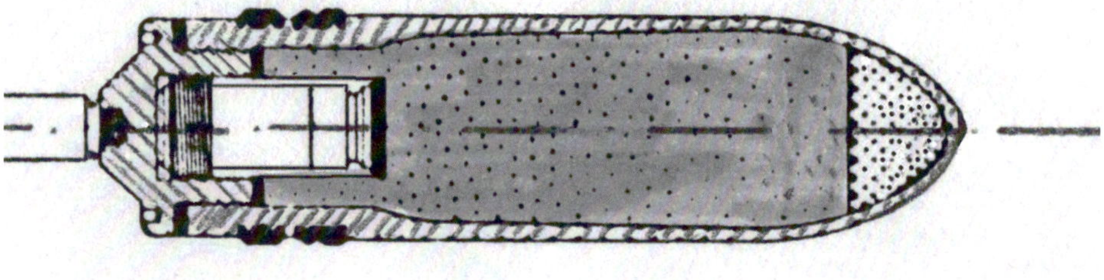

Effect of Discarding Sabot (APDS and APDSFS) Ammunition

As kinetic penetrator munitions, neither APDS nor APDSFS rounds contain explosives, since their penetrative performance is determined by their kinetic energy on impact ($E_{kin} = \frac{1}{2} m v_z^2$), with *m* equaling the mass of the penetrator and v_z the speed with which it strikes the target.

Due to the loss of velocity over the projectile's flight path, the achievable penetration performance is therefore distance-dependent. With the APDS projectile, penetration is achieved by plastic deformation of the target material. With thin plate thicknesses, the target material tears open; with thicker plate thicknesses, shearing and punching processes occur. After penetrating the armor, glowing projectile fragments and splinters from the target material enter the fighting compartment. At impact angles of less than 25 degrees, the APDS projectile tends to ricochet; the use of spaced and special armor greatly reduces penetration performance.

In the 1960s, fin-stabilized dart projectiles (often referred to simply as KE penetrator ammunition) were developed to meet the demand for higher penetration rates, even against modern armor. The transition to fin stabilization was necessary due to the lengthening of the penetrator (increase in the L/D ratio). Due to the greater penetrator mass, the transition to a tougher material (tungsten heavy metal) and the elimination of projectile spin (elimination of centrifugal forces!), the penetration performance of the dart ammunition could be significantly increased; in the best-case scenario, the penetration performance corresponds to the length of the penetrator. The higher impact velocity of KE ammunition results in different processes when penetrating the target material. The penetration occurs as a hydrodynamic penetration in which the target material is displaced and the core (penetrator) is consumed (eroded) in the process.

Dart ammunition also shows a lower loss of velocity over the flight path. The tougher penetrator material has also drastically reduced the angular sensitivity; KE projectiles are still effective at impact angles down to 15 degrees!

Effect of Hollow-Charge (HEAT) Ammunition

The penetration behavior of shaped-charge ammunition differs from that of discarding sabot ammunition in many respects. The penetration performance of a shaped-charge warhead depends, among other things, on

- the caliber,
- the mass of the explosive,
- the material of the insert,
- the quality (homogeneity) of the explosive and liner, and
- the precision of all parts (observance of rotational symmetry).

Penetration performance is independent of range. After impact of the projectile and ignition of the explosive, the detonation front runs over the insert and compresses the parts of the insert in the longitudinal axis of the projectile—this forms the hollow-charge spike (hollow-charge jet), the tip of which penetrates the target material at approximately 10,000 meters/second (!). Pressures of approximately 1 million bar are generated at the tip of the spike. Due to this high pressure, the spike particles and the target material behave like liquids—the target material is displaced to the side. No cracking or shearing takes place; thermal effects also play a subordinate role in such highly dynamic processes. It is therefore completely wrong to claim that the shaped-charge jet "cuts through the armor like a welding torch"!

The maximum penetration power is achieved by a shaped charge in homogeneous armor steel; up to four to five times the insert diameter is penetrated here. However, the hole diameter is only a few millimeters, and due to the low mass and relatively low energy content, the shaped-charge beam can easily be disrupted. In modern special armoring, appropriate measures are taken to disrupt the focusing of the jet particles, which dramatically reduces the penetration power. One of the countermeasures known to be effective against the hollow-charge threat is reactive armor, which has been used on Russian main battle tanks since 1984.

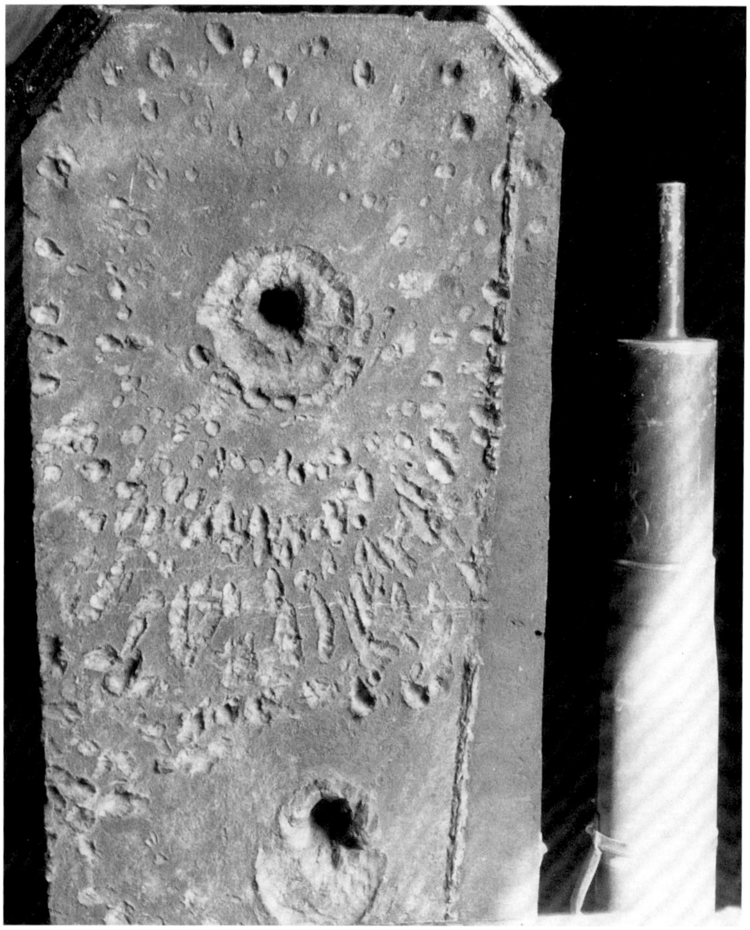

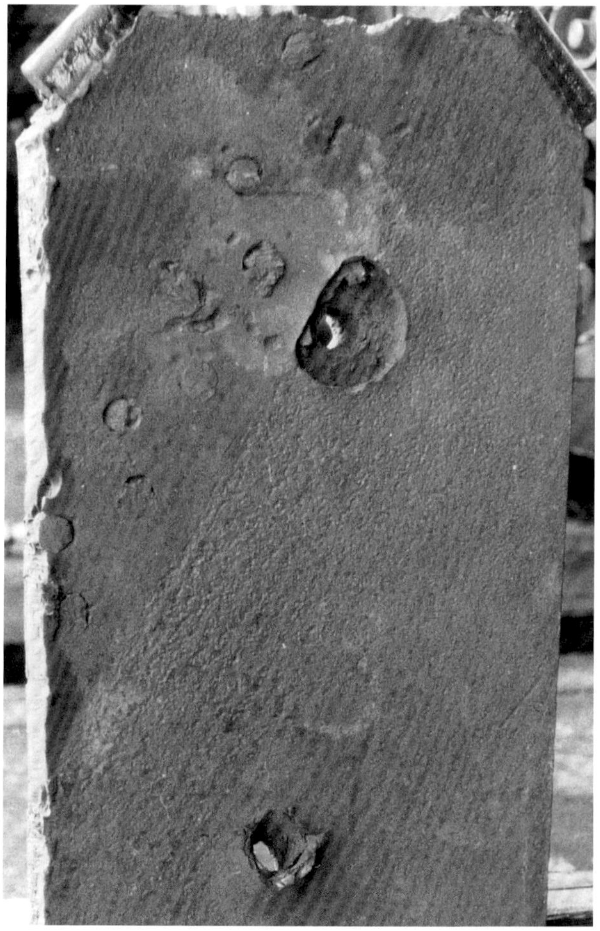

Effect of Squash-Head (HEP) Ammunition

When squash-head ammunition strikes a target, the detonating explosive causes a large gas impact effect, and a certain fragmentation effect is also achieved due to the shattering projectile casing. Squash-head ammunition is therefore primarily used against unarmored targets, area targets, field fortifications, and buildings.

When used against armored targets, armor plates up to approximately 70 mm (2.75 in.) thick are still penetrated directly by the projectile. With thicker plates, the projectile casing is destroyed on impact, so that the explosive is pressed against the armor like a pancake shortly before detonation. After detonation, a shock wave front runs through the target material. When the shock wave is reflected on the inside of the armor, the strength of the material is exceeded. This causes plate-shaped layers of material on the inside to burst off at velocities of up to 300 meters/second (Hopkinson effect). The resulting spall effect is independent of the impact velocity of the projectile; however, it decreases with greater sheet thicknesses. The spall effect is also negated by spaced or special armor.

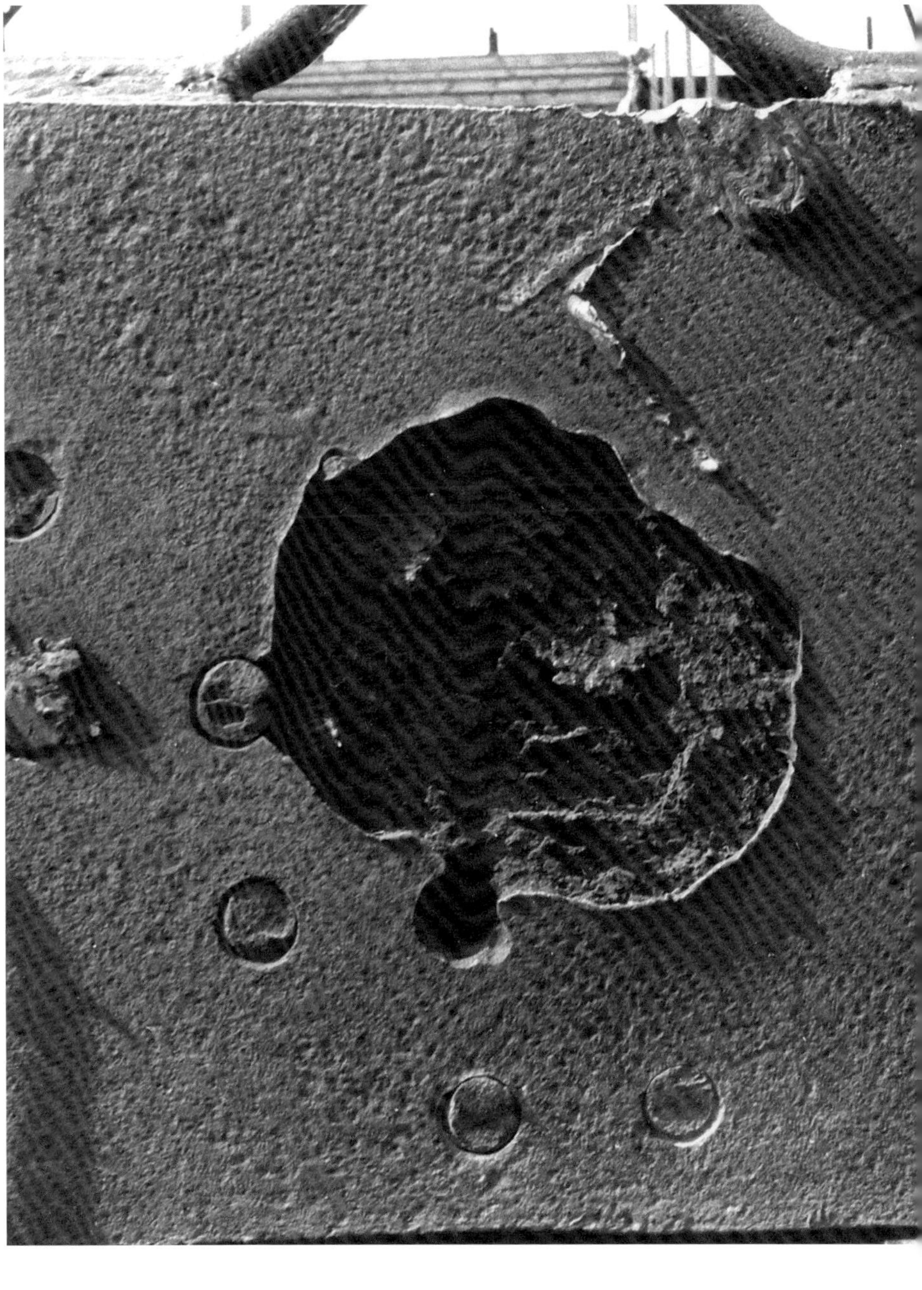

Antiaircraft Machine Gun

The antiaircraft machine gun is used for defense against tactical aircraft and for engaging surface targets. The weapon mounted on Bundeswehr Leopard 1s is the 7.62 mm MG 3, produced by Rheinmetall, which is used by many branches of the service. For use as an antiaircraft machine gun on the Leopard 1 main battle tank, a rubber cap simply has to be fitted in place of the shoulder rest.

For use, the machine gun is mounted and secured in a special upper mount. The upper mount has a spring balancer, which allows easy handling of the machine gun for the gunner at all elevation angles. The upper mount is connected to the lower mount by a bayonet catch. A swivel bearing in each of the upper and lower mounts allows the antiaircraft machine gun to be aimed upward and sideways. The lower mount can be rotated n × 360 degrees on a ring rail; a braking device allows the lower mount to be locked in any position. Both the commander's and the loader's hatch are equipped with such a ring rail. A DM 2 machine gun cartridge box with 250 rounds can be attached to the left side of the upper mount.

Turret Machine Gun

The mount for the turret (mantlet) machine gun is fitted on the left side of the 105 mm gun's cradle tube. The machine gun is mounted axially parallel (not coaxially) to the main gun and follows its movement. The recoil forces occurring during firing are absorbed by the mount. Any necessary barrel change can be carried out by the loader while the gun is still mounted. An angled trigger lever acts on the trigger, which is actuated by a solenoid when the gunner presses the firing pawls. The turret machine gun can also be fired manually by the gunner if required. After firing, the empty cartridge cases and the belt links fall into a shell-casing bag located under the mount. To remove the firing gases, a suction nozzle is located on the right-hand side above the machine gun, which is connected to the fan of the smoke extraction system in the gun cradle. Ammunition is supplied via an ammunition supply box attached to the left-hand inner wall of the turret; the box holds up to a thousand rounds. In addition to this ammunition, a further 4,500 rounds of 7.62 mm ammunition are stored in eighteen boxes in the vehicle (primarily on the hull floor under the turret's rotating platform).

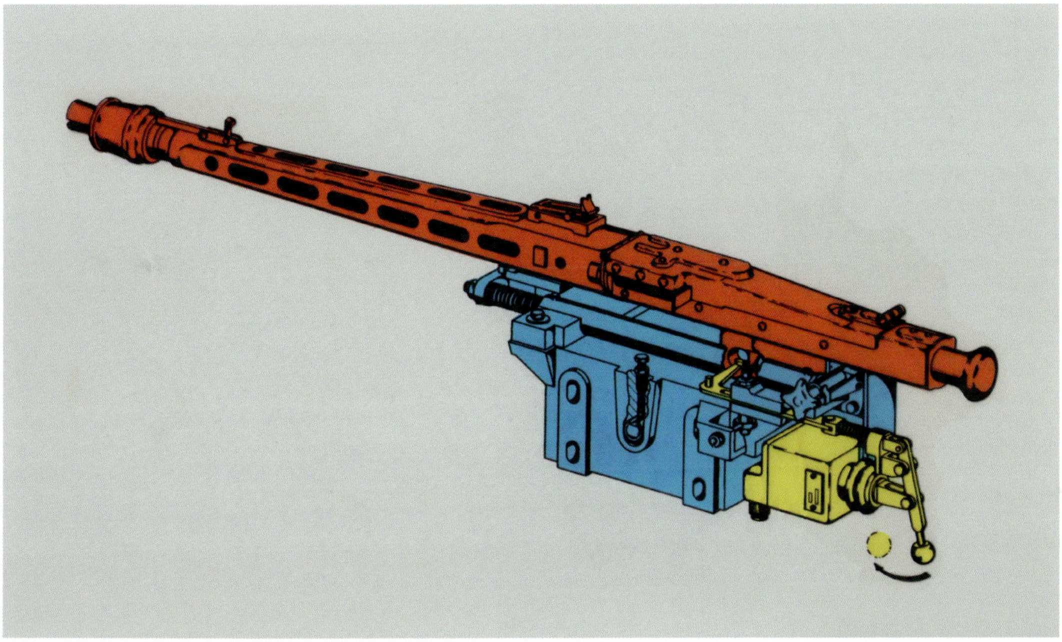

Smoke Discharger System

In the event of superior enemy forces appearing unexpectedly, the Leopard 1 main battle tank can retreat under the protection of a self-generated smoke screen. The vehicle is equipped with a smoke grenade mortar system. This consists of four 76 mm caliber smoke grenade launchers mounted on brackets on the outside of the left and right sides of the turret. The launching cups have different exit directions so that the projectiles are distributed in a fan shape in front of the vehicle. The smoke grenade launchers are fired electronically. They can be triggered by the commander using a corresponding control unit on the right-hand interior wall of the turret. In addition to the eight smoke grenades in the system, a further eight grenades can be stowed in the rear of the turret.

Smoke Grenade Discharger	Specification
Caliber	76 mm
Firing angle elevation	45 degrees
Firing angle azimuth	dependent on vehicle
Firing range	approx. 40–50 m
Start of effect after firing	≥ 4 sec.
Duration of smokescreen	≥ 40–60 sec.

TEM-2A Turret Rangefinder

The turret-mounted rangefinder sight (TEM) is used by the gunner in the Leopard 1 main battle tank both as a rangefinder and an aiming device for the gun. With a 16× magnification, it can take range measurements by using either the stereoscopic or coincidence modes. The TEM is equipped with cams for the APDS and HEAT ammunition types, which automatically take the corresponding elevation angle into account when setting the sight mark for each distance measured. The TEM consists of the base tube with a measuring base of 1.72 meters, the eyepiece arm, and the eyepiece box. A voltage transformer and the foot control are connected to the TEM. Due to the stereoscopic view required for the stereoscopic imaging method, the TEM provides the gunner with a binocular view. By adjusting the forehead support, the interpupillary distance, and the image sharpness, the gunner can create the optimum conditions for his situation.

To measure the distance, the gunner must use a rocker pedal on the floor of the rotating platform to align the two partial images in the eyepieces, using the stereoscopic mode. The stereoscopic mode also leads to usable results without the need for extensive training. With the coincidence mode, the gunner must use the foot control to bring the measuring mark into the target plane. The coincidence mode requires both the ability of the gunner to see stereoscopically and more-extensive training. However, it is more accurate than the stereoscopic mode and can also be used deep into the twilight.

If a stabilization system is retrofitted, a certain stabilization effect is achieved for the optics due to the mechanical connection of the TEM to the main gun.

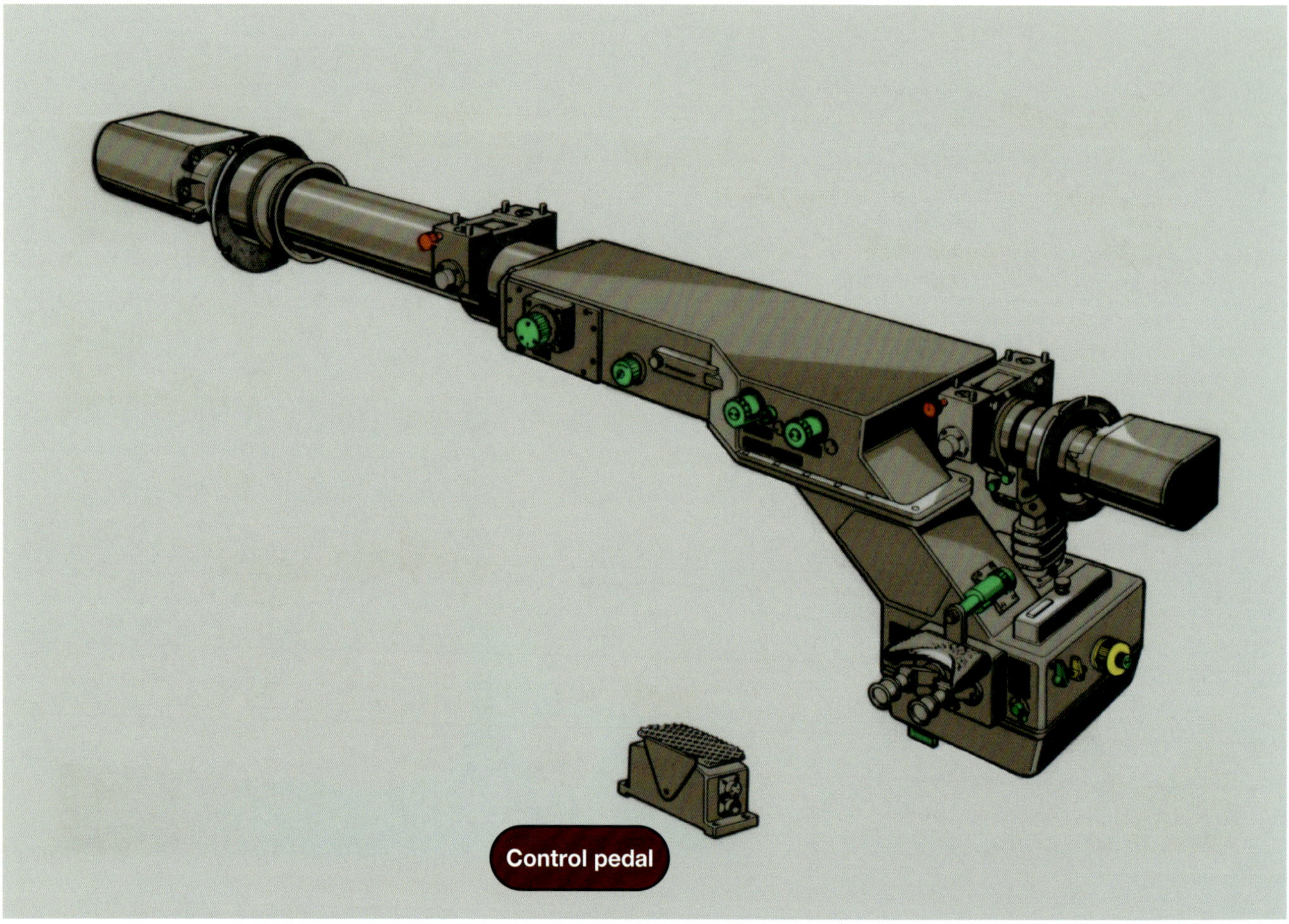

EMES 18 Fire Control System

The EMES 18 system's telescopic sight is the main aiming device of the Leopard 1 A5 main battle tank and enables the gunner and commander to effectively engage targets by using the day or thermal-imaging channel via a height- and side-stabilized mirror. Range can be precisely determined via an integrated laser transmitter and receiver. The obtained data are automatically transferred to the fire control system's computer. The gunner has a binocular view; the commander can also use the EMES 18 via an optical connection module with a monocular view.

In addition, the EMES 18, in conjunction with the collimator located at the muzzle of the barrel, enables constant monitoring of any barrel distortion (field adjustment system).

The EMES 18 system's telescopic sight is located on the right side of the turret in front of the gunner's position; an armored protective cover is mounted on the turret roof for the sight assembly. The extensive use of Leopard 2 components results in logistical advantages; the operating concept also largely corresponds to the conditions in the Leopard 2. By using the same assemblies in the EMES 18 system's telescopic sight, it was possible to achieve an adequate capability level between the Leopard 1 and Leopard 2 when engaging targets.

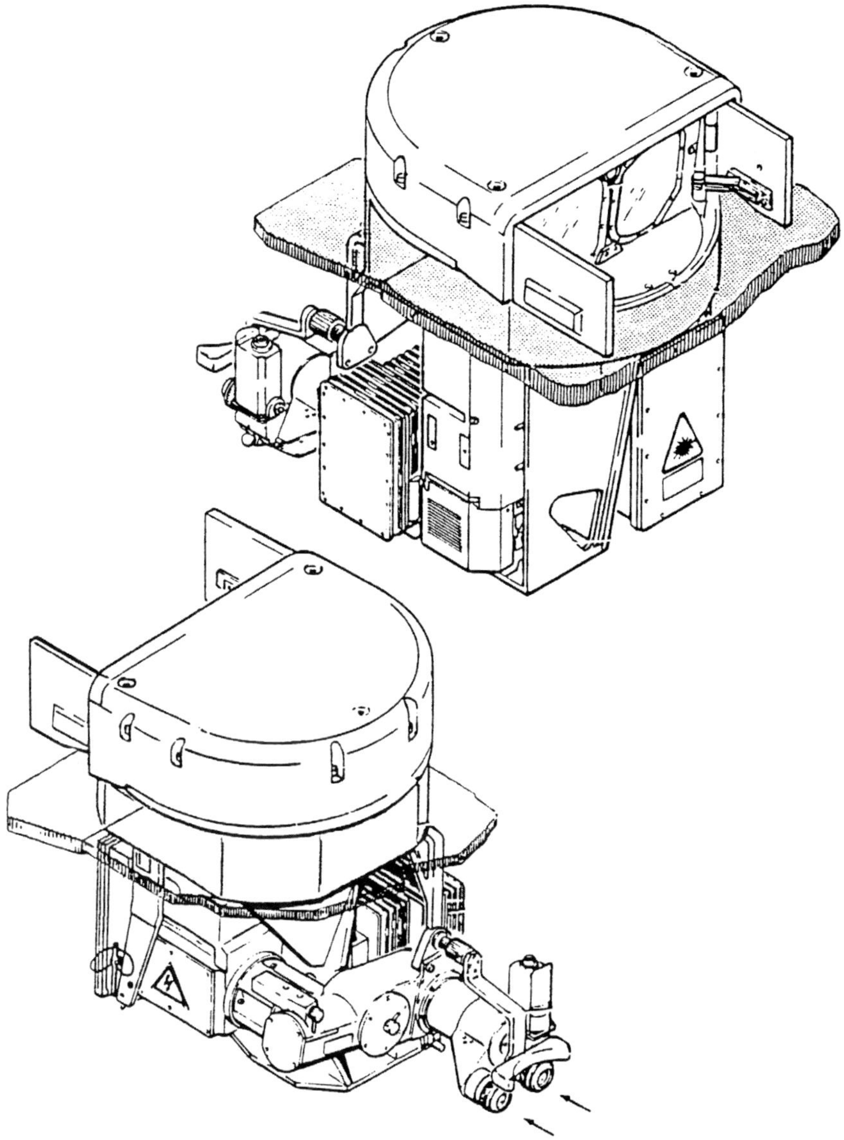

TZF 1A Telescopic Sight

The turret telescopic sight (TZF) has an 8× magnification and is used by the gunner as an aiming device for the turret machine gun and in special cases for the main gun (e.g., if the onboard power supply fails). It is located on the right-hand side of the weapon and has a monocular view. An optical joint is installed between the lens mount and the eyepiece arm. This means that the lens mount (sight) follows the vertical elevation movement of the weapon, while the eyepiece arm (sight) is fixed in the turret housing and can therefore always be held in a position favorable for the gunner. When engaging the target, the gunner must estimate the target range and set a corresponding mark on the range scale for the selected ammunition. For this purpose, the turret telescopic sight has corresponding range scales for the APDS, HEAT, and HESH types of ammunition, as well as for the ammunition of the turret machine gun. The ammunition-dependent elevation angle is incorporated into the length of the distance scale. The elevation angle is therefore considered when aligning the target with the sighting mark (holding point: target center). All other values (lead, cant, crosswind, etc.) must be estimated by the gunner himself.

If the onboard power supply fails, the turret can be aimed at the target from the side by using the side traverse hand controller, and the gun can be aimed at the target from above by using the elevation hand controller. The cartridge is fired by the shock generator located to the left of the gunner (emergency firing).

All of the Leopard 1's three aiming devices are fitted with a so-called fire aperture. This closes the sight for 0.25 seconds after firing. This measure is intended to prevent gunners and commanders from being dazzled by the muzzle flash.

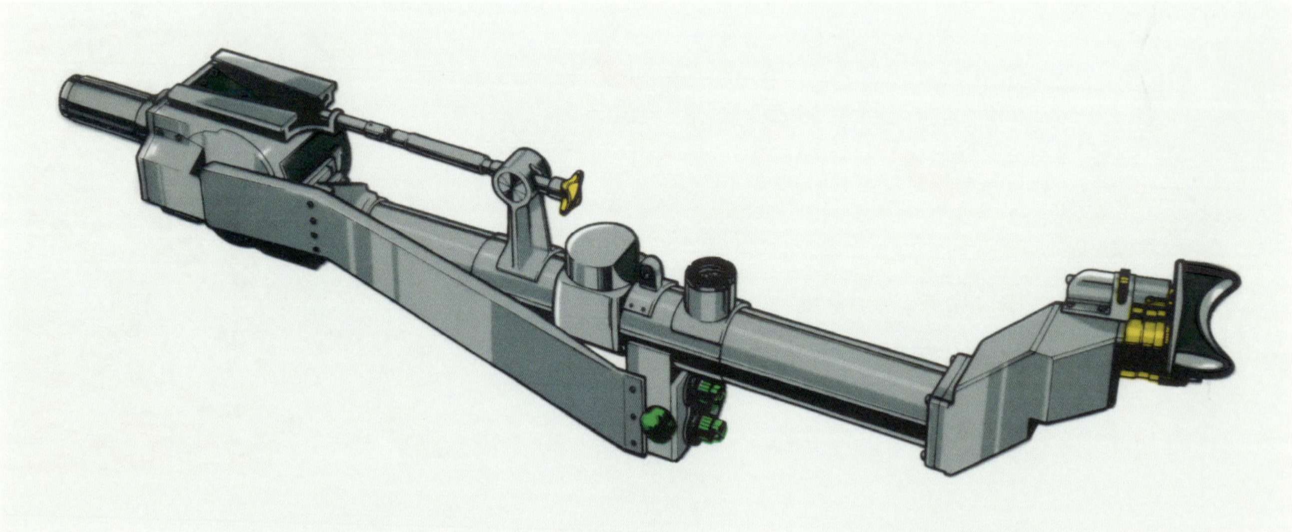

TRP 1 A Panoramic Periscope

The panoramic periscope (TRP) is used by the commander in the Leopard 1 main battle tank as an observation device, for determination of the range to the target, and as an aiming device for firing with the main gun. A flexible shaft between the TRP and the azimuth circle holds the periscope on the target when the turret is traversed. The commander can also assign a target to the gunner via the override device of the aiming system. The elevation angle of the main weapon is automatically transferred to the TRP via an electrical angle transmission system (TEW) between the TRP and the gun. If the ammunition type is set, the distance-dependent elevation angle is also considered when setting the TRP. This enables the commander to engage targets independently even in special cases.

The commander can continuously select from 6× to 20× magnification on the TRP. The variable magnification allows the device to be used optimally both as an observation device (lower magnification) and as a targeting device (higher magnification). The variable magnification setting allows the commander to use a measuring frame in the eyepiece to carry out a makeshift range determination on the basis of known target dimensions (range measurement based on the target). In vehicles with a retrofitted stabilization system, the angle transmission system also resulted in a certain stabilization effect for the TRP.

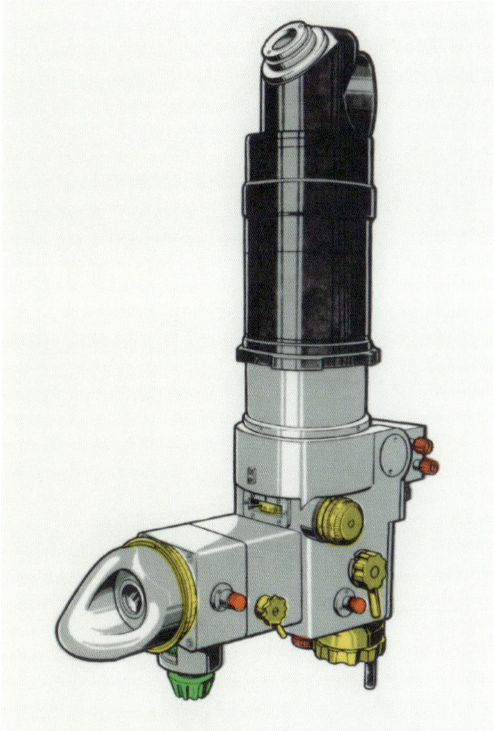

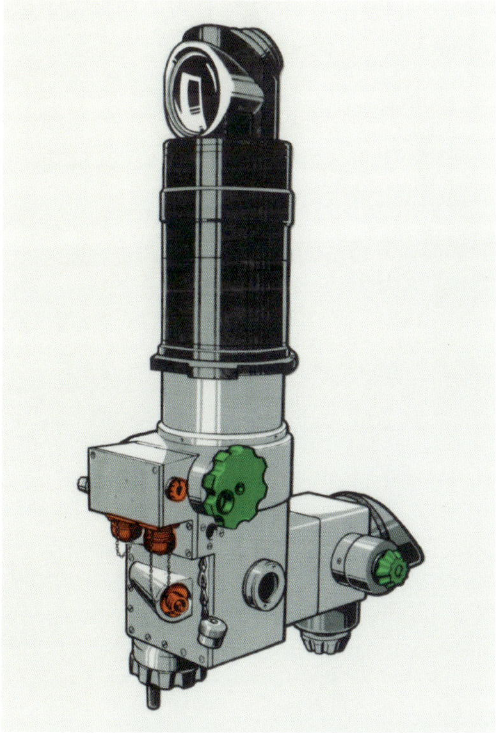

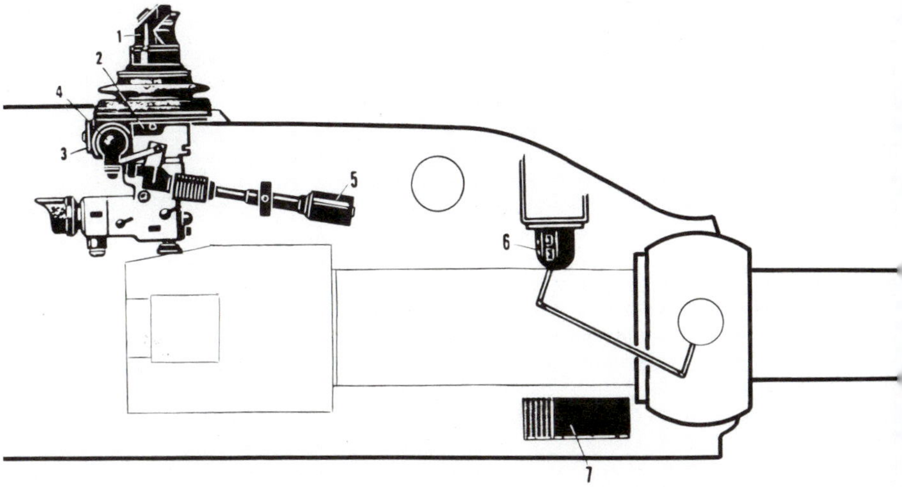

Components of the TEW-1A: A major advantage of the Leopard 1 over all other main battle tanks of its era was the ability for the commander to fire the main weapon in special situations by using his panoramic rotating periscope. The TEW-1A electrical angle transmission system was a key element in enabling this function. A high-precision position transmitter, which was connected to the main weapon via a parallelogram linkage, was used to determine the respective position of the main weapon. This value was transmitted to the telescopic sight via a feedback transmitter in conjunction with a servomotor—an angle of elevation dependent on the ammunition and distance was already considered. Using his aiming handle, the commander was able to override the gunner and aim at a target with the help of the TEW-1A.

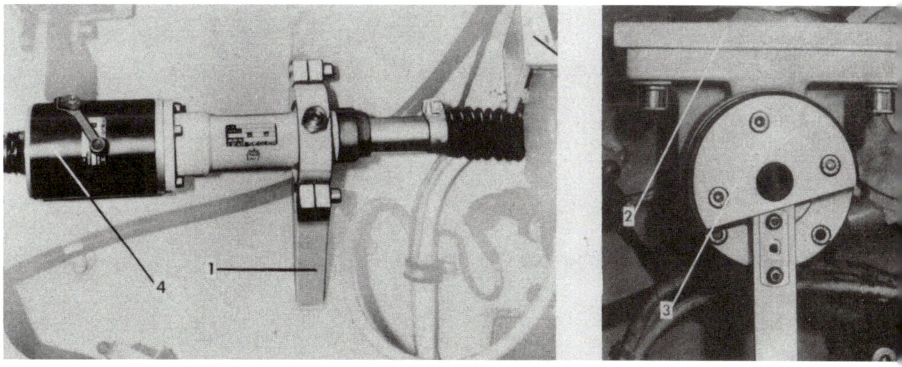

Components of the TEW-1A: The left picture shows the servomotor and the spindle drive for adjusting the panoramic telescopic sight. The picture on the right shows the position transmitter connected to the main weapon.

When the Leopard 1 main battle tank entered service, the variable magnification of the TRP and the relatively complex connecting elements of the TRP with the main weapon resulted in superiority over all other main battle tanks in terms of the commander's options for battlefield observation, target assignment, and use of the main weapon ("hunter-killer principle").

The TRP sits offset to the right in front of the commander's hatch in the so-called telescope holder. After a fastening ring is loosened, the TRP can be replaced with the IR sight for night combat.

B 171 Infrared Telescopic Sight

For night combat, the infrared telescopic sight can be inserted into the TRP-2A's mount in its place. In conjunction with the IR/white-light searchlight (IR mode), the commander can observe the battlefield and engage targets; the optics offer 8× magnification. The infrared rays emitted by the searchlight are made visible again by an image converter tube in the IR telescopic sight. To operate, the infrared image converter tube requires a DC voltage of 16,000 V, which is generated by an integrated high-voltage unit. When the searchlight is switched off, the image converter can also detect active IR sources on the battlefield.

The sighting mark in the IR telescopic sight can be set to a combat sight setting of 800, 1,000, or 1,200 meters. The infrared telescopic sight also has a firing aperture that closes the optics for 0.25 seconds after firing to prevent the IR image converter tube from being overexposed and the commander from being blinded.

AEG XSW-30-U Combined Infrared and White-Light Searchlight

The infrared/white-light searchlight is used by the commander and the gunner as a source of illumination for observing the terrain and engaging targets at night. The searchlight can be switched from IR mode to white-light mode on the control unit to the right of the commander's position. The white light can be either diffused or focused. The gunner can use the searchlight in white-light mode only in conjunction with the TEM and the TZF. In conjunction with the IR telescopic sight, the commander can use the searchlight in IR mode for terrain observation and target engagement.

The light source is a xenon high-pressure lamp, which is encased in an easily replaceable lamp cartridge. A high-voltage pulse of approximately 40,000 V is briefly required for ignition; the power consumption during operation is 950 W (for comparison: the T-55 main battle tank's firing spotlight had a power consumption of 200 W).

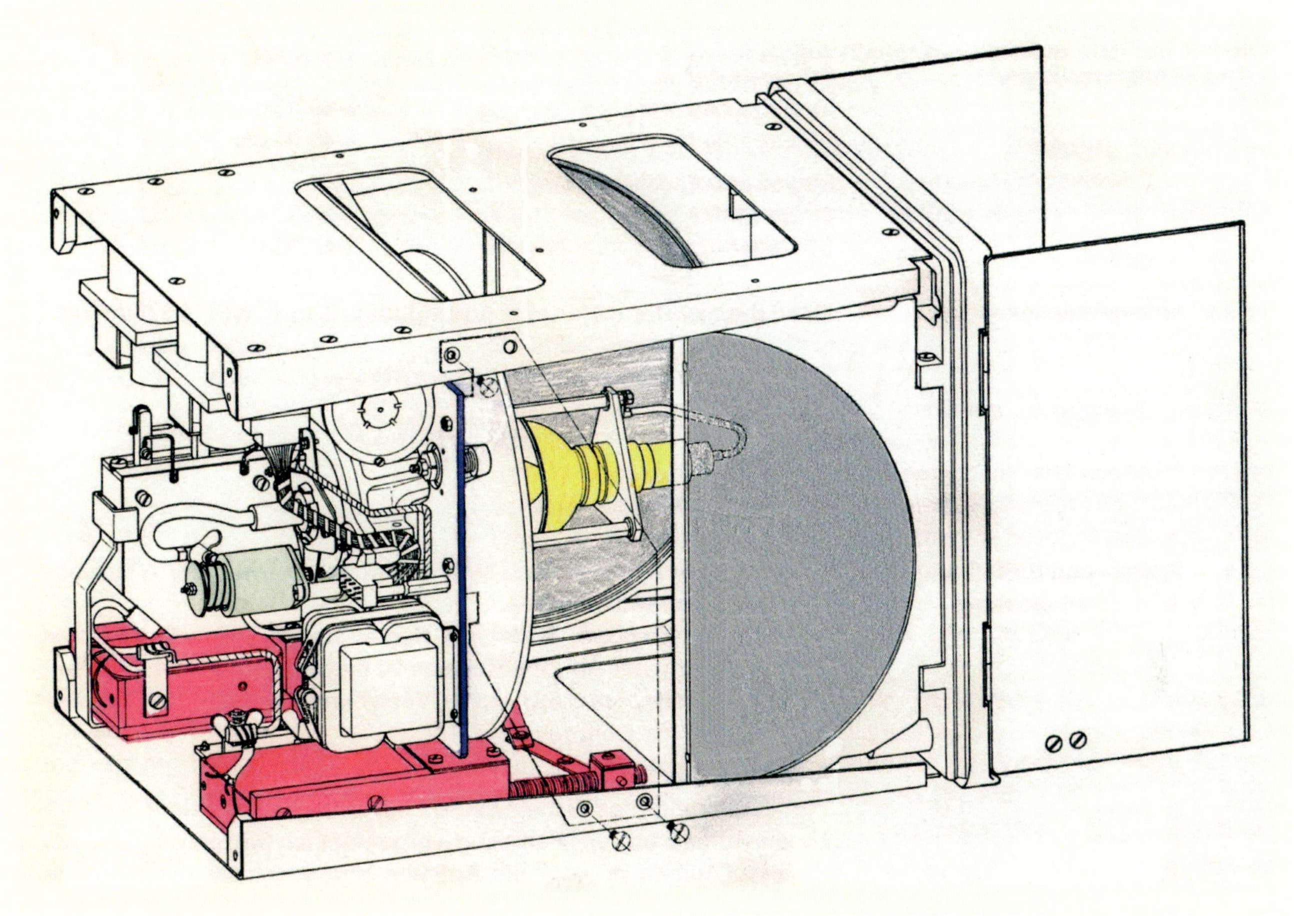

Thermal-Imaging Device

Tank development is always a struggle for superiority in terms of combat value criteria compared to the capabilities of the enemy combat vehicles. This concerns, among other things, the ability to engage the enemy at night and in poor visibility.

The technological stages of night vision technology led from active infrared systems via passive residual light amplifiers to thermal-imaging devices. The thermal-imaging device led to a revolution in the field of night combat capability, since, for example, under favorable atmospheric conditions it made it possible to detect a tank at ranges of up to 10 km! However, vehicle identification remains a problem. The identification distance (depending on the performance of the thermal-imaging device) is sometimes less than the main combat distance.

Targets or objects are detected by the thermal-imaging device due to their own thermal (waste) radiation in the wavelength range of the thermal infrared (8–14 μm); even small temperature differences are noticeable as contrast or color differences in the thermal image.

The breakthrough of thermal-imaging technology in the United States came only in the 1970s, since the mercury-doped cadmium telluride detector had to be cooled down to −197 degrees Celsius to create powerful thermal-imaging devices. It took considerable effort to create a solution suitable for armor. Introduction into the armed forces of Western nations was possible only after the basic modules (common modules) could be manufactured in large quantities. Vehicle-specific eyepiece and lens assemblies were then mounted on the basic assemblies. In the 1981–87 period, the Bundeswehr procured approximately 5,140 thermal-imaging devices for installation in the Leopard 1 and 2 main battle tanks, the Marder infantry-fighting vehicles, and Luchs armored reconnaissance vehicles (system price: approximately 250,000–300,000 DM). As a result, a clear superiority in night combat capability over the combat vehicles of the Warsaw Pact was achieved for many years.

Electrohydraulic Turret Traverse and Gun Elevation System

The main gun is aimed sideways by traversing the turret and vertically by rotating it around the trunnion axis. The turret is traversed by the traverse mechanism. The gun is raised and lowered by the elevating cylinder. The required oil flows are controlled by the gunner's or commander's aiming handles.

The hydraulic energy required for the directional movements is generated by an electric motor with an output of 6.35 kW (8.5 hp), which pumps oil from a reservoir into a pressure accumulator via a gear pump. The pressure accumulator works in an operating pressure range of 80–113 bar and supplies the required amount of oil to the control valve block. By tilting the gunner's handle around the transverse axis, the elevation cylinder is supplied with oil; the elevation cylinder can move the main weapon around the trunnion axis in an elevation range of –9 to +20 degrees. By pivoting the gunner's handle around the longitudinal axis, oil is applied to a radial piston motor in the traverse mechanism, which drives a pinion via a gearbox. The pinion in turn engages with the teeth of the turret traverse ring. The extent of the deflection of the aiming handle determines the volume flow of the oil flowing through the system; thus the extent of the deflection of the aiming handle determines the speeds when raising and lowering the gun or when traversing the turret. The turret can be traversed through 360 degrees in sixteen seconds.

The commander can override the gunner's actions at any time by operating his aiming handle and taking over the aiming of the weapon. For emergency operation (e.g., failure of the onboard power supply), the gunner has an elevation and a traverse hand controller at his disposal. A so-called rear deflector is provided to prevent damage to the gun and chassis. When the hydraulic system is switched on, this causes the gun to be raised (regardless of the position of the aiming handles), provided the turret is in a position between eight and four o'clock.

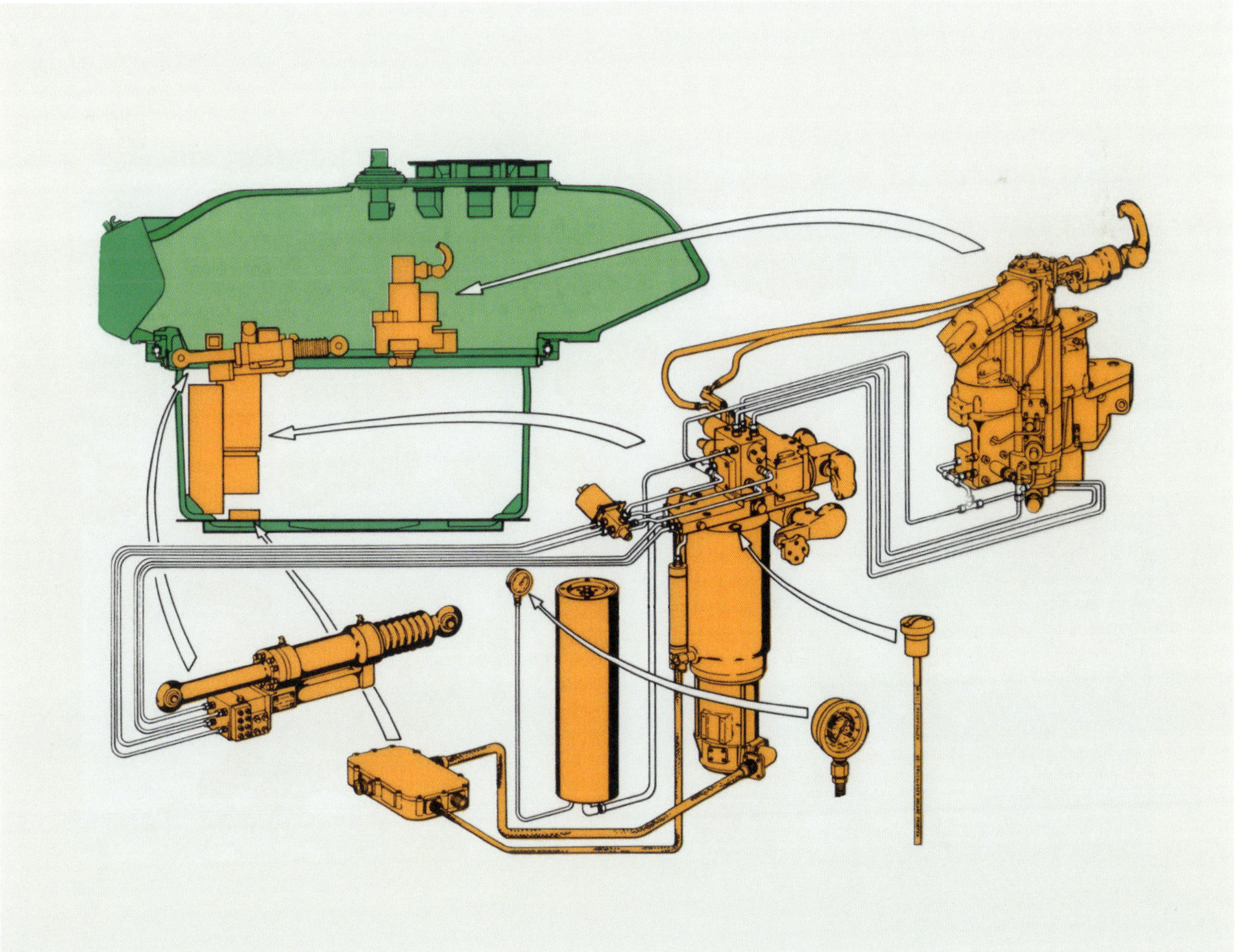

Weapon Stabilization

The ability to engage the enemy while on the move can increase the survival probability of your own vehicle—provided the enemy vehicle does not have a highly developed fire control system. A prerequisite for fighting on the move is the presence of stabilization systems for the turret, gun, and optics.

When series production of the Leopard 1 main battle tank began, the weapon stabilization system under investigation was not yet ready for introduction and could be retrofitted only from 1972 onward. A retrofit kit was developed for the Leopard 1 A1, which was subsequently adapted to the existing aiming system.

The task of the weapon stabilization system is to compensate for any disturbing movements of the chassis acting on the turret and weapon when driving off-road (i.e., the weapon should maintain its position in space). It is therefore a matter of spatial or position stabilization and not point stabilization! The weapon does not remain pointed at the target due to the stabilization—corrections by the gunner are required to achieve this. The turret and gun are stabilized by gyroscopes that detect every change in angle around the vertical and lateral axes of the vehicle and convert them into electrical signals. The signals are processed electronically and fed to so-called servo-valves. These convert the electrical signals into proportional hydraulic-flow rates that act on the corresponding actuators (traverse mechanism or elevation control cylinder).

Due to the insufficient drive power of the directional drive and the mechanical coupling of the optics to the gun, effective firefighting on the move was not yet possible with the Leopard A1–A3 main battle tanks—at best, the time for the firing stop could be shortened by the weapon stabilization system. Not until the Leopard 1 A4 was it possible to fire an accurate shot while on the move, due to the primarily stabilized optics in the PERI-R 12.

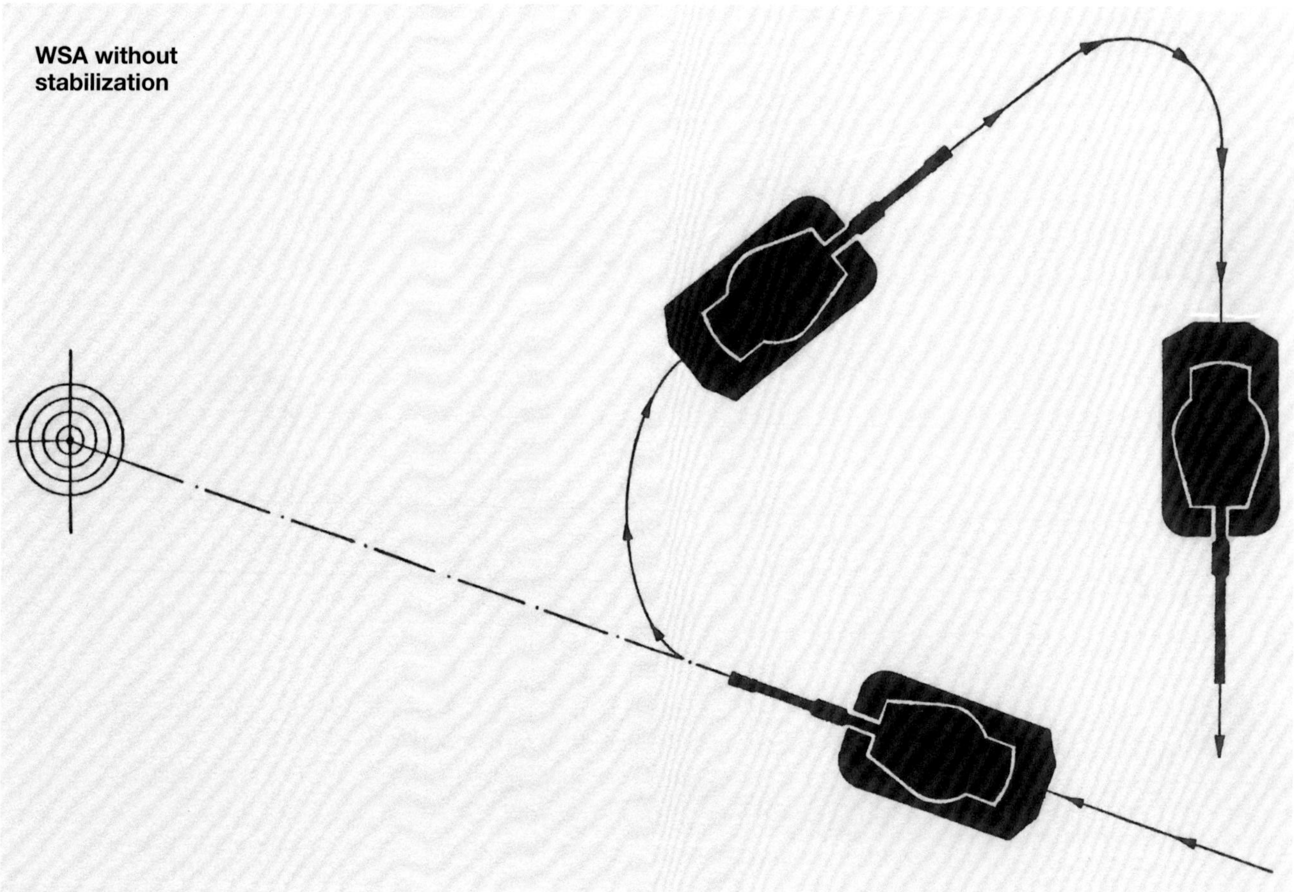

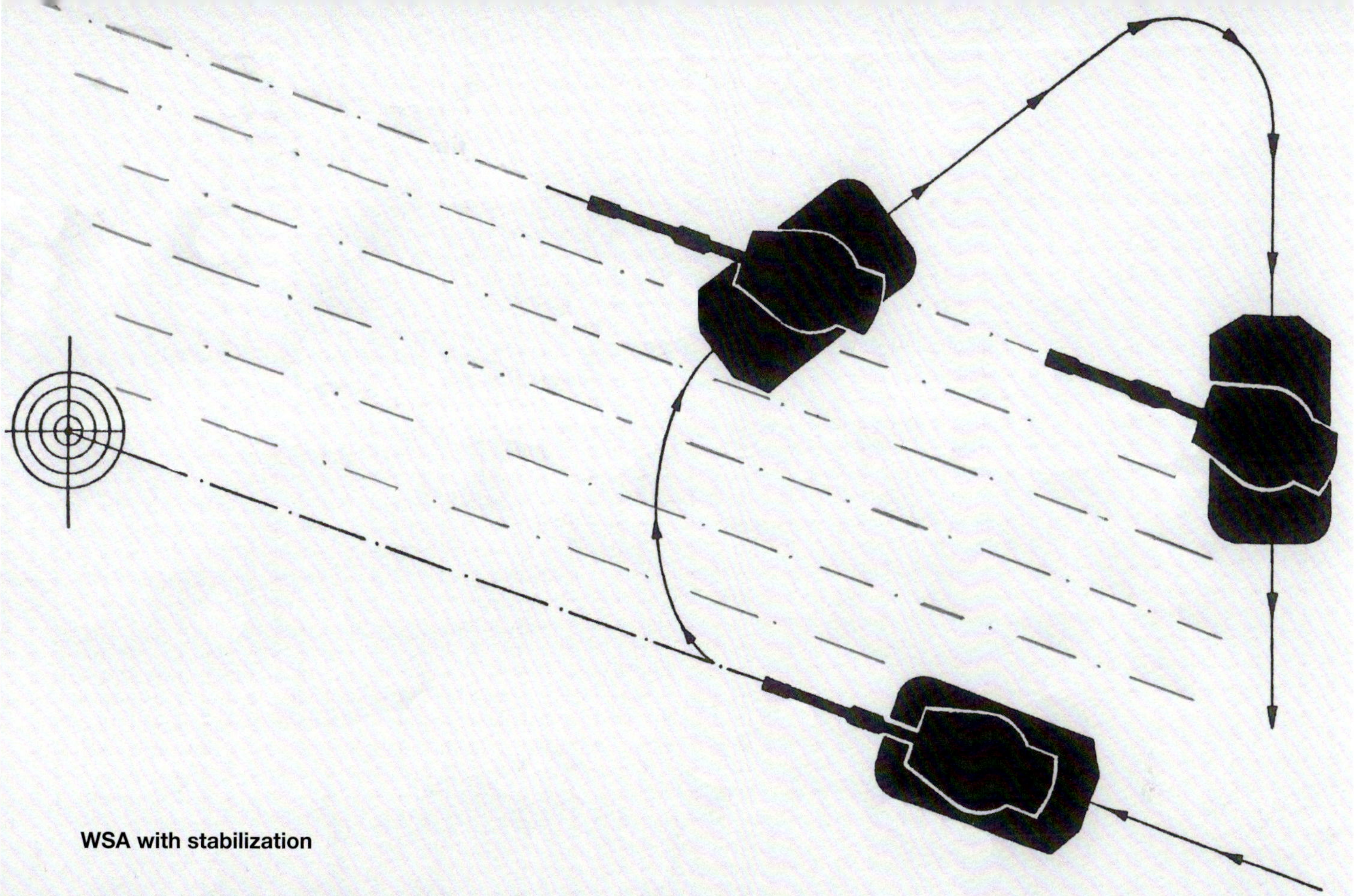
WSA with stabilization

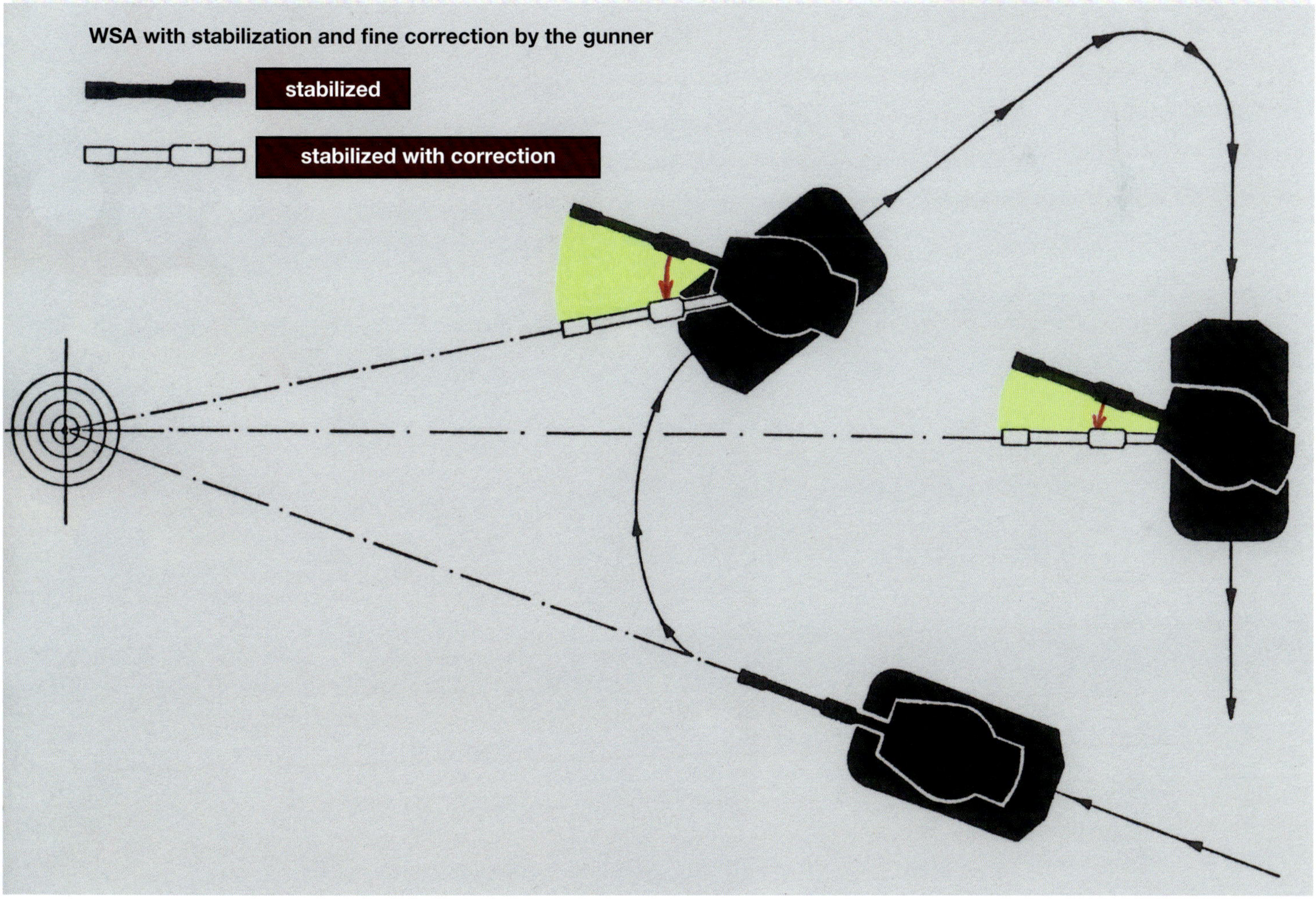
WSA with stabilization and fine correction by the gunner
stabilized
stabilized with correction

Mobility-Defining Components / Propulsion System

MB 838 CaM 500 Engine

The basic concept of the engine that powered the Leopard 1 main battle tank goes back to an initiative of the Swiss armaments authorities, which initiated the development of a compact high-performance engine for armored vehicles in the 30-metric-ton class by the then Daimler Benz AG company in 1952. As early as 1955, the first eight-cylinder engine of the MB 837 series ran on the test bench as a naturally aspirated engine. In 1957, Daimler-Benz was commissioned by the German Ministry of Defense to develop a ten-cylinder version with mechanical supercharging for the 30-metric-ton Standard Tank. To gain experience in practical driving operations, corresponding tests were carried out with a prototype engine in a modified M47. Numerous modifications and improvements had to be made before the MB 838 engine was ready for quantity production.

The use of the diesel engine in armored combat vehicles resulted in a significant improvement in fire safety and driving range and reduced the vulnerability of the older American tanks (gasoline engines). At the time of its introduction in 1965, the engine of the Leopard 1 main battle tank was characterized by its compactness, sturdiness, reliability, and durability.

Type	MB 838 CaM 500
Type of engine	4-stroke prechamber multi-fuel engine Number of cylinders/arrangement. 10-cylinder
Type of supercharging	mechanical (compressor)
Bore / stroke	165 mm / 175 mm (6.5 / 6.9 in.)
Displacement	34.7 liters (2,217.52 cubic in.)
Compression ratio	1:19.5
Average piston speed	12.8 m/sec.
Rated power/rated rpm	610 kW / 2,200 rpm
Maximum torque	2,805 Nm / 1,540 rpm
Liter output	16.3 kW/liter
Cylinder output	61 kW/cylinder
Air requirement at rated output	52.2 m3/min.
Specific fuel consumption	262 g/kWh
Oil quantity at initial filling	72 liters (19 US gal.)
Engine weight, dry	1,920 kg (4,232.87 lbs.)
Motormasse; trocken	1920 kg

The MB 838 CaM 500 engine is a liquid-cooled V ten-cylinder (90 degree) four-stroke diesel with a displacement of 37.4 liters. It achieves its rated output of 611 kW (819 hp) at 2,200 rpm. Two mechanically driven supercharger blowers powered via centrifugal clutches are used to precompress the intake air. The forged crankshaft has six bearings. Each cylinder has two intake and two exhaust valves; the valves are actuated by the two camshafts via pushrods and rocker arms. The Bosch injection pump is housed in the V-space between the two rows of cylinders to save space. To achieve a high level of engine reliability, all auxiliary units are driven by gears with helical teeth instead of V-belts or toothed belts.

MB 838 Ca-500

MB 838 Ca-500 exterior view

The engine has a dry-sump pressure circulation lubrication system to ensure a reliable oil supply to the lubrication points even when the vehicle is at extreme lean angles. There is an oil/water heat exchanger in the crankcase, which can be used to preheat the engine oil via the vehicle heater before starting the engine at extremely low temperatures. To make the starting process easier, the engine can be disconnected from the transmission by a manually operated claw clutch if required. The oil-cooled generator (9 kW, or 12 hp) and the starter (11 kW, or 14.75 hp) are flange-mounted to the side of the engine. All other units (filters, tanks, etc.) are also organically mounted on the crankcase to save space.

Air Filter

The combustion air drawn in by the engine is cleaned in two stages by two dry-air filters located in the track shoulders. In the first stage, the combustion air passes through a cyclone battery in which the combustion air is cleaned to approximately 99 percent by centrifugal action. The dirt particles that accumulate here are collected in a room and continuously conveyed to the exhaust gas outlet area by a dust extraction fan. The pre-cleaned air passes through three felt pocket elements in the second stage. The air then exits the fine-filter section with a purity level of 99.8 percent and enters the intake openings of the compressors.

During deep wading and underwater travel, the outer flaps of the combustion air intake are each closed via two cylinders of the submersible hydraulics. The engine combustion air is then drawn in via two open handhole covers in the bulkhead to the engine compartment. In this case, the combustion air is drawn in through the fighting compartment or the open commander's hatch (referred to as the deep-wading shaft or underwater-driving shaft). From 1972 onward (Leopard 1 A2), the relatively sensitive felt pocket inserts were replaced by more-robust filter cartridges in a metal housing; in older vehicles, the air filter was retrofitted accordingly.

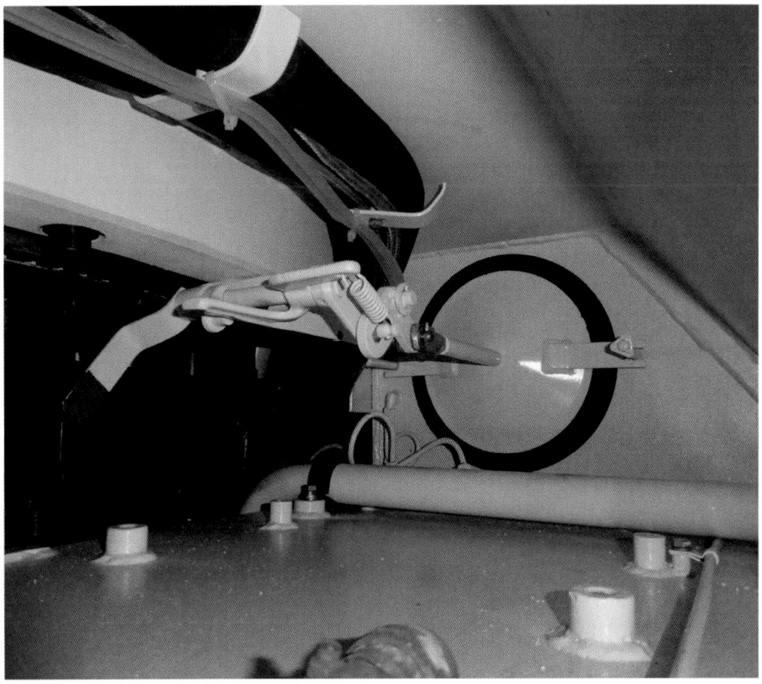

Handhole cover in the bulkhead: When the Leopard 1 is underwater, the outer air intake openings for the air filters are closed by actuating the submersible hydraulics. In this case, the two handhole covers in the side recesses in the bulkhead must be opened manually. This allows the engine to receive the necessary combustion air via the fighting compartment or via the underwater-driving shaft mounted on the commander's hatch.

Fuel System

The two main tanks of the fuel system (475 and 480 liters) are located to the left and right of the engine compartment. The fuel is pumped from the main tanks into a special extraction tank (30 liters) via a tandem fuel pump. The extraction tank is constantly filled with fuel up to the overflow point, so that the engine is reliably supplied with fuel (without air pockets) even when the vehicle is leaning at extreme angles. The heating and preheating unit in the fighting compartment is also supplied with fuel from the extraction tank. The necessary pressure equalization in the fuel tanks during refueling or draining is ensured by appropriate venting and ventilation valves. The filling status of the left or right main tank is displayed on the driver's instrument panel—depending on the position of the switchover cock.

Cooling System

The cooling circuit of the Leopard 1's power plant contains 165 liters of coolant, which consists of approximately 58 percent water; the remainder is corrosion inhibitor and antifreeze.

When the coolant temperature exceeds 83 degrees Celsius, the fan located above the gearbox is activated. The fan wheel draws in the ambient air via a grille located on the engine compartment cover and pushes it through the air duct box through the radiators located on the left and right at the rear of the vehicle. After exiting the radiators, the cooling air mixes with the exhaust gas from the engine and exits the side outlet grilles into the open air. When high cooling capacity is required, the fan wheel rotates at 2,800 rpm and requires a drive power of approximately 70 kW (93.87 hp)! The fan is driven by a hydrodynamic coupling. Depending on the cooling-capacity requirement, the fan speed is varied by regulating the amount of oil in the coupling housing.

During deep wading and underwater travel, the air duct box and radiator are flooded; this ensures reliable cooling of the engine. The air duct box and radiator are sealed off from the rest of the engine compartment by rubber bellows so that the engine, gearbox, and brakes remain dry in this operating state. There are two flaps in the air-ducting box in the area of the rear plate, through which a certain amount of air is diverted to ventilate the engine compartment during land travel. Once the engine compartment has cooled, the heated air is released through two elongated gratings on the engine compartment cover below the rear of the turret. During deep wading and underwater travel, these two flaps are closed by corresponding cylinders of the submersible hydraulics.

Cooling system / air duct box: The picture shows a rear view of the engine. The housing of the fan wheel and the air duct box below it can be seen in the center. The intake cooling air is forced into the two external radiators via the air duct box. Although the arrangement of the components makes a very pragmatic impression at first glance, it later turned out in practice that the cooling air in the air guide box is strongly swirled, resulting in an uneven flow to the radiator surfaces. The compression heats the air sucked into the fan wheel by approximately 5 degrees. The PTO connection of the 4 HP 250 transmission leading to the rear should also be noted in the picture.

Hydraulic clutch of the fan wheel (cutaway model): The hydrodynamic coupling for driving the fan wheel is a successful design. The hydrodynamic coupling consists of two housing halves with integrated blades. The lower half is driven by the motor—the upper half is connected to the fan wheel. When the engine is cold, there is no oil in the clutch housing—so no torque is transmitted to the fan wheel. As the coolant temperature increases, the oil filling in the clutch is controlled via a thermostat—until the clutch reaches its design point at maximum filling quantity and transmits a power of approximately 70 kW (93.87 hp at 2,760 rpm) at approximately 3 percent slip. Thanks to the hydraulic connection, the elements of the fan drive are not stressed by any shift shocks in the gearbox—in addition, problem-free, temperature-dependent control of the fan speed is possible.

Transmission

After careful preliminary investigations during testing, the 4 HP 250 transmission from the company Zahnradfabrik Friedrichshafen (ZF) was selected for the Leopard 1 main battle tank. It consists of a planetary gearbox with an upstream hydraulic torque converter, and a mechanical dual-wheel, superimposed steering gear. The manual transmission, with four gears, has the task of adapting the engine speed and torque to the respective road and terrain conditions; it enables starting and driving at top speed. The so-called reversing transmission enables forward and reverse travel. In principle, this type of transmission would make it possible to drive forward just as fast as backward. For safety reasons, however, only two reverse gears can be engaged; the maximum speed when reversing is approximately 25 kph.

For a tracked vehicle to corner, a speed difference must be generated between the two tracks: The drive sprocket on the inside of the curve must turn more slowly than the drive sprocket on the outside of the curve. This speed difference is generated in the steering-gear section during cornering. The transmission used in the Leopard 1 exhibits a differential effect when cornering—that is, the amount by which the number of revolutions of the inside drive wheel is reduced leads in the same way to an increase in speed by the same amount on the outside drive wheel. The steering is regenerative—that is, the braking power required to make tight turns on the inside drive wheel is not converted into heat or brake-lining wear but is fed back to the outside drive wheel as additional drive power. This largely avoids steering losses and the associated drop in speed when cornering. The transmission consists of a shift drum with four planetary gear sets connected in series. The individual gears are shifted by applying the brakes or releasing the ring gear in the respective planetary gear. The shift signals are transmitted electronically from the gear selector lever at the driver's seat to the corresponding solenoid valves

Exterior view of the transmission

in the transmission. The solenoid valves control the oil flow to the multiplate clutches in the manual gearbox. Due to the design of the transmission and the type of shifting, there is no need for a clutch pedal. The individual gears are also shifted without interrupting the tractive force, which is very advantageous when driving uphill, for example. The torque converter, located in front of the manual gearbox, increases the engine torque by a factor of 2.8 at the starting point. With this tractive power reserve, the Leopard 1 main battle tank can climb gradients of up to 80 percent (under favorable ground conditions). During fast road travel, the torque converter can be mechanically bypassed by a multiplate clutch so that the usual converter losses are avoided in this mode of operation. When driving on roads, the torque converter lockup clutch is opened only briefly for shifting, in order to avoid shift shocks. If the onboard power supply fails, the solenoid valves for second gear, forward travel, and torque converter operation can be directly actuated mechanically via an emergency circuit. The steering-control valve in the transmission is also operated mechanically from the driver's seat via a linkage due to legal-approval requirements.

In the superimposed steering gear used in the Leopard 1, the power flow coming from the engine goes through the transmission section when driving straight ahead and through the steering gear when turning around the vertical axis. When cornering, the power flow passes through both the transmission and the steering gearbox. The two power flows are then recombined in the so-called summation gearboxes and passed on to the final drives and the drive sprockets. The superimposed steering gear has the peculiarity that the minimum cornering radii are gear-dependent. This means that in fourth gear, the smallest curve radius that can still be negotiated is 22 meters, while in first gear, a curve can be negotiated down to a radius of 4.8 meters. This means that downshifting is absolutely necessary before tighter curves—this peculiarity of the transmission and steering gear is understandably an important focus in driving-school training. The superimposed steering gear also enables the vehicle to turn on the spot.

The steering gear of the Leopard 1 main battle tank is a mechanical two-wheel, superimposed steering gear, which enables safe driving and steering on the road at high speeds and leads to sufficiently high mobility and maneuverability when making tight turns off-road. The functional principle of this steering-gear design was first used in the Tiger I and Königstiger tanks of the Second World War.

Transmission wheel assembly

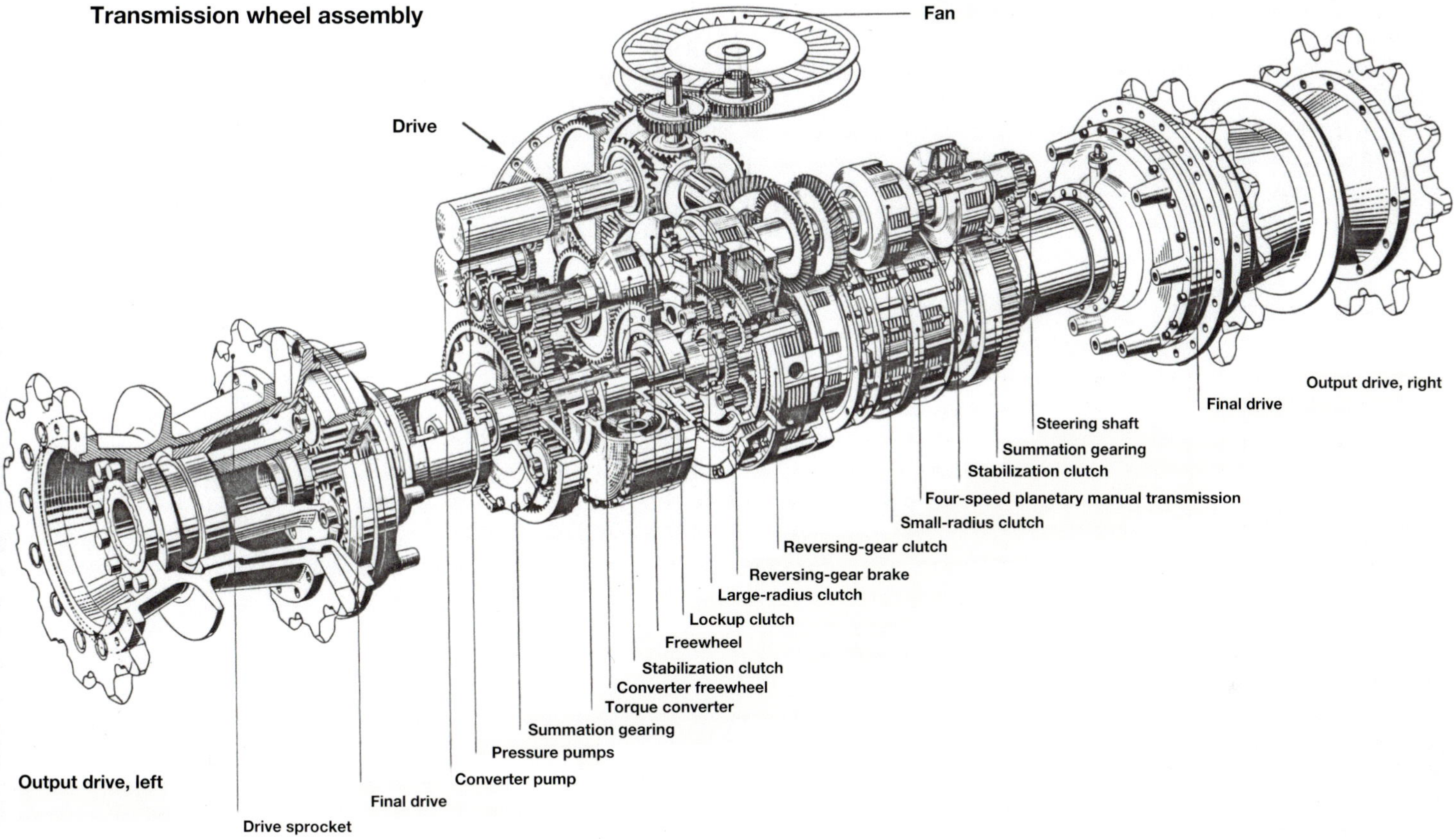

Transmission schematic

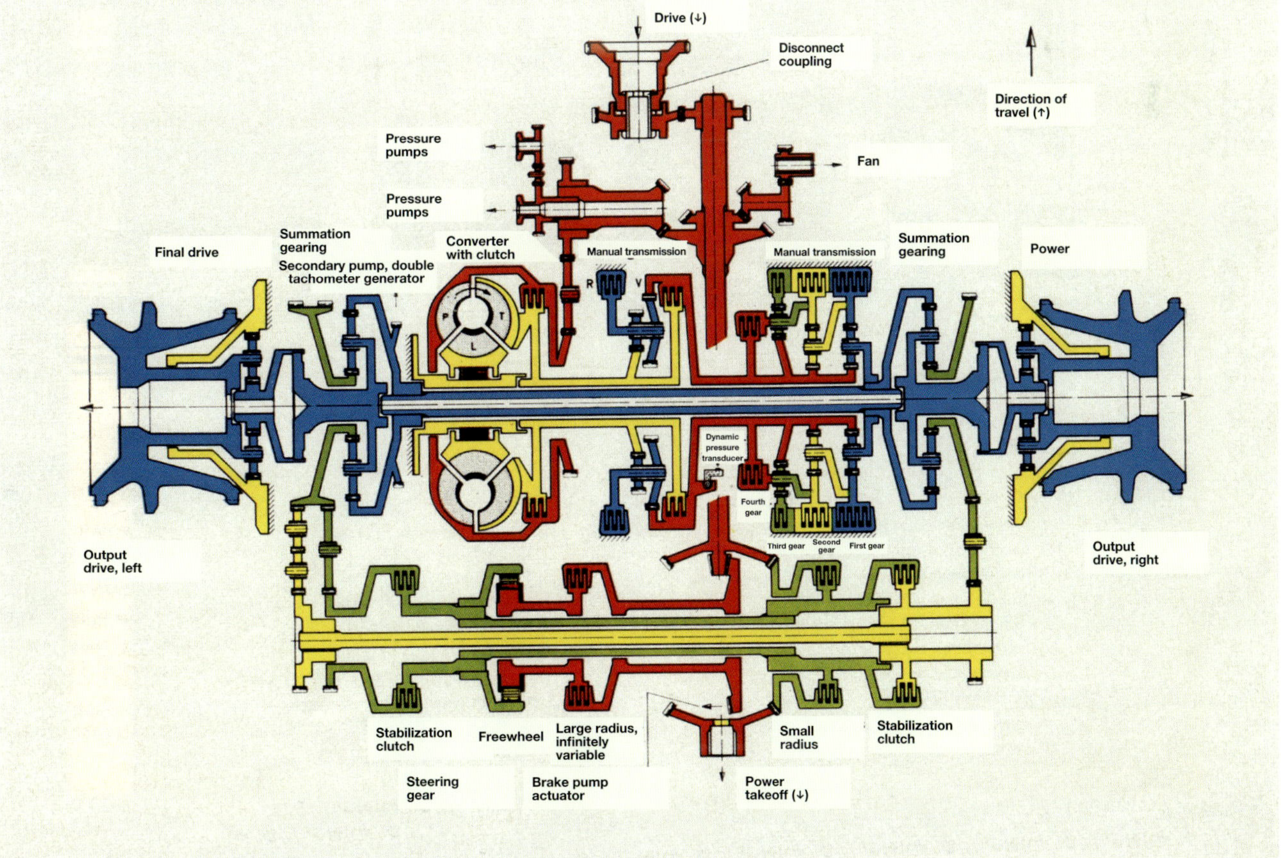

Torque converter (cutaway model): The picture shows a cutaway model of the torque converter from the 4 HP 250 transmission of the Leopard 1 main battle tank. The engine torque is transmitted by the gearwheel on the left side to the lockup clutch and at the same time to the pump wheel (*red housing parts*) located in the right half of the converter. If the speed of the pump wheel increases, the oil in the torque converter is set in rotation by the centrifugal forces and thus flows from the pump wheel into the turbine wheel on the left (*green housing parts*). At the same time, the kinetic energy of the oil transfers torque to the blades of the turbine wheel. The guide wheel located between the two wheels (*gray housing parts*) generates a supporting torque in the turbine wheel, enabling a torque boost by a factor of 2.8 to be achieved at the point the vehicle pulls away. Two freewheel rollers can be seen on the lower edge of the central shaft of the torque converter. The guide wheel is mounted on this freewheel and can rotate freely when the so-called clutch point is reached—this means that no more supporting torque is generated in this state. If the speed of the tank increases, the slip between the pump and turbine wheel is reduced. In this phase, the torque converter is no longer required. Since the remaining slip of 3–5 percent is a loss (with a corresponding fuel consumption), the torque converter is then completely bypassed by closing the lockup clutch.

Type	4 HP 250
Torque converter type	Trilok torque converter with lockup clutch
Transmission type	4-speed planetary gear-box
Steering gear type	2-radius superimposed steering gear
Weight (dry) with fans	1,875 kg (4,133.67 lbs.)
Number of forward gears	4
Number of reverse gears	2
Oil quantity at first filling	105 liters (27.73 US gal.)
Max. fan drive performance	71 kW (95.21 hp)
Max. fan speed	2,820 rpm

The emergency shift and disconnect coupling lever, located on the right-hand side hull wall in the fighting compartment. The solenoid valves in the transmission for opening the torque converter lockup clutch and for actuating second gear in forward operation can be switched via the emergency gearshift. This allows the vehicle to be moved even if the electrical transmission control system fails.
The coupling between the engine and transmission is opened manually (e.g., when starting the engine at very low ambient temperatures). After preheating the engine oil, the engine can then be started—without having to simultaneously rotate various (stiff) elements in the transmission during this difficult phase. Once the engine has reached operating temperature, it is switched off briefly and the coupling is closed manually. The engine is then restarted—now with the transmission engaged.

Engine Power Pack

The engine, transmission, and cooling system of the Leopard 1 main battle tank are combined into a power pack. The entire power pack weighs approximately 4.7 metric tons (5.18 tons) and requires a special lifting beam and a crane with a corresponding load capacity for installation/removal. The transmission is arranged transversely to the engine ("T-arrangement") and thus corresponds to the design known from the American main battle tanks ("cross-drive"). The power pack is elastically mounted four times on the hull floor. All electrical connections and couplings to the fuel and brake system as well as to the mechanical actuating elements are easily accessible and can be quickly disconnected, so that only approximately fifteen minutes are required to remove the power pack. Outside the hull, the power pack is placed on a special bearing block. With a so-called "standstill" harness, the connections to the hull-side interfaces required for a standstill can be reestablished even when the engine block is removed. In this state, the engine block can be inspected for leaks, for example, or the shift pressures on the control lines in the transmission can be checked.

In the standard armored recovery vehicle (Bergepanzer 2), the crane system is designed in such a way that the usual hangar doors can be passed through with a complete Leopard 1 engine on the hook. This was not possible with the older American M74 and M88 armored recovery vehicles.

Exhaust system / muffler: The Leopard 1 is one of the few main battle tanks with an exhaust muffler. The design of the exhaust system was not without its problems and was modified several times during the development of the prototypes and preproduction vehicles. One problem was tearing of the longitudinal weld seams of the split exhaust muffler—caused by the pulsating pressure of the exhaust gases from the engine. Furthermore, the exhaust back pressure could not be increased beyond a certain level by the muffler. Finally, the addition of the exhaust gases resulted in a larger flow volume through the grille (in addition to the cooling air), which ultimately reduced the flow area for the cooling system and required a higher fan output. To minimize the disturbance of the cooling-air flow, small scoops were welded onto the top and bottom of the muffler in the production version, which created an ejector effect for the cooling-air flow.

Brake System

A modern main battle tank not only is required to have good acceleration capabilities for the "dash out of cover" when changing position—it also needs powerful and reliable brakes. Despite the high vehicle weight, for example, all legal requirements must be met. The "hot-brake test" poses a particular challenge for the brake system; in this series of tests, the vehicle has to be braked from maximum speed several times in a short period of time. It should be noted that the brakes have to decelerate not only the translational mass of the vehicle, but also the rotational mass of the two tracks and the power transmission elements.

The brake system of the Leopard 1 main battle tank consists of two internally ventilated disk brakes. Eight hydraulically actuated brake pistons act on each of the two discs as service brakes. A mechanically actuated caliper body acts on the same brake disk as the parking brake. The brakes are attached to the inside of the side rail and remain in the vehicle when the power pack is removed. The service brake is actuated by the brake pedal on the driver's seat. A hydraulic control circuit actuates a servo-valve located on the rear wall of the vehicle, which—depending on the brake pedal position—releases the pressure from the brake circuit to the pistons. The maximum operating pressure in the main circuit is 135 bar. Under optimum ground conditions, a deceleration of up to 8 meters/second^2 can be achieved. The caliper bodies of the parking brake are also actuated from the driver's seat by pulling the brake levers via mechanical cable pulls.

Final Drives and Drive Sprockets

The drive sprockets and reduction gearing (final drives) are at the end of the power transmission chain. As is usual in heavy-vehicle construction, the drive power in the transmission of the Leopard 1 main battle tank is transmitted at a relatively high speed level, while the corresponding drive torque is kept at a relatively low level. This means that the power-transmitting components can be designed to be smaller and lighter. Only shortly before the drive sprockets is the speed level reduced by a reduction gear (here: final drive) and the corresponding drive torque increased in order to achieve the necessary tractive force. The final drives on the Leopard 1 main battle tank consist of a planetary set with a reduction ratio of 3.8:1. The drive sprocket drum is driven directly by the planetary gear carrier (web). Two sprockets are bolted to each drive wheel drum; the sprockets engage in the spaces between the track end connectors. When the tank pulls away, a torque of up to 10,500 Nm is reached at the drive sprocket; at maximum speed, the speed of a drive wheel is approximately 525 rpm. The high forces and torques require a robust mounting of the drive sprocket drum as well as appropriate reinforcements and ribbing on the inside of the trough in the area of the side lays. To remove the power plant, the connection between the gearbox output and the final drive must be loosened. This is achieved elegantly on the Leopard 1 by pulling an internally toothed sliding sleeve in the brake body.

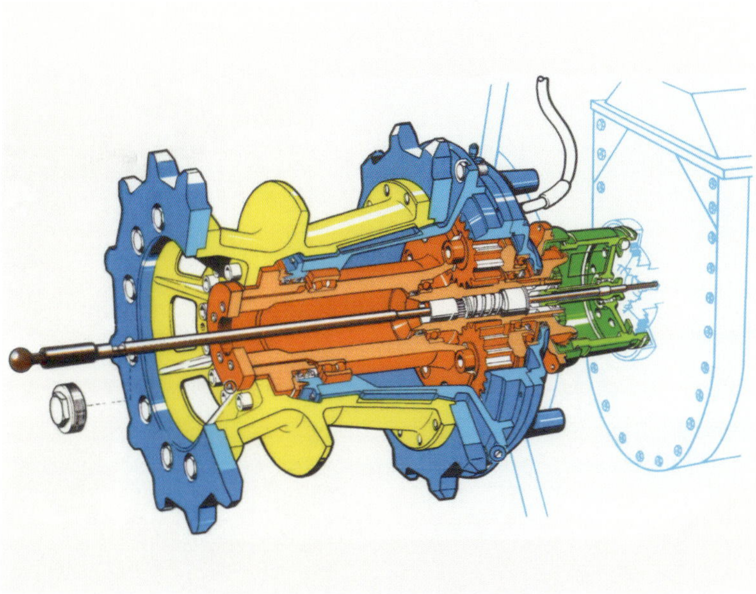

Drive sprocket of the Leopard 1: On the prototypes, the drive sprocket drum still consisted of welded steel parts; for the production version, the drive sprocket drum was made of cast steel for cost reasons. From the second-generation prototypes onward, the drive sprocket drum was provided with openings to enable self-cleaning. The two sprockets are bolted to the drive sprocket drum to enable replacement. During development, the shape of the sprockets was changed several times to optimize the running in of the end connectors and to prevent the track from climbing up as far as possible. The sprockets are subject to high levels of wear, especially when the vehicle is operated on sandy ground (Lüneburg Heath, Fraulautern, etc.). Two small holes can be seen on three of the teeth in the picture. These are wear marks. The tooth flanks can be worn down to the holes. The drive sprockets on both sides must then be replaced so that the other side of the teeth is subjected to wear.

Mobility-Defining Components / Running Gear

Complete Running Gear

The running gear of the Leopard 1 main battle tank consists of seven road wheels with torsion bar suspension, four return rollers, an idler wheel, and one drive sprocket per side. Each of the three forward and two rear road-wheel stations has a hydraulic shock absorber to limit pitching vibrations when driving fast off-road. A truncated cone spring is fitted to each track road-wheel station to limit the spring deflection and protect the torsion bars. For logistical reasons, the idler wheel is identical to the road wheels—the necessary compromise in driving dynamics was accepted. The idler wheel is mounted on a crank rocker in the nose and can be adjusted in its position to set the chain tension by using a mechanical chain tensioner. The four return rollers support the upper track run; they are arranged offset to each other and alternately carry the inner or outer half of the track. This arrangement is intended to utilize the torsional elasticity of the track during track whipping, in order to avoid excessive load peaks on the return rollers. All the hubs of the road wheels and return rollers are filled with motor oil and are maintenance-free. The torsion bar suspension results in a design-related offset of 337 mm (13.26 in.) between the road wheels on the right and left side—however, this is not important from a driving-dynamics point of view. Compared to a wheeled vehicle, the tracked running gear has a relatively high internal resistance. A force of 8.4 kN = 855 kp is required per side just to move the parts of the running gear. When traveling at top speed, 530 kW (390 hp) is required to overcome the resistance of the transmission and running gear alone!

Work being carried out on the running gear of a Leopard 1 main battle tank: Due to the weight of the components, work on the tank's running gear is extremely unpopular with the crews. The crowning glory is the replacement of track pads when the two tracks have to be opened and removed, and then 336 worn track pads have to be replaced per vehicle.

In the picture, the drive sprocket has been removed so that it is obviously planned to replace it with the drive wheel on the other side of the running gear. The picture was taken in 1968 in the Hessen barracks (town of Allendorf); the vehicle belongs to PzBtl 64 (64th Armored Battalion).

Leopard 1 in the mud: On the terrain course of the Wehr-Technischen Dienststelle 41 (WTD 41) in Trier, people and technology are frequently pushed to their limits. The picture shows a Leopard 1 main battle tank after driving through the mud track on the Grüneberg several times. All parts of the running gear are completely mud covered—but all bearing points of the track and return rollers must be carefully sealed! The self-cleaning system of the running gear (including drive sprocket) must also function properly to maintain perfect track guidance. Finally, in such situations, attention must be paid to issues such as cleaning the optics and periscopes and keeping air intake openings (combustion air for the engine) clear.

Torsion Bars and Shock Absorbers

As part of the development of the Leopard 1 main battle tank, torsion bars, disk springs, and hydropneumatic spring elements were tested and examined in the prototypes. In the end, the principle of torsion bar suspension proved to be the most reliable and, viewed over the life cycle of the weapon system, also the most cost-effective system offering the required performance.

The torsion bars lie transversely in the hull; they have a length of 2,266 mm (89.2 in.) and a diameter of 56 mm (2.2 in.). Both ends of the torsion bar have serrations. One end of the torsion bar is fixed in the hull, while the other end is connected to a swing arm. This end of the torsion bar is rotatably mounted in roller bearings in the hull. When the road wheels are placed under load, the torsion bar is twisted over its entire length (elastic deformation) and allows a twisting angle of up to 60 degrees. With a swing arm length of 400 mm (15.75 in.), this results in a total spring travel of 400 mm (15.75 in.).

To dampen pitching vibrations, five hydraulic shock absorbers are installed on each side of the running gear on the swing arms. The damping force increases with increasing compression and extension speed. During compression, the hydraulic oil is pressed through throttle valves and heats up in the process. The generated thermal energy corresponds to the kinetic energy removed from the excited system. A sufficiently high damping performance allows the vehicle to pass through the resonance phase without the crew being exposed to unacceptably high accelerations.

With a good system design, the functional running-gear performance and the available drive power are harmoniously matched to each other.

Removing a torsion bar

Torsion bar breakage: When properly designed, a torsion bar can withstand over 20,000 load cycles without breaking. As a rule, no replacement is required during its service life. In rare cases, torsion bar breakage may occur at the first road wheel, which is subjected to high loads. Since the highest torsional stresses occur on the outside under load, the surface reacts sensitively to damage—this can lead to premature breakage of the torsion bar.

Torsion bars in the Leopard 1 main battle tank: During prototype trials, the torsion bar suspension (vehicles of Company Group A) prevailed relatively quickly over the vehicles of Company Group B with hydropneumatic or disk suspension. Compared to the other suspension technologies, torsion bars are simple in design, are absolutely maintenance- and wear-free, and have no thermal problems. Special manufacturing processes (e.g., presetting, shot peening) enable high material utilization to be achieved—resulting in favorable weight ratios for a given workload capacity. The torsion bars are protected inside the hull and can be easily installed. They have only a minor influence on the vehicle, since (as can be seen in the picture)—in addition to the torsion bars—further beads must be added to reinforce the floor of the hull. Since the torsion bar has no inherent damping and a linear spring characteristic, additional elements (e.g., end stop dampers) must be installed for damping and to achieve a progressive characteristic.

Road Wheels

The Leopard 1 has seven road wheels per side. Each road wheel consists of two identical halves, which are placed on the stud bolts of the hub and bolted together. The track's center guide teeth run in the gap between the roller halves. The center guide teeth absorb the lateral forces generated when cornering or driving on an incline and transfer them to the ground via the track. Since this results in high frictional forces between the center guide teeth and the road wheels, the inner sides of the road-wheel halves are provided with a hardened layer in this area. The road wheels are part of the unsprung masses of the vehicle and are therefore made of a light metal alloy to reduce weight. The weight of a complete wheel half is approximately 80 kg; the diameter with drum is 680 mm (26.77 in.). The wheel rims are fitted with 35 mm thick (1.38 in.) rubber tires to improve running smoothness, especially when driving on roads and hard surfaces. The critical factor here is the vibration excitation of the entire system, which occurs when the gaps between the chain links roll over.

The hardening layer and the tire are the parts of the track road wheel subject to wear; these can be reapplied to the road-wheel rim and renewed as part of an industrial repair. Unfortunately, in the 1960s it was not possible to achieve logistical equivalence with the road wheels of the Marder infantry-fighting vehicle (diameter: 690 mm, or 27.16 in.).

Track

The track must transfer the propulsive power or force of the engine to the ground. In practice, there is often an excess of drive power, while the traction capacity of the track—depending on the ground conditions—does not always allow the drive power to be transferred. The result is that the track slips. In order to improve traction and lateral guidance, the track is profiled in a similar way to tires.

For the production version of the Leopard 1 main battle tank, the decision was made to use a track with a basic design, similar to the tracks of the American main battle tanks of the time. It is a rubber-bushed end connector track with bolted-on center guide teeth. The track pins are rubber-bushed in the tubular bodies. The track pins of two adjacent track links are connected by the external end connectors. This type D 139 track met the most-important requirements for reliability, durability, and road protection. The low traction capacity in wintry conditions and the fact that the entire track had to be discarded after the tread became worn down were problematic.

Starting in 1972, the new D 640 A system track from Diehl was available for the Leopard 1 main battle tank. This is also a single link track, the track pins of which are mounted in the tubular body with rubber elements. In contrast to the D 139 track, however, the new track had replaceable track pads. In winter, the rubber pads on every eighth to tenth track link could be replaced with snow grousers to improve traction. In the early version of the D 640 chain, additional ice grousers could be hammered into the corresponding holders in the tube body if necessary. This track represents a relative optimum considering the various requirements and is still produced today for the vehicles of the Leopard family. While the track pads and end connectors have to be replaced after a mileage of approximately 3,000 km, the tubular body can reach up to 12,000 km.

D 139 track

D 640 track

Survivability-Defining Components

Hull and Turret Shells in General

The hull and turret shells of the Leopard 1 main battle tank were manufactured using different technologies in accordance with the conventions of battle tank construction at the time. As with British and Russian main battle tanks of the 1960s, the hull shell consists of welded rolled steel plates, while the turret (in the first versions) is a cast construction. Since the welded seams are less strong than those of homogeneous armor, the hull casing was designed to increase projectile resistance by supporting the plates against one another (positive locking). Thanks to the existing casting technology, the wall thicknesses of the turret could be easily adapted to the different requirements. The casting technology also proved to be advantageous for realizing the complicated shape of the front part of the turret, including the integration of the rangefinder blisters, as cost-effectively as possible.

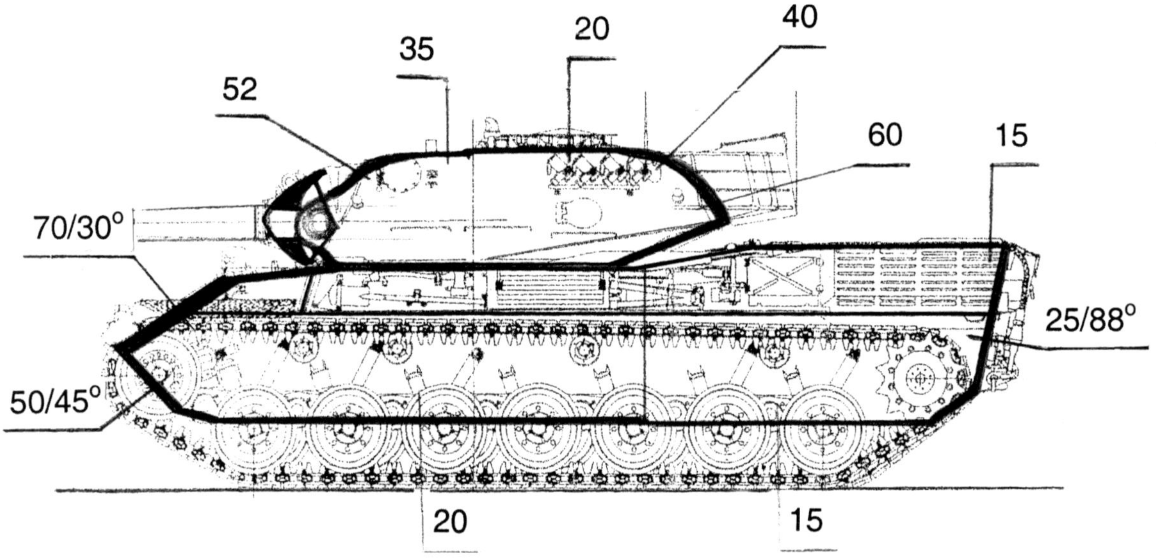

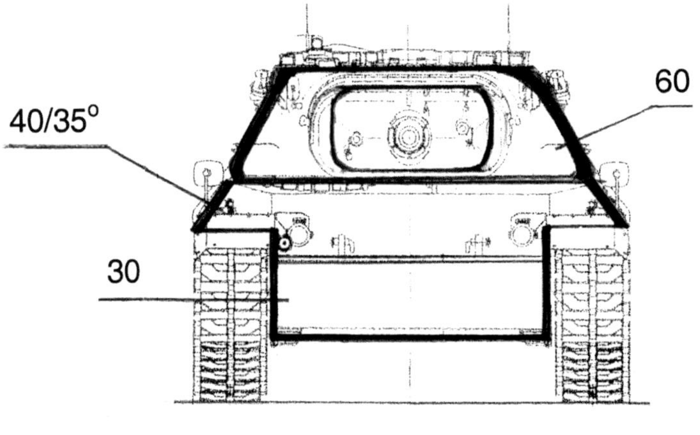

Hull Shell

The hull of the Leopard 1 main battle tank is welded together from rolled armor steel plates of different thicknesses. To prevent voids in the weld metal and to ensure a perfect joint between the welded plates, the hull shell is welded in large rotating stands. This avoids so-called overhead seams.

By sloping the plates in the front and side areas, the armor penetration distances are increased. For example, the upper front plate is 70 mm (2.75 in.) thick—against horizontal fire, the 30 degrees of slope results in a penetration distance of 140 mm (5.5 in.). The driver's hatch is protected against horizontal fire due to its position. Firing at the hull-turret joint, even with small-caliber ammunition, can cause the turret to jam. For this reason, eight segments of cast armor steel were welded onto the hull roof in the front and side areas of the turret from the second batch onward to protect the hull-turret joint; older vehicles were not retrofitted.

The hull is divided into the fighting compartment and engine compartment by a bulkhead. To ensure NBC protection, a hermetic (gas- and watertight) seal to the engine compartment can be achieved once all flaps and parts have been fitted to the bulkhead.

In the area of the fighting compartment, the hull roof has a clear opening of 2,200 mm (86.61 in.) to accommodate the turret ring frame. The rear part of the hull roof also has a large opening in the area of the engine compartment for installing and removing the engine. These large openings considerably reduce the torsional rigidity of the hull casing in the longitudinal direction. The gross weight of the hull shell is 11.12 metric tons (12.25 tons).

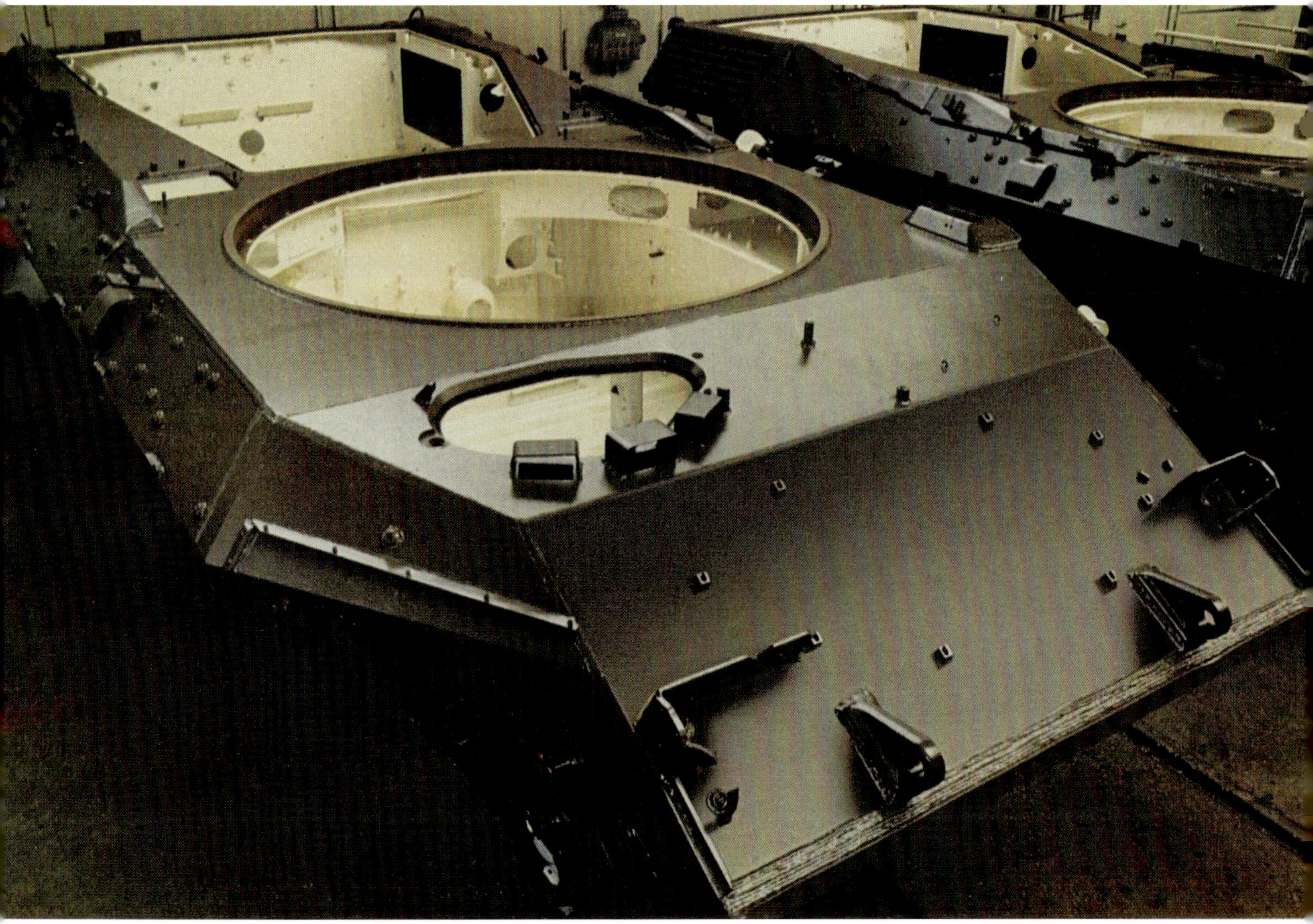

Protection for the hull-turret joint: In the design of turret and hull shells, small details in the structural design can make the difference between surviving or failing in the face of a threat. One detailed aspect is the protection of the turret joint against small-caliber ammunition. Without such protection, fire from small-caliber machine guns can cause the turret to jam. Many armored vehicles of the former German Wehrmacht as well as Russian main battle tanks were equipped with such protective elements. In the case of the Leopard 1, the turret-hull joint protection was initially forgotten—elements of the turret-joint protection system were welded in place only on vehicles from the second-production batch onward.

Gratings are parts of the hull shell that allow air to flow, on the one hand, but also provide a certain degree of ballistic protection, on the other hand. Gratings are used as air inlets for the engine combustion air, for the cooling air, and for the NBC protective ventilation system, and, if necessary, for engine compartment ventilation. They can be used as air outlets for cooling air, for the exhaust system, for engine compartment ventilation, and for openings for dust discharge in NBC protective ventilation systems and air filters. When designing the grille blades, a compromise must be found in terms of pressure loss coefficient and protection level. The grille surface should have the same level of protection as the neighboring shell surfaces. The picture shows a cross section through the exhaust air / exhaust gas grille of the Leopard 1 (cast turret version).

Turret Shell

Although German tanks had welded turrets during the Second World War, the decision was made to use a cast turret at the beginning of Leopard 1 development. The casting technology offered the advantage of relatively free shaping and continual variation of the wall thicknesses. A relatively high production rate could also be achieved once the casting molds had been created. These were certainly the reasons why American, British, and Russian main battle tanks of this era were also fitted with cast turrets. However, the homogeneous armor available at the time had a lower protective performance than rolled steel plates of the same thickness.

The production of the one-piece-casting turret required an upper and lower mold. A core had to be inserted between the two casting molds due to the undercut in the area of the turret bustle. The turret bustle served as a counterbalance for the more massive front armor. This allowed the center of gravity of the turret to be shifted to the vertical axis, which was particularly beneficial for stabilization. In the area of the turret roof, the cast turret had a large opening, which was closed during the manufacturing process by welding a homogeneous steel plate in place. All the mechanical processing required to accommodate the two hatches, including the angled transom, was carried out in the homogeneous steel plate. The gross weight of the cast turret was approximately 6 metric tons (6.6 tons).

In the early 1970s, improvements in welding technology made it possible to improve the projectile resistance of the seams, so that the decision was made to use a welded turret for the vehicles of the fifth and sixth production batches. At the same time, the principle of spaced armor was implemented, which tended to offer better armor protection with the same surface weight.

Mantlet seal: Not visible to the outside observer is the mantlet seal, which closes the opening between the gun cradle and the turret shell so that it is gas- and watertight. The seal is a plastic plate between the gun cradle and the mantlet and is also attached to the turret mouth via a metal frame with a large number of smaller screws. To consider the range of elevation of the main gun, a bellows provides the necessary freedom of movement for these two elements. The pictures show the plastic plate on the gun cradle and the mounting frame (metal) on the turret opening. The gray bellows is located between the plastic plate and the mounting frame.

This cutaway model of a preproduction vehicle shows the overlapping of the elements of the turret opening and mantlet to ensure the necessary ballistic protection over the entire elevation range of the main gun. The mantlet seal between the gun cradle and the turret mouth has been omitted from the cutaway model. The picture shows one of the four expansion screws in the lower area of the gun cradle with which the mantlet is attached to the gun cradle.

Side Skirts (Track Skirts)

Although side skirts had already been used on tanks in the Second World War due to their protection-enhancing effect, and the Centurion main battle tank also had side skirts in the 1950s, the first production batches of the Leopard 1 main battle tank were delivered without them. Possible reasons for this decision may have been their hindrance to self-cleaning of the running gear or the difficult access to the running gear during maintenance work (e.g., tensioning the track).

At the beginning of the 1970s, however, the vehicles of the fifth production batch (Leopard 1 A2 version) were delivered with the side skirts that had been tested in the meantime. The vehicles of the first four production batches were also retrofitted with side skirts starting in 1972. The skirts consisted of sections in which perforated plates made of high-strength homogeneous steel were embedded in rubber. The skirt elements improved protection against hollow-charge projectiles in particular, since the hollow-charge warhead was triggered prematurely by the skirt before striking the main armor if it hit the main armor at an angle, and the hollow-charge spike no longer had the optimum penetration performance by the time it reached the main armor. The protective effect of the skirts was also improved in the face of bullets of up to medium caliber, since the perforated structure of the armor steel plates often led to deformation or destruction and destabilization of the projectiles.

Drawing illustrating the effect of track skirts

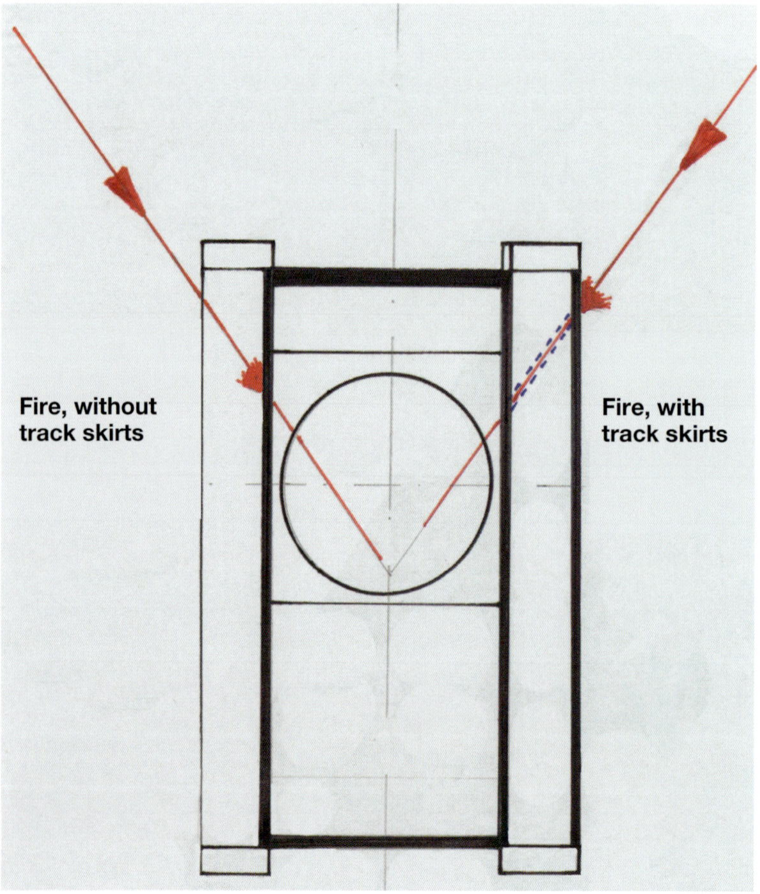

Track skirts

Shock-Absorbing Supplementary Turret Armor

Beginning in 1975, vehicles of the first four production batches were retrofitted with supplementary turret armor and designated Leopard 1 A1A1. The elements of the additional armor on the front and turret sides were attached to the basic shell using so-called shock mounts (rubber blocks).

Even if projectiles do not penetrate the armor, they transfer their kinetic energy to the target on impact. Even 20 mm shells can generate accelerations of up to 6,000 g. Firing with 40 to 57 mm ammunition (even without penetration) often leads to irreversible damage to optical devices (detached prisms) or causes misalignment of the optical devices or damage to parts of the onboard electrical system (e.g., fuse boxes).

The shock-absorbing mounting of the outer plates is intended to prevent the basic shell from being subjected to a shock load in the event of a hit, or to reduce the shock effect in the basic shell by means of the rubber-elastic mounting.

Supplemental turret armor

Shock mounts

Other Components and Systems

Ventilation and NBC Protection System

The ventilation and NBC protection system supplies the hermetically sealed fighting compartment with filtered air and generates an overpressure of approximately 30 mm (1.18 in.) WS (water column) in the fighting compartment. The overpressure ensures that no contaminated outside air can penetrate into the fighting compartment even if there are leaks in the hull (e.g., in the area of the turret ring or the torsion bar bearings). The NBC filter section is located on the left-hand side in the front of the hull. It contains a HEPA filter for any aerosol components in the outside air and four gas filters. The outside air supplied to the filter section is first precleaned in a cyclone coarse-dust filter. The filter effect of the ABC filters lasts for approximately ten hours. When the filters are changed, the contaminated filters have to be transported to the outside through the fighting compartment. This disadvantage was avoided in the design of the NBC protective ventilation system of the Leopard 2 main battle tank. In front of the filter section, there is a changeover valve to be operated by the driver. This allows the filter section to be bypassed during normal ventilation of the fighting compartment.

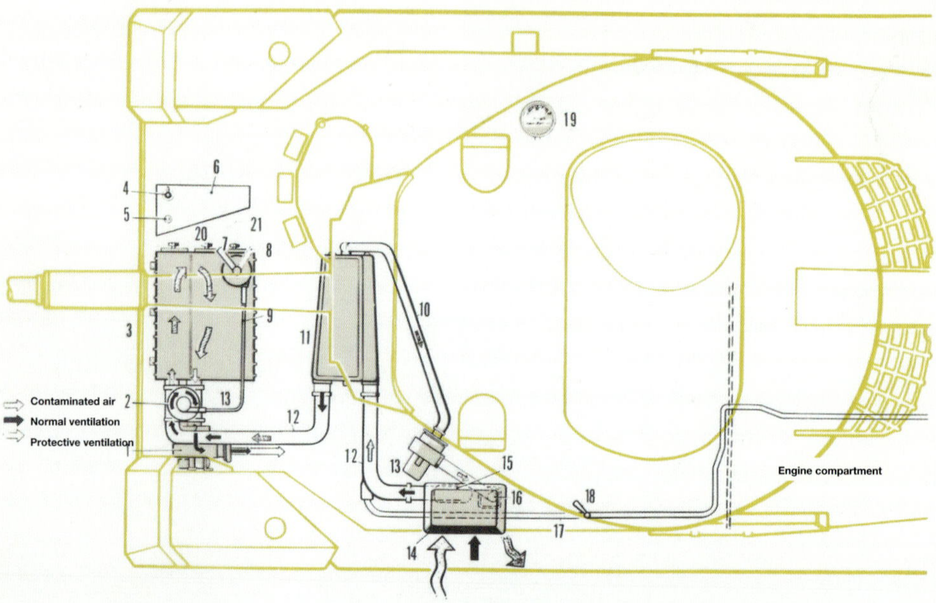

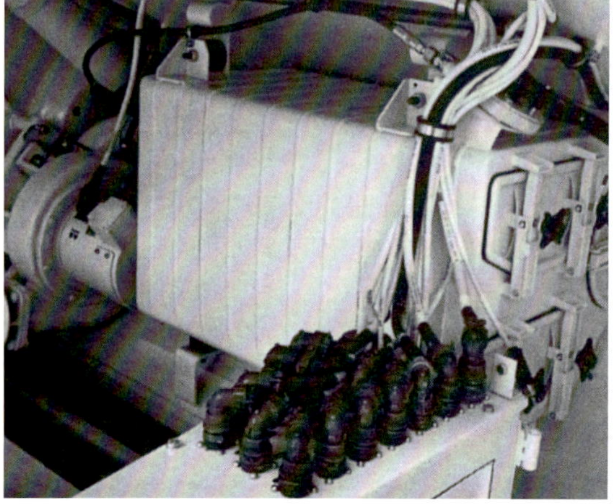

NBC protective ventilation system: The picture shows the position of the ventilation and NBC protective ventilation system on the left-hand side in the forward hull. The two maintenance openings for the gas filters and the (round) maintenance opening for the HEPA filter can be seen in the housing. The normal/protective ventilation switch is located on the filter housing; it is operated by the driver at the direction of the commander. The main blower can be seen to the left of the filter housing. From the fifth production batch onward, a so-called compact system was installed, which contained only a HEPA filter. The disadvantage was that contaminated filter elements had to be disposed of through the fighting compartment via the driver's hatch. This problem was avoided with the Leopard 2 main battle tank.

Heating System

The heating system consists of an external heater located in the right-hand track shoulder in the area of the fighting compartment; it operates independently of the engine. Finely atomized diesel fuel is burned in a combustion chamber. The hot exhaust gases heat the air extracted from the fighting compartment in an air-to-air heat exchanger. The hot air can be used to heat the fighting compartment or to preheat the batteries. The exhaust gases are passed through an air/water heat exchanger before being discharged to the outside. At very low outside temperatures, the coolant can be fed through the air/water heat exchanger of the heater via a circulation pump on the engine to preheat the engine—in this operating mode, the batteries are also warmed up in parallel via the hot air. Both the starting process and the cooling process after the heater is switched off take place in an automatic sequence. Safety circuits ensure that operation is interrupted in the event of faults or overheating. At high outside temperatures, the heater's fresh-air blower can be used as a fan to circulate the fighting-compartment air.

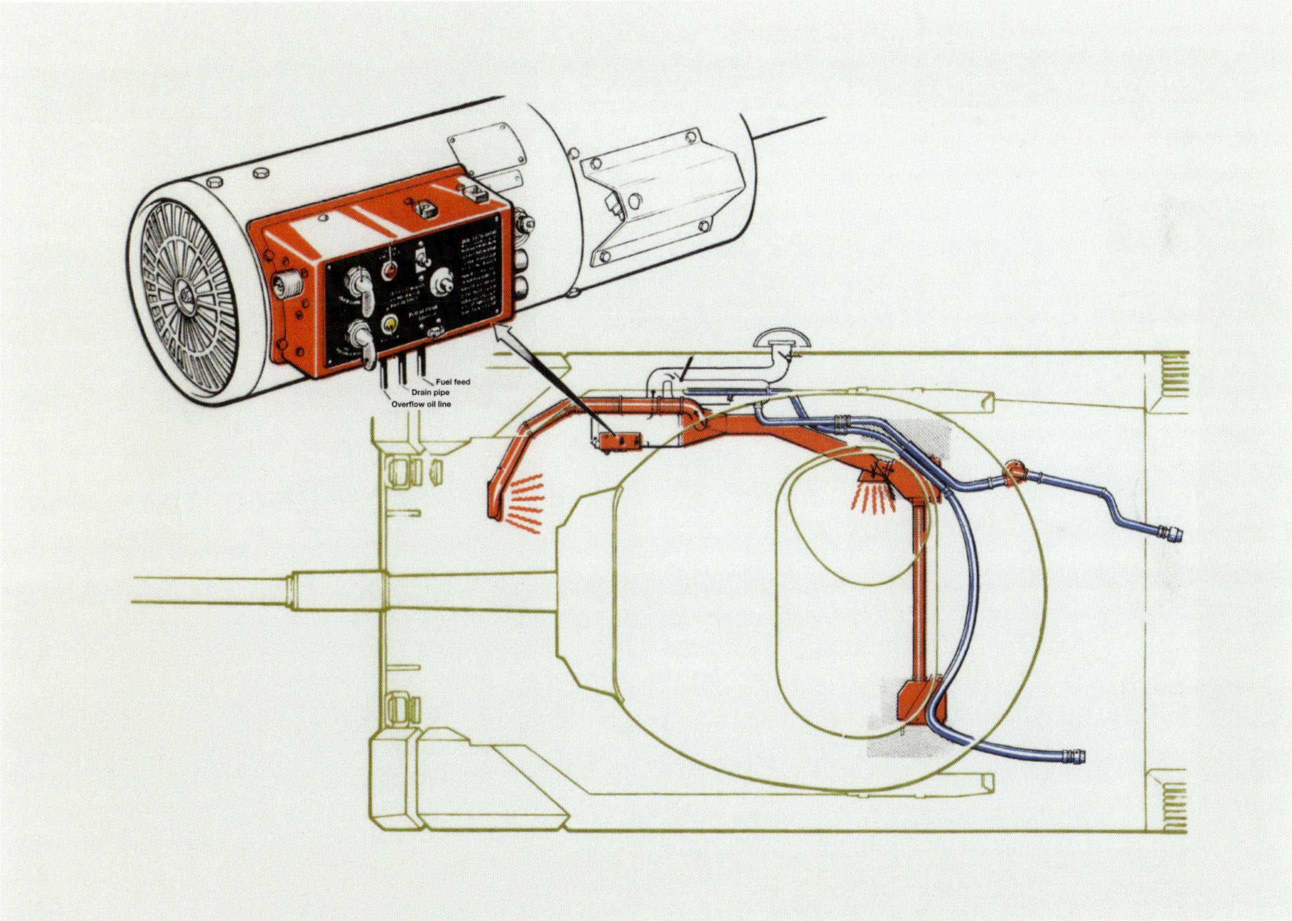

Submersible Hydraulics

The purpose of the submersible hydraulics is to close the intake and exhaust flaps in the hull before deep wading or underwater travel and then to open them again. The pressure of approximately 45 bar required to close the individual flaps can be generated by a hand pump located on the loader's side. After the pressure is released, the individual flaps are opened again by springs. In addition to the submersible hydraulics, the crew must inflate a sealing gasket located in the turret ring frame to approximately 2 bar by using a manually operated air pump before deep wading or submerged travel. As the pressure builds up in the submersible hydraulics, the hydraulic traversing system is automatically switched off so that the ring seal in the turret ring frame is not damaged by traversing the turret. While sixteen flaps are closed by the diving hydraulics, the crew must open two handholes in the bulkhead to the engine room before deep wading and underwater travel.

Since the air intake grilles of the air filters on the hull roof were closed by the submersible hydraulics, in this state the engine receives combustion air via the fighting compartment or the open commander's hatch (with the deep-wading shaft or submerged-driving shaft fitted).

Regardless of the diving hydraulics, the openings for the turret machine gun and the turret telescopic sight in the mantlet as well as the muzzle of the main gun must be sealed by the crew before deep wading or submerged travel.

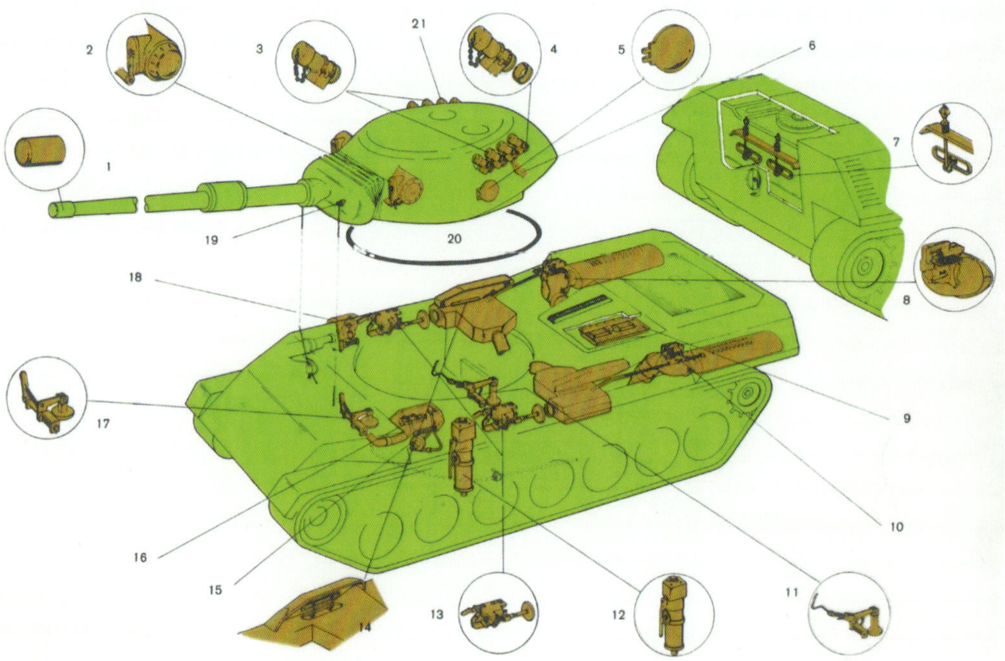

Fire-Extinguishing System

The fire-extinguishing system is designed to protect the assemblies in the engine compartment from major damage in the event of a fire by means of an electrically triggered extinguishing process. For this purpose, pipes with spray nozzles are installed in the engine compartment, and these distribute the extinguishing agent from four extinguishing-agent bottles to possible sources of fire. In the event of a fire, two extinguishing-agent cylinders are triggered automatically by a fire-warning wire (linear detector element), which is laid throughout the engine compartment. If the "fire wire" is heated to above 180 degrees Celsius at one point, the electrical resistance is reduced there—and this opens the valve of the first extinguishing-agent bottle. If the fire is not extinguished after emptying the first extinguishing-agent bottle, the second extinguishing-agent bottle is also emptied automatically. The four extinguishing-agent bottles are located on the right-hand side wall of the tank behind the driver's seat.

The two remaining extinguishing-agent bottles can be activated manually only at the control box of the fire-extinguishing system. The fire-monitoring system in the engine compartment is also in operation when the vehicle is parked and the main switch is turned off. Initially, monochlorobromomethane was used as an extinguishing agent, which was soon replaced by Halon 1211. Due to the CFC 161 agreement, the halon had to be replaced by a nitrogenous mixture (Deugen-N) in recent years.

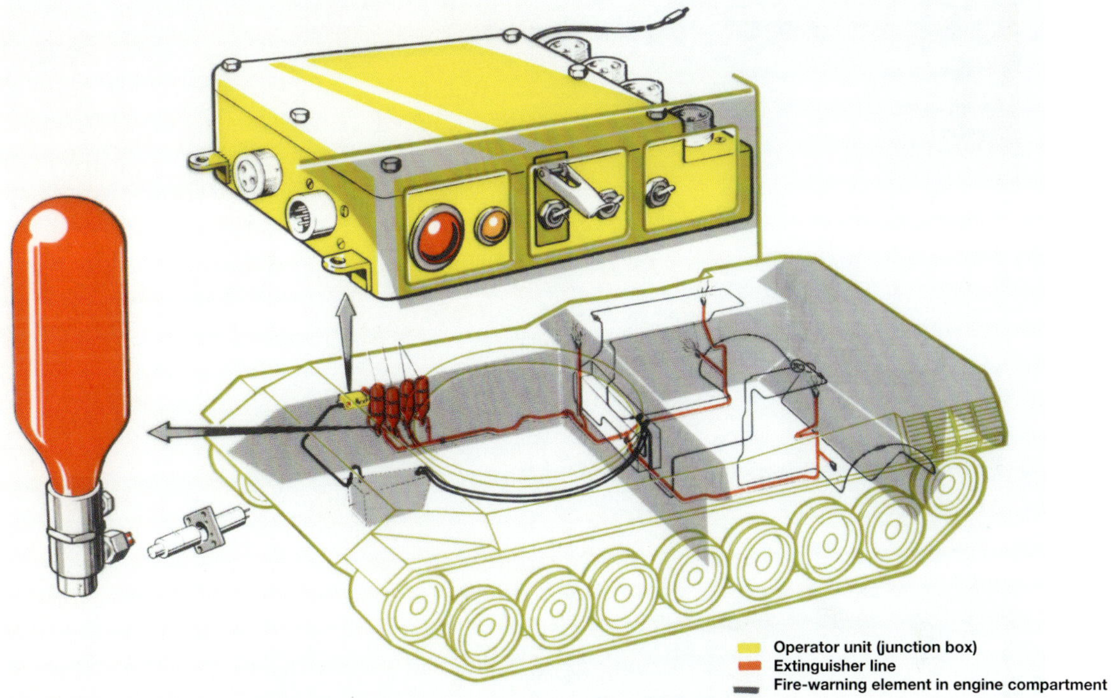

Electrical System / Generator / Batteries

The electrical system of the Leopard 1 is designed for 24 V direct current (charging voltage of the batteries: 28 V). The electrical energy is stored in eight 12 V batteries, which are connected in parallel in four groups—resulting in a total capacity of 400 ampere-hours. Four batteries are positioned on the left and four on the right in front of the bulkhead in the fighting compartment. The batteries are charged by an air-cooled three-phase generator, which can supply a maximum current of 320 A at 28 V (equivalent to an output of almost 9 kW, or 12 hp). A liquid-cooled rectifier with silicon diodes is connected to the generator. A regulator controls the voltage of the generator, depending on the load from consumers and the charge status of the batteries. The entire onboard electrical system is switched on and off via the master switch on the driver's instrument panel (with the exception of the fire-extinguishing system, which is always supplied with power). If the batteries fail (low state of charge), the engine can be started by a second vehicle via an external power cable and an external power source. Up to 3,200 A flows briefly during the starting process!

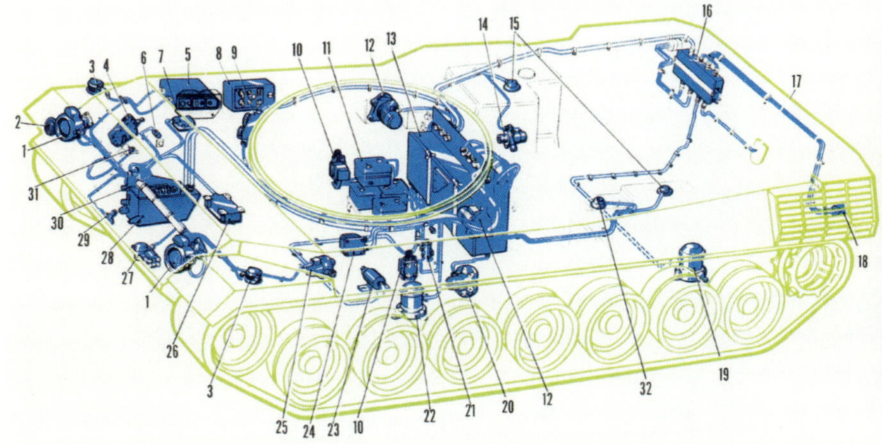

Turret Ring Bearing

Although not visible from the outside, the turret ring bearing is also one of the most important components without which a turret tank would not function. From the turret designer's point of view, the ring bearing should have the largest-possible diameter so that there is enough space inside to accommodate the crew and components. An external diameter of 2,200 mm (86.61 in.) was specified for the Leopard 1 and Leopard 2 main battle tanks, considering the railroad-loading gauge. The turret ring bearing has to meet a wide range of requirements. Conventional roller bearings made of steel would be far too heavy for such dimensions. Therefore, a four-point wire-race ball bearing was selected for the Leopard 1 (A1–A3). The steel bearings (diameter approximately 30 mm, or 1.18 in.) run in four hardened-steel races. The four wire races are embedded in two bearing rings made of light metal. The use of a weapon stabilization system requires that the rotational resistance of the bearing—even in the event of deformation and thermal expansion—does not change as much as possible. Another problem is that the forces resulting from the turret weight (approximately 10.8 metric tons, or 11.9 tons) cannot be transferred evenly around the circumference into the race. Instead, the forces are concentrated on the side and rear areas of the turret ring bearing. To further reduce the change in rotational resistance in the event of hull deformation, a three-race roller bearing was used on the Leopard 1 A4 main battle tank—this resulted in a significant improvement in the stabilization quality.

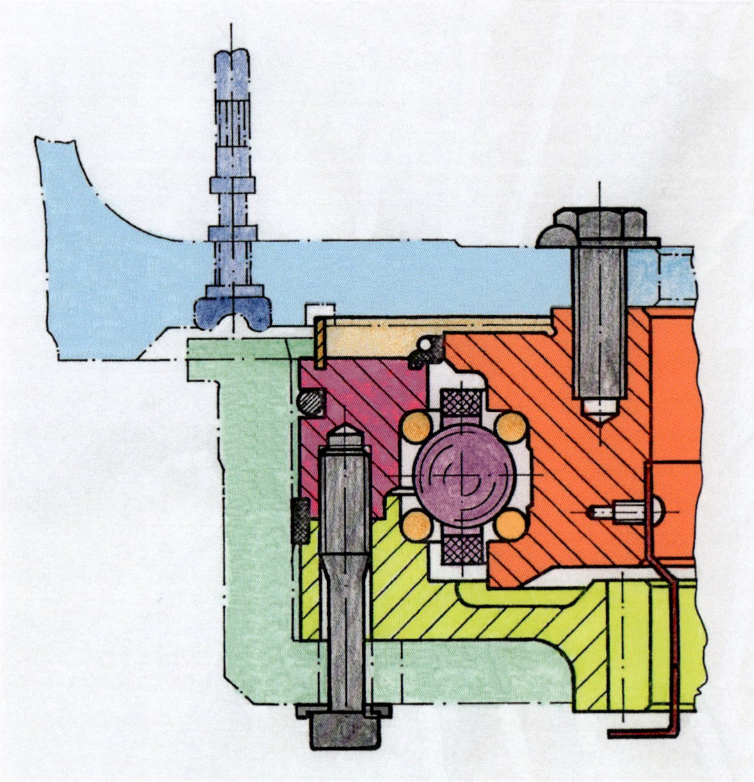

Slip-ring transmitter

Slip Ring Transmitter

The slip ring assembly is a relatively small component, but a turreted tank would not function without it. It is located in the center on the floor of the turret basket; the upper part is attached to the turret basket floor; the lower part is attached to the hull floor (chassis). The slip ring assembly thus provides the connection between the chassis and the turret for the transmission of electrical power, control signals, and signals from the onboard communication (intercom) system. Since different requirements are placed on the individual transmission paths, thirty-six transmission paths are provided in the slip ring transmitter of the Leopard 1 (for comparison, the slip ring transmitter of the Puma infantry-fighting vehicle has 174 paths). The two DC supply lines for the electrical consumers in the turret can withstand short-term loads of up to 800 A.

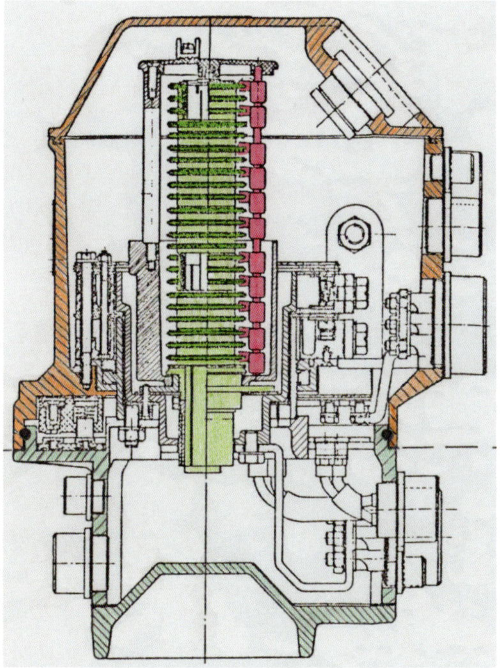

Slip-ring transmitter, cutaway drawing

Vehicle Radio System

In 1965 the Leopard 1 main battle tank was delivered with the SEM 25 vehicle radio system, which operates in the 26–70 MHz frequency range. Compared to the older radios from American stocks, the SEM 25 transceiver was characterized by simpler operation. Ten frequencies from the total of 880 available channels could be preset (programmed). This made life considerably easier for the commander and significantly improved his ability to command the Leopard 1. As a rule, a vehicle had two SEM 25s, so that each transceiver operated on one of the 2.5-meter-long whip antennas. Each antenna had an antenna-tuning device that automatically adjusted to the selected transmission power (1 watt or 15 watts). Under favorable transmission conditions, a range of up to 35 km could be expected. Each crew member had a control unit that could be used to choose between internal or external voice communication. Accompanying infantry could communicate with the tank crew via an outboard intercom on the vehicle's rear plate. The entire system was supplied with 24 V from the onboard power supply—transient protection was installed upstream to protect sensitive semiconductor elements in the radios from overvoltage.

From around 1986, a large proportion of the remaining Leopard 1 vehicles in the army were converted to third-generation SEM 80/90 radios.

Onboard Equipment, Tools, and Accessories

The crew of the Leopard 1 main battle tank has a comprehensive range of onboard equipment at its disposal for carrying out care and maintenance work and for operating the vehicle. There are special tools and tool kits for the main weapon, for the smoke grenade launcher, and for the optical devices for care and maintenance work. There are also special tools on board for working on the running gear and for work on the engine. This category includes

- barrel-cleaning rods (eight pieces) with cleaning tool,
- a ring wrench or ratchet ring wrench for track tensioning,
- a special tool for track assembly,
- a special tool for lifting one side of the engine compartment cover, and
- a special spindle tool for loosening the sliding sleeve from the transmission output.

For "life in the field," the crew has a wide range of tools and equipment at its disposal, including

- a small hatchet and a woodcutter's axe;
- two shovels, hacksaw, crowbar, cross-hatchet, and sledgehammer (5 kg);

• a wire cutter;
• tow cables (two pieces) and shackles;
• an external power cable;
• several refueling funnels; and
• tarpaulin and camouflage netting.

Spare parts:

• spare track links (three pieces)
• spare periscopes (five pieces)

Finally, other parts are included in the onboard equipment (e.g.,

• a manually operated fire extinguisher (6 kg);
• a set of flags and a flashlight;
• a warning triangle, trowel, first-aid kit; and
• a hotplate and water can).

Chapter 7

Maintenance

Engine Change

To be able to make a vehicle with a defective engine available to the troop commander again as quickly as possible, the engine, transmission, and cooling system of the Leopard 1 main battle tank were combined into a power pack. A power pack can be replaced in approximately twenty-five minutes with the aid of a 5-metric-ton crane. All connections to the chassis (coolant lines, fuel lines, electrical connections, and operating/transmission parts) have quick-disconnect couplings. This means that changing the engine of a Leopard 1 requires only a very short time compared to other main battle tanks. For the power pack, the repair team has a special lifting harness that is matched to the attachment points on the engine and in the fan hub; the lifting cable engages precisely above the power pack's center of gravity.

To perform a stationary run, the unit is equipped with a so-called stationary stand, the mounting points of which engage precisely with the engine mounts on the engine and transmission housing. The connections between the hull and engine interfaces can be established in a short space of time by using a so-called stationary harness. The quick installation and removal of the engine is also necessary, since almost all maintenance points are accessible only when the engine is removed.

Removal of the Main Gun and Turret

If necessary, a worn barrel can be removed within fifteen minutes, thanks to the bayonet connection to the base piece. The complete weapon system can be removed in approximately thirty minutes due to the corresponding size of the turret opening. On Russian main battle tanks, the turret must be loosened and lifted or tilted at the rear. It takes several days to replace the gun on these vehicles!

On the Leopard 1 main battle tank, the mantlet (weight: 820 kg) can be removed with the aid of a crane after loosening four expansion screws on the gun cradle and then loosening sealing elements (NBC protection; waterproofing). After the mantlet is removed, the two trunnion bearings are accessible, and their bearing rings can then be removed axially outward. Now the height-adjustable parts of the weapon system (weight: approximately 2,300 kg) can be pulled forward out of the turret opening.

To remove the turret—which is only very rarely necessary—the screw connection with the upper ring of the ring bearing and the cable connections on the slip ring transmitter must be loosened. A 13-metric-ton crane is required to lift out the turret; the work involved can be estimated at approximately three hours.

The design of the Leopard 1 main battle tank considered the requirements of material durability and ensured good accessibility and interchangeability of the assemblies. Compared to other vehicles, the Leopard 1 main battle tank is thus characterized by much more favorable material preservation properties. In conjunction with the reliability and durability of the components, the Leopard 1 has below-average utilization and operating costs compared to other main battle tanks.

Chapter 8

The Leopard 1 in Service

The Leopard 1 Main Battle Tank in Service with the Bundeswehr

The Leopard 1 main battle tank has enjoyed great popularity among the troops since its introduction. The fact that after approximately twenty years of use in training, certain signs of wear and tear on some assemblies required increased effort (e.g., for setting and adjustment work) does not change this. Compared to the types that preceded it (M47 / M48), the Leopard 1 was significantly faster, more agile, more powerful, more reliable, and more precise to drive. As a technically interested tanker in PzBtl 64, the author was lucky enough to switch to the Leopard 1 after a few months of training on the M48 main battle tank. This direct switch meant that the technical changes and improvements between the two vehicles were particularly easy to recognize. The space available to the crew was better than on the M47—but less than on the M48 main battle tank. Despite the relatively limited space available for the crew, great importance was attached to ergonomic design elements when designing the Leopard 1. These included the seat design, the accessibility of the controls and the hydraulic raising device on the commander's seat, and the presence of an electric hot plate for warming up food for the crew. The relocation of the rangefinder from the commander's position (in the M47/48) to the gunner's on the Leopard 1 main battle tank enabled the commander to concentrate on commanding the vehicle and on battlefield observation and target reconnaissance. With the panoramic periscope, the commander had a universally deployable means of observation and targeting; unfortunately, it was initially not stabilized and later only secondarily stabilized (mechanical coupling with the primarily stabilized weapon).

With a specific power-to-weight ratio of just under 15.3 kW/ton (21 hp/ton), the Leopard 1 main battle tank had an excellent power-to-weight ratio for its time. This encouraged

Leopards of the 3rd Company, 64th Armored Battalion, photographed during a movement exercise on the ring road of the Wildflecken training area (1968)

individual units to declare the so-called Heeres-Weitflugmeisterschaften (army long-distance-flying championships). The record is said to be 15 meters (49.2 ft.) in free flight. However, some drivers sustained significant injuries in this questionable competition when their Leopards landed on the road wheels without shock absorbers. Otherwise, there were relatively few accidents involving the Leopard 1, especially since its steering was precise and its brakes powerful and reliable. However, some Leopards did leave the road

Leopard 1 A4 after deep wading: Although this vehicle is equipped with the underwater-driving shaft, the open loader's hatch suggests that it has probably just completed a deep-wading run in the water-training facility on the Panzer-Ringstraße in Munster. Apparently, the mud flaps in the area of the forward track shields (rubberized parts) sustained damaged caused by a very rapid entry into the water.

A Leopard of the 3rd Company, 64th Armored Battalion, after going off the right path on a downhill section of the Baumholder training area

Prototype of the "Beo-Leo" (July 1998)

on bends because "guest drivers" who had not been properly trained and instructed on the vehicle did not shift into a lower gear in tight turns. In driving school, they had learned that the steering gear allowed only a minimum turning radius in each gear position. If the turn radius of the road was tighter, you had to downshift by one gear.

In another official competition—the Canadian Army Trophy (CAT)—crews of the Leopard 1 were often the winners and frequently relegated the M60 and Chieftain main battle tanks to the back of the field. The CAT competition was a shooting competition between NATO countries and was regarded as the "Olympics" of tank gunnery.

A high drive power and a high engine torque (which was increased by a factor of 2.8 by the torque converter when pulling away) are the basic prerequisites for being able to drive at relatively high speeds off-road and on inclines. However, the drive-side forces also had to be able to be transferred to the ground. This is where the fully rubberized D 139 track that was initially used always set the limits. Particularly in wintry conditions (e.g., on a hard-packed layer of snow), traction was very poor. It was only with the introduction of the D 640 A system chain in 1972 that the troops had a tank track suitable for use in winter, since the rubber pads could be replaced with snow grousers if necessary. However,

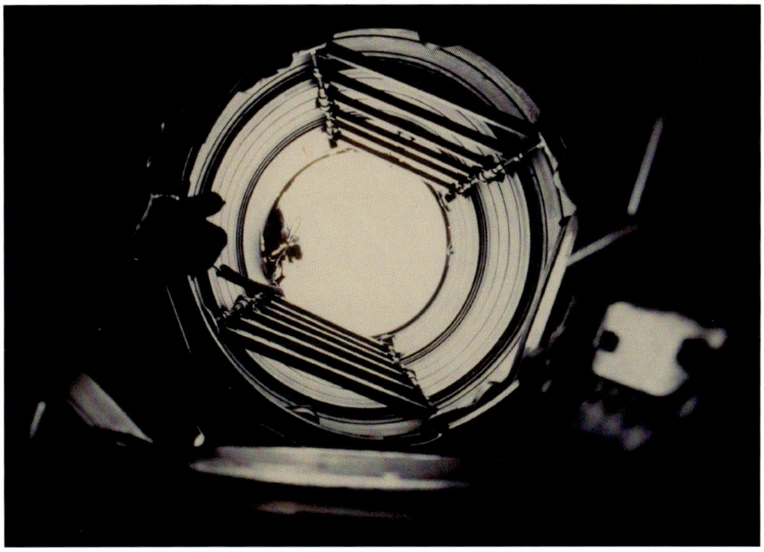

The underwater-driving shaft seen from the inside

the introduction of the D 640 A system track brought with it a weight increase of approximately 800 kg per vehicle. And the D 640 A track led to greater vibration excitation. This was particularly noticeable in the welded turret versions, since the optics were occasionally subject to strong vibrations under certain driving conditions. Interestingly, this effect was less pronounced in the cast turrets due to the inherent damping of the cast homogeneous steel.

Under today's legal requirements, the Leopard 1 main battle tank in its original version

Leopard main battle tank at a technical stop: On longer movements, a technical stop by the marching column must be planned at suitable sections of the route. Each crew member has specific tasks: One controls traffic around the vehicle in coordination with the other traffic lookouts. Furthermore, checks are carried out on various parts of the running gear (temperatures, possible oil leaks; anomalies on the tracks); items of equipment must also be checked to ensure that they are secured.

Leopard 1 main battle tank in the deep-wading pool: The picture shows a Leopard 1 of the 3rd Company, 64th Armored Battalion, in the deepwater basin of the driving-school area in the town of Allendorf. The photo was taken in the winter of 1969—so the first vehicle still had to break through a thin layer of ice in the deep-wading pool. The submersible hydraulics were activated for deep wading, and the turret traverse ring seal was inflated. While in the water, it was possible to check the watertightness of the driver's hatch and the engine compartment cover as well as that of all the flaps, which were closed hydraulically by the submersible hydraulic system.

would no longer receive approval. One critical component is the braking system, which was designed as a single-circuit system and would also no longer pass the hot-braking test required today (this problem is solved in the Leopard 2 by using the hydrodynamic retarder). Another critical component from today's perspective is the heating system, whose exhaust gas routing ran through the fighting compartment (there was a risk of carbon monoxide escaping into the fighting compartment in the event of leaks). Partly due to these problems, the planned conversion of 165 vehicles (originally 335 vehicles were planned) into self-propelled artillery observation tanks or Leopard 1 ("Beo Leo") was dropped in 2000. With the observation tanks based on the Leopard 1 chassis, the artillery force would have received a vehicle whose mobility would have matched the performance of the PzH 2000 self-propelled howitzer.

Submerged travel posed a special challenge for crews and vehicles. A considerable amount of training, including safety instructions for the crew, was required before an underwater journey could be carried out. This included the proper use of the diving rescuer, which each crew member had at their disposal (the diving rescuer produced oxygen chemically for a longer period of time). The next step was to explore the bottom of the water for obstacles or shallows. The final step was to prepare the vehicle. This included cleaning and checking all the seals on hatches and flaps, placing the submerged-travel shaft on the commander's hatch, and preparing the tow ropes for an emergency recovery of a vehicle that had broken down while in the water. If the nonreturn flap in the exhaust pipes had been functioning properly, the engine could have been switched off underwater and restarted. Should water nevertheless enter the vehicle during deep wading or underwater travel, a bilge pump (maximum flow rate: 125 liters/minute) is available in both the fighting compartment and the engine compartment. Considering safety and environmental problems, underwater driving was largely practiced in suitable pools in Munster or at WTD 41 in Trier. With the reduction in the duration of military service, this special training section in the tank battalions had to be dropped.

A Leopard company on the firing range. The photo shows the vehicles of two platoons (2nd Company, 64th Armored Battalion) on the range. Before the start of the gunnery exercise, the weapon team has already checked all weapon systems (barrel brakes, recuperators, contact bridges, breech wedges, etc.) at the site. After the point adjustment on an adjustment target (1,500 meters), the first shot is fired with no crew in the vehicle, via a remote firing system for safety reasons. The commander must signal the status of the vehicle (safe/ready to fire) by putting up flags—firing with a green flag raised costs the offenders a crate of beer in the evening.

Leopard 1 immobile: During movements on military training areas, it is common for armored vehicles to get stuck. In "simple cases," the comradely assistance of another battle tank is sufficient. Particularly in these situations, the torque boost provided by the torque converter when the tank begins to move helps. If the ground is extremely soft in the wider area around the bogged-down vehicle, a recovery tank must be called in to recover the vehicle from a safe location by using its long towing cable. In practice, such an exercise is a relatively lengthy operation. In peacetime, getting a tank stuck is unpleasant and labor-intensive for the crews. Life-threatening situations, on the other hand, occur when there is a real threat. In borderline cases, a vehicle has to be abandoned. Destructive charges (thermite sticks) were provided for the Leopard 1 for this purpose, with which to render the vehicle or gun unusable by the crew before abandoning it.

Chapter 9

The End of the Leopards

As a result of the CSCE Treaty on disarmament in the European states, Germany was granted a maximum of 3,500 main battle tanks. Before reunification, the Bundeswehr had 2,225 Leopard 2, 2,437 Leopard 1, and 650 M48 A2 G A2 main battle tanks—a total of 5,312. As a result, a large proportion of the main battle tanks had to be sold or scrapped, beginning in the 1990s. For this purpose, a recycling and scrapping center was established in 1991 at a disused industrial site in Rockensußra (Thuringia). In 2004 the company changed its name to Battle Tank Dismantling GmbH Koch. Over the next few years, the company was to scrap over 14,000 armored vehicles. The majority came from the stock of the former NVA (East German army), but there were also Leopard 1s, Marders, Lynxes, Scorpions, Rolands, and Jaguar 1s or 2s among them.

The company works strictly according to the rules of the CSCE Treaty and in compliance with the War Weapons Control Act. All vehicle movements on the company premises are monitored by satellite. The regulations of the CSCE stipulate that a main battle tank is considered unusable if, among other things, the left side of the hull with the mount for the side skirt and the left trunnion mount of the main weapon have been burned out over a large area. Unless the Leopard 1s were used in a foreign country, they met their final end in Rockensußra—after a stopover in the Siegelsbach storage depot.

Scrapping of the hull

Leopard 1A5 chassis ready for scrapping.

Due to the CSCE agreement of November 1990, the Bundeswehr subsequently scrapped all M48 A2GA2 and Leopard 1 main battle tanks. The Leopard 1A5 version, in particular, was highly sought after by other countries due to its modern fire control system. As a result, from 2002 onward, around 920 Leopard 1 A5 main battle tanks (in some cases only the turrets) were sold by the Bundeswehr to other nations (including Brazil, Greece, Italy, Denmark, Brazil, Canada, and Belgium) as well as to industry. A few vehicles survived in museums—while around three hundred vehicles (in some cases only chassis) were scrapped in Rockensußra.

When a main battle tank is scrapped, various types of steel, light metal alloys, copper, brass, and bronze, as well as tin, lead, and small amounts of gold, are produced in the blanks. The disposal of some types of plastic (containing phenol, chloride), materials containing asbestos, and paints is problematic. The environmentally friendly disposal of all types of oils, lubricants, and coolants is relatively costly. Overall, hardly any profit could be made by scrapping a main battle tank in the end, since the mass scrapping of armored vehicles in the early 1990s, for example, saturated the capacity for steel in Germany (maximum of 500 tons/year)—and thus the price of steel scrap fell. This was offset by the high personnel, energy, and disposal costs of around 40–50,000 DM per vehicle (1992 prices).

Scrapping of the turret

Conclusion

The Leopard 1 main battle tank was the first major tank project for German industry after the end of the Second World War. After the war, many companies were understandably reluctant to reenter armaments development and production. Initially, generous contractual arrangements by the client increased the motivation for such a reentry—which ultimately proved successful.

With the Leopard 1 project, including other vehicles of the Leopard family, and the SPz-neu project that followed later, the foundations were laid in the 1960s for a successful tank industry in Germany. A solid overall system design and extensive and thorough testing were the key to the success of the products, which were later also widely used on the international market. The Leopard 1 program thus laid the foundation for many years of successful tank development in Germany. This starting point also ensured that the Leopard 2 main battle tank is still in production in 2020, while the production lines for comparable Western main battle tanks had to be closed years ago due to a lack of demand.

Members of the Bundeswehr on a camouflaged Leopard 1 during Exercise Reforger 83. *Photo: Aerospace Av Service on behalf of the US Army*

THE AUTHOR

As a reserve officer in the Panzertruppe, Rolf Hilmes was trained on the Bundeswehr's most important main battle tank, the Leopard. After his military service, he worked in the armaments field as a tank technology consultant, before accepting a position as a lecturer and department head at the Bundeswehr Academy. Since his retirement, he has been able to devote more time to his hobbies—which include preparing presentations, articles, and books on the subject of tank technology.